World Climate Change

World Climate Change
The Role of International Law and Institutions

edited by Ved P. Nanda

Routledge
Taylor & Francis Group

NEW YORK AND LONDON

First published 1983 by Westview Press, Inc.

Published 2021 by Routledge
605 Third Avenue, New York, NY 10017
2 Park Square, Milton Park, Abingdon, Oxon OX14 4RN

Routledge is an imprint of the Taylor & Francis Group, an informa business

Library of Congress Cataloging in Publication Data
Main entry under title:
World climate change.
   (A Westview special study)
   Bibliography: p.
   Includes index.
   1. Climatology--International cooperation--Addresses, essays, lectures.
2. Air--Pollution--Law and legislation--Addresses, essays, lectures. 3. Cli-
matology--Addresses, essays, lectures. I. Nanda, Ved P.
K3775.W4W67   1983   341.7'6755   82-21810

ISBN13: 978-0-367-21403-6 (hbk)
ISBN13: 978-0-367-21684-9 (pbk)

Printed in the United Kingdom
by Henry Ling Limited

Contents

Preface

The book, a collection of fourteen essays, provides a comprehensive discussion and analysis of the legal and institutional aspects of world climate change and weather-related activities and problems. Its authors -- lawyers, social scientists, and academicians -- are experts on the subject, many of them having served as consultants to the U.S. government and various United Nations agencies. They discuss the problems and challenges posed by climate and weather changes in a political context, appraise several options for atmospheric management -- unilateral, bilateral and multilateral -- and make specific recommendations to reduce and ameliorate the adverse global effects of climate fluctuations and changes.

Ved P. Nanda
Denver, Colorado

Acknowledgments

I owe a debt of gratitude to many friends, but I shall mention only a few names. First, I appreciate Robert Schware's initiative in suggesting and working toward a two-day conference on World Climate Change in the summer of 1980 at the University of Denver College of Law. The contents of this book comprise, with two exceptions, papers prepared for the conference and later revised.

The Aspen Institute of Humanistic Studies and the International Legal Studies Program of the University of Denver College of Law jointly assumed responsibility for the selection of the participants and for the program. Walter Orr Roberts and the undersigned co-chaired the conference. Dr. Roberts and Dean Daniel Hoffman of the College of Law were of immense help with their advice and assistance which ensured the success of the conference.

Mrs. Nancy Nones, administrator of the International Legal Studies Program, ably attended to the conference logistics and subsequently supervised proper typing and preparation for publication of the edited manuscript. I am especially thankful to her and to Richard Nelson and John Works, Jr., editors of the Denver Journal of International Law and Policy, for reading the manuscript and for their assistance with technical accuracy on four chapters which initially appeared in the Journal.

I deeply appreciate unfailing courtesies and wise counsel of two good friends at Westview -- Frederick Praeger and Lynne Rienner.

As editor and a contributor I am grateful to my colleagues at the University of Denver Law Library, Alfred Coco and Sue Weinstein, and, at the Denver Public Library, to Robert Shaklee and Sue Yoneda, for the use of their collections, especially their assistance with official documents of the United States and the United Nations.

V.P.N.

1
Social Resiliency and Carbon Dioxide: Preliminary Remarks

Walter Orr Roberts

I am told that there is an old joke in the Soviet Union: "What are the greatest enemies of socialism?" The answer: "Capitalist imperialism, spring, summer, fall and winter." There is a point to this that applies to nations of all ideologies or economic systems. The living world everywhere stands vulnerable to the inconstancies and the excesses of climate. The source of ultimate bounty, climate and weather are also, at times, a powerful force against human well-being. A clear, worldwide perception of this fact is now emerging.

Human societies can, however, be strongly vectored over the coming 30 to 50 years, towards a state of greatly enhanced resiliency to climate. There are specific measures that can be taken to reduce the adverse effects of whatever climate fluctuations and changes we may face. These measures are, in my view, the best social and economic strategies we have to avert or ameliorate the adverse impact of the probable future global climate warming expected by most experts as a consequence of the still exponentially rising burden of man-made atmospheric carbon dioxide.

Fossil fuel usage is, by most estimates, the largest single contributor to the projected warming. Though some futurists are more optimistic, I foresee a continued rise of the fossil fuel exploitation over the next 50 to 75 years, until all the readily mined coal has been exhausted. Several recent reports[1] support my fear that the carbon dioxide levels in the atmosphere will double, and perhaps redouble again before the level stabilizes, and will not retreat significantly for perhaps 500 to 1000 years.

The average global warming is best estimated at $3.5° + 1.5°$ C. for a carbon dioxide doubling. My opinion is that this doubling will occur between 2030 A.D. and 2050 A.D. The warming will, if it occurs, be the largest in the past hundreds of thousands of years. It will be far more extreme in the highest latitudes, and least in the tropics. However, for agricultural and most other human concerns, the change in rainfall and snowfall patterns will have far more impact than the temperature change itself. The distribution of precipitation cannot yet be predicted with any credible accuracy. Some evidence suggests, however, a weakening of the general weather circulation and more severe drought stress in a number of the world's most productive agricultural regions. Moreover, the best evidence from climatologists today is that other human activities, such as deforestation, urban-expansion, soil degradation, dust generation, hydro-fluorocarbon emission and the like are additive to carbon dioxide in their effect, rather than being a countering influence.

In my own view, there is no hope nor justification, considering all of the forces at play in the global problematique, for seeking to control the carbon dioxide effluents by collecting and sequestering them. I feel it is better to take affirmative steps designed to build resiliency in our social and economic systems that will allow us to escape the worst of the consequences of the global warming if and when it comes. To do so will have a host of rewards, for most of the measures are positively beneficial, quite aside from the question of a carbon dioxide climate change. We know from the whole course of human history that climate vagaries are forever causing human troubles. Examples are legion: the Soviet wheat shortfalls in 1972, 1975 and 1979; the Sahel drought in 1968-1972; the U.S. "Dust Bowl" in the 1930's; and the frequent India monsoon failures -- just to name a few.

The impact of all such climate-induced disasters will be reduced if we build agriculture and other human systems with an eye to making them more resilient to climate anomalies. Irrigation systems are one example, if they are fed by a secure water resource. But there are dozens of others: energy conservation is one whose benefits are obvious even if the climate does not change with carbon dioxide. Another example is building human settlements on land less susceptible to flooding by hurricanes or typhoons. Reforestation is still another, since trees and all green living matter help to control atmospheric carbon dioxide, and wood is a previous renewable resource for humanity.

There are many open avenues for highly productive research to enhance the resiliency options for nation states, regional zones, and the globe. World publics have had a surfeit of doom and gloom forecasts and hunger for realistic hope of a better world to come. The stage is set, in my opinion for a new, "can-do," affirmative approach to carbon dioxide, climate, food, and energy, with emphasis on values of things that are "good for their own sake" but also that promote the resilience of

human societies to climate vagaries of whatever origin.
I believe, moreover, that a project on this can contribute affirmatively in respect to ethical issues, too. We
need to think more responsibly about what we owe to
future generations by way of leaving them a healthy
planet -- even though straight economic analysis might
suggest discounting benefits that are as far in the
future as the global warming we now gamble with.

NOTES

1. See, e.g., International Institute for Applied
Systems Analysis, Energy Systems Analysis, Energy Sys-
tems Group, Energy in a Finite World, Vols. I and II
(Ballinger Pub. Co., 1981).

2
The Challenge of
World Climate Change

Ved P. Nanda

Two recent reports--The Global 2000 Report to the
[U.S.] President[1] and World Conservation Strategy[2] prepared for the United Nations Environment Programme
(UNEP)--contain a sober warning that the world environment and resources currently are under severe stresses
which could seriously damage the Earth's carrying capacity. The Global 2000 report projects long-term trends
and concludes that unless urgent actions throughout the
world are taken now, human suffering and environmental
damage will worsen with a consequent potential for international strife. The World Conservation Strategy book
warns that the "planet's capacity to support people is
being irreversibly reduced in both developed and developing countries,"[3] and recommends institutional and planning guidelines for better management and conservation
of living resources.
    These reports are useful in enhancing public aware-
ness of the nature and immensity of the problem which
modern civilization faces. The gravity of the situation
was dramatized in the early 1970's in the Club of Rome's
controversial but valuable study, The Limits to Growth,[4]
which painted a rather grim picture of man's future.
Since then there has grown a genuine interest and concern
in studying the various aspects of the problem, exploring
available alternatives, and fashioning innovative approaches toward amelioration of the existing conditions.
    One such exploratory effort was made in the summer
of 1980 when the Aspen Institute of Humanistic Studies
and the International Legal Studies Program of the University of Denver College of Law assembled a group of
distinguished scientists, international lawyers, and
social scientists in Denver to discuss selected issues
of world climate change. The Denver meeting followed the
World Climate Conference which had met earlier in Geneva
and had "flashed some ominous signals about the number of
disturbing trends relating to the world climate which
could have disastrous effects on the biosphere and on

4

humanity."[5] Two of the participants at the Denver meeting, William Kellogg and Robert Schware, have also concluded after a recent year-long study: "If the consensus of the international climatological community is correct, and if worldwide use of fossil fuels continues to increase atmospheric carbon dioxide, mankind is likely to cause a significant average warming of the Earth's surface--a greenhouse effect--within the next 50 years."[6]

Although the damaging effects of coal smoke and auto emission in combination with other compounds in the atmosphere are not fully understood, it is widely recognized that acid precipitation has killed fish in many lakes in the United States, Canada, and in the Scandinavian countries.[7] According to a recent news story,

> not until the state [of New York] reported last December that hundreds of Adirondack lakes were dead or dying from acid precipitation was the gravity of the threat clear. And even that report did not convey what several days of interviews with several residents and state conservation officials established: Not only fish, but also other species are starting to disappear in one of the nation's wildest places.[8]

Recognizing the seriousness of the situation, the Eighth World Meteorological Congress in 1979 established the world climate program, one of whose four major components is its Impact Studies Programme.[9] The first phase of the program, to last from 1980 to 1983, includes efforts to: (1) reduce the vulnerability of food systems to climate change, (2) anticipate the impact of climate change caused by human activity, (3) improve the science of climate impact studies, and (4) identify human activities that are most sensitive to climate.[10]

At the two-day Denver meeting, on July 10 and 11, 1980, papers were presented identifying the nature of the problem, exploring the existing and alternative public and private international law institutions as responses to weather and climate problems, and discussing policy implications of the various feasible remedies.

The papers prepared for the conference and later revised, with two additions, comprise the chapters that follow.

Dr. Walter Roberts sets the stage by urging that the world community "take affirmative steps designed to build resiliency in our social and economic systems that will allow us to escape the worst of the consequences of the global warming if and when it comes."[11] The second essay in the introductory part calls upon international lawyers to make special contribution by working toward

the enhancement of the awareness of environmental challenges, the refinement of norms and the strengthening of
institutional structures, and the exploration of preventive and adaptive strategies in cooperation with
scientists and social scientists.[12]

Part I of the book consists of six chapters, all by
noted authorities on the subject. In discussing climate
and climate impacts, Mr. Robert Chen considers that our
understanding of present-day climate variations and
their impacts have to be improved before we could learn
more about the nature and impacts of climate changes.[13]
He suggests that suitable adjustment alternatives be
developed and the necessary mechanisms established in
order to ensure that when necessary such alternatives
are acted upon effectively.[14]

Mr. Chen's essay is followed by two chapters on the
role of international organizations in resolving the
issues raised by man's possible impact on climate.
Dr. William Kellogg focuses primarily on the recent international cooperative efforts in meteorology.[15] He
suggests that international collaboration on climatic
change and variability should be seen in the context of
global cooperative measures on environmental problems
in general.[16] In contrast, Dr. John Perry casts his net
wider -- he discusses the problems international organizations in general face in resolving these issues.[17]
Although he begins his essay on a pessimistic note, he
concludes: "The international structure evolved in this
century cannot produce any magical solutions. However,
by gradually injecting the issues into the international
agendas, we can set in motion a global process of en-
volvement entrainment, consciousness-raising, and consensus-formation that will lay the groundwork for whatever we must do for our global condominium."[18]

Dr. Stephen Schneider's focus is on food-climate
interactions.[19] He offers specific recommendations to
minimize the human impacts of climatic fluctuations.
These include building food reserves and establishing
effective distribution systems, creating diversity in
cropping patterns, and maintaining the long-term productive potential of existing or new croplands through
proper farming practices.[20]

The final two chapters in Part I discuss respec-
tively the responsibility of developed and developing
countries and the concept of national security in a
changed international environment. Doctors Robert
Schware and Edward Friedman conclude that the developed
countries, as suppliers of fuel to the world, the major
consumers, and the primary cumulative contributors of
carbon dioxide to the atmosphere, are primarily responsible for new climatic regimes.[21] In the concluding
chapter, Mr. Thomas Wilson, Jr. calls upon nation states

to adapt their political thinking, especially their
traditional concepts about national security, in light of
the changed context which demands creative participation
and collaboration on issues that are no longer national
or regional, but are truly global.[22]

Part II, consisting of seven chapters, is an inquiry
into the existing and alternative inter- and nongovernmental institutions and international legal norms as
responses to climate challenges. The lead chapter by
Doctors Robert Schware and William Kellogg provides an
overview of the various international strategies and
institutions which could be used for coping with climate
change.[23] They discuss the existing and potentially
effective international mechanisms, emphasizing the role
of international agreements, international commissions,
and international conferences. This is followed by a
discussion of the various available strategies for mitigating the carbon dioxide-induced changes.[24] The focus
is on strategies that increase resilience to climate
change,[25] strategies that slow world-wide carbon dioxide
emissions,[26] and strategies that lead to improved
choices.[27] They call upon nation states to implement
these and similar strategies even if there be no global
climate change, concluding that "there is no need to
delay action and wait for firmer scientific evidence
about the carbon dioxide threat."[28]

The next six essays focus on various options of
atmospheric management. Professor Ved Nanda and Peter
Moore, Esq., discuss regional and multilateral initiatives, while George Sherk, Esq., studies unilateral
actions. Professors Edith Brown Weiss and Ray Jay Davis
are concerned primarily with the management itself.
Professor Howard J. Taubenfeld surveys the legal responses, and Armin Rosencranz, Esq. raises questions
regarding feasibility of actual international cooperation.

Ved Nanda and Peter Moore critically evaluate the
recent contributions of UNEP and other inter- and non-
governmental organizations and discuss the initiatives
taken on regional levels to prevent environmental degradation and to provide remedies.[29] They conclude that
"it seems imperative that more attention be paid simultaneously on several fronts, such as: environmental
education; environmental research and training; the development of both preventive and remedial policies, norms
and institutional experimentation with both regional and
international mechanisms; and improved and strengthened
measures of coordination."[30] To make the nascent environmental law effective, they consider it essential that
there be enhanced awareness in every country of the need
for environmental action, for it is equally imperative
that strengthened means of implementation on national,

regional, and international levels be established. They urge action on all fronts now.

George Sherk, Esq., focuses on unilateral approaches in an historical context.[31] He studies obstacles as well as options affecting unilateral action and concludes that although unilateral action alone is incapable of controlling all aspects of planned and inadvertent climate modification, multilateral mechanisms would have "little effect unless supported by nation-states."[32] Thus he urges that, in addition to the establishment of multilateral mechanisms, unilateral actions be encouraged for controlling climate modification.[33]

Professor Taubenfeld provides a broad survey of the legal implications of controversies created by human responses to and manipulation of atmospheric change, with the underlying sense that "[i]n many instances, the nature of the problems is already discernible and action is already necessary, for the effects of a failure to act immediately may not be felt for decades, and when these effects are felt, they may have become irreversible."[34] He raises the problem of national endeavors to the benefit of such interests as agriculture and industry, such as the reversal of river flow and conversion and harvestation of the great forests that are proving to have massive impacts on the cycles of nature. Against these practices, considered "domestic" issues by the actors and thus without the province of international regulation, international law has little authority. "Even raising the question may be considered an unwarranted interference with domestic concerns."[35]

Taubenfeld then discusses radical but inadvertent changes wrought upon the environment by the interaction of modern human activity and the workings of nature, and contemporary legal reactions to these problems. With respect to acid rain, for example, the ECE's recently made Convention on Transboundary Air Pollution calls for the joint development of control strategies in opposition to CO_2 pollution. While many nations accept the need for action, "[f]ew support any kind of international management or controls."[36] On the subject of chlorofluorocarbons -- a problem of uncertain, but global, consequences -- action has centered in the individual nations. A change in the behavior of those most responsible industrialized nations would have a substantial ameliorative effect.

Considering the 1972 Declaration of the United Nations Conference on the Human Environment,[37] Taubenfeld recognizes that, although the Declaration states useful norms and goals of the world community to salvage and recover the environment, yet there is not at present any mechanism for "resolving disputes as to scientific facts, for evaluating claims of injury and making binding awards, or for dealing with activities which affect the environment generally."[38] Taubenfeld concludes his essay by briefly analyzing several of the existing bilateral and multilateral arrangements for curbing the overwhelming dangers of unchecked abuse of the environment, urging the wider use of intergovernmental agreements and agencies, to the ultimate extent of "a responsible world government with the ability to assure the equitable distribution of the rights to life, to material welfare, and to security."[39]

Professor Weiss considers the carbon dioxide problem to be a challenge for the international community which can be met by breaking "new ground to handle [CO_2's] unique blend of political, economic, legal, and scientific issues."[40] After describing the predicament Weiss draws upon pertinent past prescriptions in international law for the management of carbon dioxide accumulations -- agreements on international rivers and international basins, air pollution, and the evolving law on the use of shared resources. It is in this historical context that she presents national and international preventive and adaptive strategies for carbon dioxide pollution. She deems it essential that "the CO_2 problem should be viewed foremost as a problem in developing the appropriate transition strategy for moving from a fossil fuel to a nonfossil fuel economy in the next fifty to one hundred years."[41]

While an intensified search is likely "for technical solutions, such as ways to expand the capacity of oceans to absorb carbon dioxide or to limit carbon dioxide emissions,"[42] she considers it essential to anticipate and address "the effects of possible climate change, particularly upon water supplies and migration patterns, and upon the general dislocation of a country's economy . . . ."[43] She advises "countries that are likely to be adversely affected to join together in measures to alleviate the stress and damage caused by climatic changes."[44]

Mr. Rosencranz draws the reader's attention to the inadequacy of the existing norms of international law and the available institutional structures in abating SO_x emissions sufficiently to remedy the problems caused by transboundary acid rain. The major causes are the unwillingness of nation states to comply with such norms unless it is in their national interests, and the ineffectiveness of the institutional structures to compel compliance. Rosencranz, too, broaches the subject of the ECE convention and its implications for air pollution control, but he sees in this "breakthrough" that ultimately "[n]o country has to alter its status quo unless it chooses to."[45] As a particular example of the obstacles to international cooperation, he discusses the Canada-United States SO_x treaty negotiations, based

essentially on mutual self-interest and yielding no
alleviation of the problem.

Optimistically, Rosencranz postulates a bright
picture will emerge when a nation's courts first use the
principles of the Stockholm Declaration in enforcement
against its offending nationals. Despite the unpromis-
ing current outlook, Rosencranz sees the greatest advantage of the Declaration and efforts like it as being
their effect in raising the world consciousness in
environmental protection, particularly the danger of
acid rain.

Professor Davis discusses the subject of weather
modification and legal options for governmental management of atmospheric resources. Among the means discussed is incidental control, or the control exercised
over weather modification activity, absent legislation
directed at such activity, by application of existing
regulation in related areas. For example: Because much
of cloud seeding is done from federally owned land,
"[i]ssuance or denial of permits [for special use of the
land] would be a form of control over cloud seeding
incidental to the general permit granting authority."[46]
Under this section Davis also deals with the applicability of traditional legal rules of resource rights and
tort liability.

He proceeds to discuss regulatory consequences of
the flow of information, permitting and licensing of
modification operations, the government's contract
capacity and its own modification activity, and, ultimately, outright prohibition of modification by governments. Davis' assessment of these elements of governmental control on weather modification culminates in a
recommendation that "there be careful consideration of
control devices so that a proper combination of them
will protect against indiscriminate weather modification
programs, and secure an atmospheric environment favorably affecting the quality of life."[47]

The conclusion seems inescapable that while further
study is required on the part of scientists and social
scientists into the technical issues of environmental
pollution and ways to alleviate it, it is essential
that international lawyers contribute to the future
of control in three particular areas: (1) enhancing
awareness, (2) refining norms and strengthening institutional structures, and (3) exploring preventive and
adaptive strategies in cooperation with science and
social sciences. This thrust is manifest in the concluding chapter of the book by Professor Ved Nanda.[48]
He, however, perceives that notwithstanding the global
nature of the CO_2 problem, regional and national
measures are likely to "provide the essential first steps
for both preventive and adaptive management strate-

gies."[49] He concludes on a sobering note: "In the final analysis, we in the latter part of the twentieth century must have the vision and the will to find creative solutions to this formidable problem."[50]

NOTES

1. Council on Environment Quality and U.S. Dept. of State, The Global 2000 Report to the President: Entering the Twenty-First Century, Summary Report (1980) [hereinafter cited as Global 2000].
2. International Union for the Conservation of Nature and Natural Resources, World Conservation Strategy: Living Resource Conservation for Sustainable Development (1980).
3. Id., Introduction.
4. D. Meadows, D. Meadows, J. Randers & W. Behrens, The Limits to Growth (Report to the Club of Rome 1972).
5. U.N. Dept. Public Information, Non-Governmental Organizations Section, World Environment, U.N. Doc. DPI/NGO/SA/80/6 (1980), at 1.
6. W. Kellogg & R. Schware, Climate Change and Society 1 (1980).
7. U.S. EPA Research Summary, Acid Rain 674 (1979). See also Global 2000 at 336.
8. Blumenthal, "Acid Rainfall in the Adirondacks Disrupting the Chain of Life," N.Y. Times, June 8, 1981, at 11, col. 1.
9. See World Meteorological Organization, Outline Plan and Basis for the World Climate Programme 1980-1983, WMO No. 540 (1979). See also W. Kellogg & R. Schware, Climate Change and Society 125 (1981).
10. Id., Appendix C.
11. P. 2 supra.
12. Pp. 4 to 12.
13. See p. 14 infra.
14. Id. at pp. 20-21 infra.
15. See p. 26 infra.
16. Id. at pp. 27-32 infra.
17. See at p. 33 infra.
18. Id. at p. 45 infra.
19. See p. 46 infra.
20. Id. at pp. 62-63 infra.
21. See p. 64 infra.
22. See p. 71 infra.
23. See p. 79 infra.
24. Id. at p. 85 infra.
25. Id. at p. 86 infra.
26. Id. at p. 87 infra.
27. Id. at p. 88 infra.
28. Id. at p. 89 infra.
29. See p. 93 infra.

30. Id. at pp. 116-117 infra.
31. See p. 124 infra.
32. Id. at p. 135 infra.
33. Id.
34. P. 145 infra.
35. Id. at p. 149 infra.
36. Id. at p. 153 infra.
37. Report of the United Nations Conference on the Human Environment (Stockholm, 5-16 June 1972), 1 U.N. GAOR (21st plen. mtg.), U.N. Doc. A/CONF.48/14 Rev. 1 (1972), reprinted in 11 Int'l Legal Mat. 1416 (1972).
38. Id. at p. 156 infra.
39. Id. at p. 161 infra.
40. P. 169 infra.
41. Id. at p. 167 infra.
42. Id. at p. 186 infra.
43. Id.
44. Id.
45. P. 198 infra.
46. P. 212 infra.
47. Id. at p. 220 infra.
48. See p. 227 infra.
49. Id. at p. 237 infra.
50. Id.

1
Climate and Climate Impacts

Robert S. Chen

I.

One often hears of the "global" nature of the
earth's climate, a reference to the obvious fact that the
atmosphere envelopes our entire planet. Less often emphasized, however, but perhaps more important, is the
pervasive nature of climate--the also obvious fact (once
stated) that the climate affects each and every one of us
in virtually everything we do. We wear clothing, construct buildings, and consume energy in large part to
shelter ourselves from the variable, sometimes adverse,
and often capricious conditions that characterize the
natural climate. The climate both permits and constrains
our cultivation of land, raising of livestock, and use of
water. It often determines our mode and route of travel,
whether by foot, bicycle, automobile, train, ship, or
aircraft. Climatic extremes such as storms, droughts,
and floods inflict many casualties and considerable damage
every year worldwide. These pervasive impacts of climate
on human activities, irrespective of nationality, race,
sex, or technological development, make international
consideration of climate fluctuations and their impacts
particularly critical.

II.

One of the most striking characteristics of our
climate is its great variability, both predictable and
unpredictable in nature. Temperature and other atmospheric conditions undergo regular daily and seasonal
fluctuations on local, regional, and hemispheric scales.
On the other hand. we experience many different and hard-
to-predict combinations of temperature, rain, snow, wind,
clouds, and so on--in any particular location for varying
periods of time. Occasionally, we encounter episodes of
anomalous climatic conditions that might be termed "climatic extremes" or "climatic hazards", such as floods,

droughts, hurricanes, tornadoes, windstorms, and hailstorms. Although these environmental phenomena are
sometimes themselves affected locally or regionally by
such human activities as the development of urban "heat
islands", deforestation, or water diversions, they are
almost entirely beyond our direct conscious control, that
is, through weather or climate modification.[1] Instead,
throughout history, humanity has adapted to its environment, depending on its artifacts and ingenuity for its
comfort and survival.[2]

As mammals, humans have the ability to maintain
internal physiological environments that are markedly
different from the outside environment. This ability is
of course limited in many respects--excessive cold or
warmth, cold combined with wind, extreme dryness or wet-
ness, or lack of food or water can, for example, tax the
unprotected human body beycnd its ability to cope. To
avoid these limits, we have learned either to modify our
local environment by wearing clothes and building shelt-
ers or to adapt our lifestyle and practices, for example,
or by planting different crops, transporting food and
other goods, or migrating. In essence, we engineer a
"human climate" around ourselves in which we can live and
work generally in greater comfort and safety than in the
natural climate. The difference between the "human" and
"natural" climates might be viewed as the climate's
impact--that is, the adjustments we must make to ensure
our survival and welfare amidst a constantly changing
and sometimes hostile environment.

A room is a good example of the human climate we
construct for ourselves. Among other things, we build
walls to stop the wind and help insulate from the cold or
warmth (or pollution) of the outside. We add a roof to
shelter from rain and snow, completing the enclosure. To
provide for light and fresh air when we desire them, we
place windows in our walls or skylights in our ceilings.
As we often require more light than available naturally
from the sun at particular times of the day or night, we
generate "artifical" light. In higher latitudes, we find
it necessary to burn fuels during some or all seasons to
provide heat for our comfort; in equatorial latitudes, we
have discovered that comfort, efficiency, and sometimes
even survival depend on protection from the heat through
ventilation or perhaps air conditioning. Since not every
location receives adequate amounts of precipitation, we
store and transport water, usually through a massive
infrastructure of reservoirs, wells, and pipes. Many of
the materials we use or consume last longer or have
greater appeal if stored in an environment different from
that normally found in a room; we therefore create "mini-
environments" such as refrigerators, root and wine cel-
lars, water heaters, and greenhouses that incorporate

different combinations of temperature, humidity, and
illumination.

Obviously, rooms also have a variety of purposes
beyond that of providing physiological shelter, including
the creation of additional usable space when we stack
them in a building and the psychological and cultural
functions of privacy and decoration, to name two. But in
large part, the energy, resources, and effort we devote
to shelter are an important component of the substantial
costs we incur in adjusting to climate. In the United
States, for example, space heating and air conditioning
constituted about 19 percent of gross energy consumption
in 1973, lighting and refrigeration were another 8 percent and water heating just under 4 percent.[3] Much
energy is also used to help equalize climatic differences
between regions--for example, many agricultural products
in the United States are transported across long distances from areas of good climatic conditions for particular crops to their markets. Thus, at least one-third,
and probably much more, of U.S. energy use is directly
attributable to the climate. This does not include
energy used indirectly, such as that involved in making
clothes, building houses, or constructing dams.

Major costs also arise because of our imperfect
ability to adjust to climate. Climatic extremes such as
storms, floods, droughts, and heat waves entail considerable direct losses. In the United States, for example,
damages from floods and frost each result in over a
billion dollars annually on average. Over five hundred
deaths per year on average are caused by climatic hazards
such as hurricanes, tornadoes, windstorms, snow in urban
areas, and lightning.[4] The combined heat wave and
drought during the spring and summer of 1980 led to over
1300 heat-related deaths and over $18 billion in agri-
cultural losses according to federal government estimates.[5] The droughts of the 1890's and 1930's had even
more devastating impacts, including the mass exodus of
one-half to three-fourths of the population from large
areas of the Great Plains in the 1890's and one-fourth
to one-half of the population in the 1930's. However, it
is notable that less migration has occurred during recent
droughts, perhaps due to society's increasing ability to
absorb and distribute adverse impacts.[6]

A significant part of the costs of climate stems
from the uncertainty inherent in natural climate variations. If we knew exactly when and where storms were
going to hit and droughts and cold spells occur, we
could in many instances take steps to minimize or ameliorate the impacts, for example, by conserving water or
fuel, shifting supplies, evacuating vulnerable popula-
tions, or even not bothering to plant crops. Although
such steps would not be "cost-less", they would most

likely be less than the costs of death, damage, and/or
disruption that might otherwise ensue. Unfortunately,
our ability to predict weather or extended episodes of
climatic extremes is extremely limited.[7] We must instead
rely on past experience to furnish us with some inkling
of the likely future variations of climate.[8]

Even if we did have perfect knowledge of future
climatic variations, we might still incur large costs in
maintaining our human climate. Obviously, the need to
heat, cool or otherwise modify undesired climatic conditions would still remain, although we might be able to
use our resources more efficiently. But more importantly,
adjustments to climate may require steps that are economically, socially, or politically difficult. The 1980
heat wave provided a simple but graphic example of this
in the United States--many elderly people in urban areas
suffered more than others from the heat because they kept
their windows closed for fear of crime. At an institutional level, various existing agreements that apportion
water rights among users in major U.S. river basins have
constrained efforts to conserve water and provide minimal
supplies to some during times of shortages.[9] In many
developing countries, the basic food transportation and
storage infrastructure is extremely primitive, so that
the establishment of food reserves or the distribution of
foreign food aid is difficult and may be of only limited
benefit.[10] Indeed, some experts claim that much of what
is usually considered to be the impacts of climate, such
as starvation and malnutrition during drought, may in
reality stem from the inability of some members of
society to obtain basic human needs; climatic hazards or
adverse episodes may aggravate this inability, but are
not the root cause. These experts cite a number of instances in which large exports of grain, meat, and cash
crops continued and even grew despite widespread drought
and famine conditions, as in the case of many Sahelian
nations in 1970-73 and India during the massive Bengal
famines of 1943-44 in which millions of people died.[11]
Such examples illustrate further that some groups in
society, e.g., the poor and elderly, may be more vulnerable to climatic variations than others.

Without adequate understanding of and information
about climate, our ability to adjust to climate variations is likely to be even worse. In the case of the
Colorado River Basin, water-management agreements were
based on incomplete streamflow records that failed to
show the true long-term climatic variability characteristic of the river system--much less water is now known
to be available on average than was apparent when the
agreements were reached.[12] In building the Tacoma
Narrows Bridge and the Hood Canal Bridge in Washington
state, engineers failed to account adequately for the

likelihood and effect of extreme wind conditions: both
bridges collapsed due to high winds.[13] We are also just
beginning to realize that there may be subtle intercon-
nections between climatic episodes worldwide that could
have important implications for society. For example,
Table 1 illustrates quantitatively the statistical
relationship between good or bad weather in one crop-
growing region and good or bad weather in others for
major grains of the world. Interestingly, bad weather--
and therefore reduced yields--in, say, a wheat-growing
area is more likely to be accompanied by bad weather in
other wheat-growing areas than one might expect if the
weather in these areas were totally independent. This
effect is more pronounced for all grains together. In an
area of increasing reliance on international food trade
to balance national "food budgets," such correlations
could have significant international ramifications.[14]

Whether individuals, groups, nations, or the world
as a whole view climate impacts as either beneficial or
adverse depends largely on personal values, perceptions,
priorities, and paradigms. An unusually warm winter, for
instance, might be considered beneficial by homeowners
and government inflation-fighters, but adverse by the
insulation industry, fuel companies, and oil-exporting
nations. Although the net impact might be small from a
macroeconomic perspective, the redistributive implications could be significant from a policy viewpoint.
Moreover, the pervasive nature of climate ensures that
each individual is likely to experience more than one
kind of impact, say a decrease in heating bills but an
increase in food prices (stemming perhaps from greater
insect damages due to reduced destruction of their eggs
during a warmer winter). Residents of cold climates
might assign extra importance to changes in heating costs
while those in warm climates might be more concerned
about food price fluctuations.

III.

It is clear from the previous discussions that any
analysis of climate's impact on society needs to recognize the degree to which climatic factors are embedded in
society's structure and adjustment processes, including
our rooms and buildings, our agricultural, transportation
and energy systems, our economic and institutional arrangements, and our values and decisions. Indeed, subtle
interrelationships and feedbacks between climatic phenomena and social processes may greatly influence, if not
dominate, the ensuing impacts. For example, although the
more benign climate of the so-called "sunbelt" regions of
the United States may be an important factor that drives
the continuing migration of people from northern to

southern states,[15] other social factors such as growing
population mobility and an increasing number of retirees
certainly play key roles, since climatic differences
existed long before the migratory trend emerged. This
complex and dynamic interaction of climatic factors,
social structure and process, and values suggests that
policies to reduce or ameliorate climate impacts must
explicitly take into account both the physical and social
systems involved, as a number of authors and groups have
recognized.[16]

Thus far, the focus has been on climatic variability
and relatively short-term natural fluctuations of climate (days to a few years at most). We have seen that
such variability interacts with human activities and
social organization in a variety of ways. What if the
earth's climate were to undergo long-term changes (on the
order of decades to centuries)?

First, we should note that such changes could take
different forms, including shifts in mean climatic conditions (e.g., a warmer or colder or a wetter or drier
climate on average), changes in variability (e.g., more
or less frequent climatic extremes), alterations in
regional or temporal patterns (e.g., shifts in desert
areas, earlier or later monsoons, and milder or harsher
seasons), and changes in the "mix" of climatic phenomena
(e.g., more or less clouds, rain, snow, mail, sea ice,
glaciers, storms and lightning). Any of these, or some
combination of them could conceivably occur and in some
cases are known to have occurred. Moreover, the time
pattern of changes could range from a very slow, gradual
shift to sudden alterations as thresholds are surpassed
or perhaps even oscillatory behavior.

Second, any climatic changes may be extremely hard
to detect, given the natural variability of "noise" of
climate, the limited climatic data available, and our
present lack of understanding of the climate system and
the mechanisms of climate change.[17] For example, air
temperatures at the earth's surface have been directly
measured (using thermometers) at only a few locations for
more than a century and even now are not monitored
regularly over much of the globe, especially the oceans.
Measurements of other climatic parameters such as precipitation, cloudiness, humidity, and solar insolation
are often subject to large errors, limited in geographic
coverage, and short in duration. Such limitations could
make it difficult to distinguish between temporary
anomalies and long-term trends, between global mean
changes and shifts in regional patterns, or between
various possible causes of climatic change, whether natural or anthropogenic. Proxy methods to help determine
the nature of past climates and satellite remote sensing
to provide more complete worldwide monitoring are among

the techniques that could improve our ability to detect potential climatic changes and ascertain their origin.

Third, society may also change substantially on comparable time scales, as evidenced by the swift growth of the world's population in recent years, some 75 percent from 1950 to 1980.[18] The rapid societal transformation implicit in this statistic could itself radically alter the ability of society to adjust to environmental or other changes. A further complication is that rapid and uncontrolled growth of this kind might well be accompanied by widespread environmental changes such as deforestation, dust and carbon dioxide emissions, and river diversions that could significantly affect climate on regional or global scales.[19]

Despite these (and other) complexities, it is clear that long-term changes in climate could have very important impacts on society and human welfare. Such changes would certainly disrupt present patterns of adjustment to climatic variability and, unless our understanding of climate improves dramatically, increase the uncertainty associated with future climate fluctuations. As with present-day climate impacts, redistributive impacts could be immense, even if the climate improves on average for the world's population. For example, a scenario that garners much attention in the United States is the suggestion that a warmer climate could lead to a northward shift of the "climatic zone" that is suitable for growing wheat, possibly endangering American pre-eminence as the world's leading grain exporter.[20] If the poor are generally more vulnerable to disruption than others, as some have suggested,[21] existing problems such as famine or international mass migration now associated with current climate variations could substantially worsen. This might aggravate national instabilities or international tensions. More optimistically, certain climate changes might well improve agricultural or other opportunities for large segments of the world's population. Unfortunately, we now lack the ability to make credible predictions of the magnitude or even direction of these kinds of impacts.

IV.

It is evident that, whatever their precise form, climate changes, like present-day climate variations, will have pervasive impacts. The nature and magnitude of these impacts will depend greatly on the degree of our understanding of climate and the capability for and constraints on adjustment of individuals and groups within society. Two imperatives emerge from this discussion that are especially relevant for any international actions to deal with the possibility of climate change.

First, improvements in our understanding of present-day
climate variations and their impacts are a prerequisite
to learning more about the nature and impacts of climate
changes. Second, suitable adjustment alternatives must
be developed and the mechanisms established to ensure
that such alternatives are acted upon effectively when
necessary. Both of these tasks will require thoughtful
and self-critical analysis by those now involved in
international scientific and political activities. Both
will require extraordinary worldwide collaboration and
effort. Yet the challenge is clear: our response to
climate must be as pervasive as climate's influence is,
since we are all in this together. As Adlai E. Stevenson
has aptly stated: "We all travel together, passengers on
a little space ship, dependent on its vulnerable supplies
of air and soil; all committed for our safety to its
security and peace, preserved from annihilation only by
the care, the work, and I will say the love we give our
fragile craft."[22]

NOTES

 The views expressed in this paper are those of the
author and do not necessarily represent the views of the
Climate Board or the National Academy of Sciences.

 1. Present efforts at weather or climate modification are primitive and at best marginal in success. See,
for example, Chapter 6 of S. H. Schneider, with L. E.
Mesirow (1977), The Genesis Strategy (New York: Delta).
 2. This environmental paradigm is gaining greater
recognition among social scientists recently; see, e.g.,
R. E. Dunlap (1980), "Paradigmatic Change in Social
Science," Am. Behav. Sci. 24:5-14 and K. Butzer (1980),
"Adaptation to Global Environmental Change," Prof.
Geographer 32:269-78. It is distinct from the environmental determinism suggested by some such as E. Hunting-
ton (1915), Climate and Civilization (New Haven: Yale
Univ.).
 3. These figures include both residential and commercial sectors. See Tables 2-3 of S. H. Schurr, J.
Darmstadter, H. Perry, W. Ramsay, and M. Russell (1979),
Energy in America's Future: The Choices Before Us (Baltimore: Johns Hopkins Univ.).
 4. White, G. F., and J. E. Haas (1975), Assessment
of Research on Natural Hazards (Cambridge, MA: M.I.T.
Press), p. 68.
 5. Center for Environmental Assessment Services
(1980), Climate Impact Assessment, United States--Annual
Summary 1980, National Oceanic and Atmospheric Administration, Washington, D. C.

6. Warrick, R. A. (1980), "Drought in the Great Plains: A Case Study of Research on Climate and Society in the USA," in Climatic Constraints and Human Activities, IIASA Proceedings Series Vol. 10, J. Ausubel and A. K. Biswas, Eds. (New York: Pergamon), pp. 93-123.

7. See, for example, N. Nicholls (1980), "Long-Range Weather Forecasting: Value, Status, and Prospects," Rev. Geophys. Space Phys. 18:771-788 for a recent review.

8. For a more detailed discussion of the use of climate data and information, see Climate Board (1981), Managing Climatic Resources and Risks, Report of the Panel on the Effective Use of Climate Information in Decision Making (Washington, D. C.: National Academy Press), 51 pp.

9. See, for example, R. G. Fleagle and A. H. Murphy, "The Use of Climate Information in Management of the Columbia River," in Climate Board, id. note 8, at 23-35, and C. W. Howe and A. H. Murphy, "The Utilization and Impacts of Climate Information on the Development and Operations of the Colorado River System," in Climate Board, id. note 8, at 36-44.

10. Glantz, M. H. (1977), "The Value of a Long-Range Weather Forecast for the West African Sahel," Bull. Am. Meteorol. Soc., 58:150-158.

11. See, for example, R. Garcia (1978), "Climate Impacts and Socioeconomic Conditions--Edited Transcript of Remarks Delivered at the Workshop" in International Perspectives on the Study of Climate and Society, Climate Research Board, National Academy of Sciences, Washington, D. C., pp. 43-47; and F. M. Lappe and J. Collins (1978), Food First: Beyond the Myth of Scarcity, revised ed. (New York: Ballantine), pp. 79-96.

12. Howe and Murphy, supra note 9, at 36-44.

13. The Tacoma Narrows Bridge collapsed due to standing waves induced in the suspension-type bridge by winds. For a detailed analysis of the destruction of the Hood Canal Bridge, see R. J. Reed (1980), "Destructive Winds Caused by an Orographically Induced Mesoscale Cyclone," Bull. Am. Meteorol. Soc. 61: 1346-1355.

14. Data from Economic Research Service (1975), "The World Food Situation and Prospects to 1985," Foreign Agricultural Economic Report No. 98, U.S. Department of Agriculture, Washington, D.C., p. 73. Time series of individual crop production for the period 1953-73 in the different regions were used in this analysis.

15. See, for example, Bureau of the Census (1976), U.S. Statistical Abstract, 1976 (Washington, D.C.: Government Printing Office), p. 14, or more recent versions.

16. For example, Scientific Committee on Problems of the Environment (1978), "SCOPE Workshop on Climate/ Society Interface," SCOPE Secretariat, International

Council of Scientific Unions, Paris, 36 pp.; Panel IV
(1980), "Social and Institutional Responses" in Workshop
on Environmental and Societal Consequences of a Possible
CO2-Induced Climate Change, CONF-7904143, Carbon Dioxide
Effects Research and Assessment Program, U.S. Dept. of
Energy, Washington, D.C., pp. 79-103; and R. Kates
(1980), "Improving the Science of Impact Study," proposal
by the Scientific Committee on Problems of the Environment, International Council of Scientific Unions, Paris,
19 pp. See also note 6 supra.
    17. See, for example, R. A. Madden and V. Ramanathan
(1980), "Detecting Climate Change Due to Increasing Car-
bon Dioxide," Science 209:763-768; and A. D. Hecht and
J. Imbrie (1979), "Toward a Comprehensive Theory of
Climatic Change (Editorial Introduction)," Quat. Res.
12:2-5.
    18. Mauldin, W. P. (1980), "Population Trends and
Prospects," Science 209:148-157.
    19. See, for example, SMIC (1971), Inadvertent
Climate Modification: Report of the Study of Man's
Impact on Climate (Cambridge, MA: M.I.T. Press); or,
more recently, R. E. Munn and L. Machta (1979), "Human
Activities that Affect Climate" in Proceedings of the
World Climate Conference, World Meteorological Organiza-
tion Rept. No. 537, Geneva, pp. 170-209. For an inter-
esting discussion of river diversion proposals in the
USSR, see T. Gustafson (1980), "Technology Assessment,
Soviet Style," Science 208:1343-1348.
    20. For example, see Panel V (1980), "Issues Assoc-
iated with Analysis of Economic and Geopolitical Conse-
quences of a Potential CO2-Induced Climate Change," in
Carbon Dioxide Effects Research and Assiessment Program,
supra note 16, at 107.
    21. Ad Hoc Study Panel on Economic and Social
Aspects of Carbon Dioxide Increase, Letter Report to the
Office of Science and Technology Policy (available from
Climate Board, National Academy of Sciences, Washington,
D. C.), 11 pp.
    22. Stevenson, A. E. (1965), speech given before the
U.N. Economic and Social Council, Geneva, Switzerland,
July 9, 1965, as quoted by R. Dubos (1968), So Human an
Animal (New York: Scribner's), pp. 261-262.

TABLE 1. Changes in Grain Production Due to Weather in 25 Major World Grain-Producing Regions. Source: Economic Research Service (14).

Grain	Without covaria- tion[1]	With covaria- tion[2]	Percent differ- ence
	million metric tons		
Wheat	11.59	13.28	+15
Rice	4.58	4.81	+5
Corn	5.68	6.24	+10
Barley	5.13	5.42	+6
Oats	i.95	2.23	+14
Sorghum-millet	2.06	2.23	+8
Rye	0.91	1.03	+13
Coarse grains (incl. rye)	8.22	10.04	+22
All grains (incl. rice)	14.74	21.08	+43

[1] Assumes that yield fluctuations are not related.
[2] Includes interrelation between yield fluctuations.

2
International Climate Program Planning and Research

William W. Kellogg

I. A TRADITION OF COOPERATION IN METEOROLOGY

In order to understand the recent developments in international cooperation regarding weather and climate, it is useful to review briefly the history of this co-operation. Collaboration in exchanging weather and climate data goes back many centuries, for during the age of exploration seafarers made a point of collecting and exchanging their observations of winds, weather, ocean currents, and magnetic field directions. However, it was only during the last century the need was clearly recognized for some more systematic arrangements. Thus, in 1872 in Leipsig and the following year in Vienna, the International Meteorological Organization (IMO), led by the American Naval Officer Matthew Maury, was organized. Its first Chairman was the head of the Dutch Weather Service, C.H.D. Buys Ballot.

The history of the IMO is marked by a succession of efforts by the weather services of the world to create a permanent system for data exchanges. This became increasingly possible with the advent of the telegraph and then, after the turn of the century, by radio. During the sixty-year period of its existence (1891-1951) this very active collaboration between weather services and scientists continued through a nongovernmental organization; indeed it was not until the IMO changed its name and became a specialized agency of the United Nations that it became an intergovernmental body.

It is interesting to inquire why this active and operationally-oriented organization preserved its non-governmental character so long. It appears that there was a sincere desire on the part of the governing committee of the IMO to involve nongovernment (non-weather service) meteorologists and to preserve the organization as a truly scientific forum. The weather service directors, starting in 1891, were nevertheless invited to the IMO meetings as private "experts."

25

Following World War I two other organizations were established that also dealt internationally with weather and climate information. These were the International Commission for Air Navigation (ICAN), an intergovernmental body, and the International Union of Geodesy and Geophysics (IUGG), a nongovernmental body.

During this period there were two important developments in the history of the IMO: one was the creation of a permanent Secretariat in DeBilt in 1926--the IMO president then was Dr. Van Everdingen. Another important move came in 1935 when regional commissions (later called "associations") were established. These associations have continued to be very active, and demonstrate the value of such regional cooperation in the field of meteorology and climatology.

When the IMO became a specialized agency of the U.N. in 1951 and moved its Secretariat to Geneva, there was a problem of deciding how the IMO, now called the World Meteorological Organization (WMO), and the IUGG would function vis-a-vis each other. Both organizations were anxious to guide international research in meteorology and climatology, and there was a considerable amount of rivalry some of which still lingers on today. However, during the International Geophysical Year (1957-1958) a set of working arrangements were agreed upon, whereby the WMO recognized IUGG "as an international forum for the achievement of meteorology as a science," while the IUGG in turn recognized WMO as having "the primary responsibility for the international organization of meteorology."

It seems that these vague statements provided enough oil on the troubled waters of international politics to allow the two organizations to work together through the years. Further arrangements followed between the WMO and the IUGG, and also the IUGG's parent organization, the International Council of Scientific Unions (ICSU), which will be discussed later.

II. THE SATELLITE ERA

The earliest efforts to work together internationally in meteorology were largely devoted to exchanging climatological information. However, with the advent of aviation and radio communication, the emphasis rapidly shifted to making weather forecasts, which was a new kind of game. Nothing has influenced the field of meteorology and high-speed global communications more than the advent of earth satellites, starting in 1957.

The advantages to meteorology of satellites not only looking down at the earth as a whole but also in communicating information from place to place rapidly were quickly perceived, even before the first satellite was

ever launched. In 1961 President Kennedy, speaking to
the U.N. General Assembly, called upon all countries to
mount a new international initiative to improve the
science of weather forecasting "in the light of developments in outer space." The U.N. General Assembly
adopted resolutions asking WMO, together with ICSU, to
work out a plan for this new thrust.

A program plan was hurriedly worked out by two
eminent consultants, Dr. Harry Wexler (U.S.) and Dr. Vic-
tor Bugaev (S.U.), and in 1963 the WMO Congress endorsed
the new concept of a world meteorological forecast and
communication system called the World Weather Watch
(WWW).

These developments in outer space led a number of
scientists to consider new techniques to obtain a complete three-dimensional and continuous picture of the
atmosphere, based on both ground-based and satellite
observations. In 1967, after a lengthy negotiation
between the WMO and ICSU, the proposed Global Atmospheric
Research Program (GARP) was agreed upon. The formula for
cooperation between the WMO and ICSU was fairly elaborate, but it involved a Joint Organizing Committee (JOC)
that was appointed jointly by the two organizations, and
a Joint Planning Staff (JPS) that was housed and largely
supported by the WMO Secretariat. The GARP was subsequently adopted by the WMO as an essential part of the
WWW, and the WMO Congress called it "an entirely research-oriented cooperative international meteorological
and analytical program with the goal of producing a
vastly improved understanding of the general circulation
of the global atmosphere--a goal thus shared with the
WWW." In this way the operationally-oriented WWW and the
research-oriented GARP were declared as united, at least
for the time being.

The GARP proved to be a great success, and has often
been termed a model of scientific collaboration. There
were a number of major efforts under this program, one
being the GARP Atlantic Tropical Experiment (GATE, 1974)
and the First GARP Global Experiment (FGGE, 1978-1979).
Data from both of these major field programs, especially
the FGGE, are still being analyzed and have provided a
definite increase in our scientific knowledge and in our
ability to test forecast and climate models against a
detailed description of the real atmosphere.

III. ADOPTION OF THE WORLD CLIMATE PROGRAM

As noted earlier, the emphasis in the decades following World War I was mostly in the direction of improved short-range weather forecasts and the communication system to allow these forecasts to be made. However,
there was a growing realization that along with the day-

to-day weather climate was an important consideration as well.

In May 1979 the Congress of the WMO, with most of the more than 140 member states voting, enthusiastically adopted the World Climate Programme (WCP). This new program then became official on January 1, 1980, with the WMO assuming responsibility for its overall direction and coordination. While the action taken by the WMO Congress will be reviewed at its next meeting in 1983, it seems likely that the WCP will continue as an established intergovernmental program for many years to come.

This action is significant for a number of reasons, the most obvious being that it is tangible evidence that climate--its variability and changes--is now clearly recognized as an important factor governing the affairs of society, both in the developed and developing countries. This action also calls attention to the fact that climate is a universal concern, and that the application of climatic knowledge in planning national socioeconomic development has created the need for more effective international cooperation in this field. Furthermore, the growing realization that human activities, especially the release of carbon dioxide into the atmosphere from the worldwide use of fossil fuels, will probably affect the global climate in the next few decades places a heavy responsibility on the community of nations and the scientific community to understand the impending climatic change and prepare for it.

With all these considerations in mind the architects of the WCP (of which the author was one) proposed that it have two general objectives:

> To improve knowledge of the natural variability of climate and the effects of climatic changes due either to natural causes or to mankind's activities;

> To assist decision-makers in planning and coordinating climate-sensitive activities of economic, environmental, and social significance, so that these become less vulnerable to climatic variations and change.

In line with these objectives, it was decided to identify four components or subprograms of the WCP, namely:

World Climate Data Programme (WCDP)
World Climate Applications Programme (WCAP)
World Climate Research Programme (WCRP)
World Climate Impact Studies Programme (WCIP)

Although the titles are fairly descriptive, a description

of each of these components follows.

The WCDP is devoted to improvement in the organization and archiving of the many kinds of climate-related data needed for both research and applications. It is recognized that the great mass of twice-daily synoptic meteorological observations that are made routinely for weather forecasting and flight operations (under WMO's World Weather Watch program) are already being exchanged and archived in the three World Data Centers for Meteorology (in Washington, and Asheville, in Moscow, and in Melbourne). The WCDP is especially directed at helping developing countries organize their own local or regional climatic data banks.

If the WCAP receives the support it deserves, through it the developing countries will obtain help in applying a knowledge of climate and climate statistics to everyday activities of operations and planning for development. This will be arranged by the WMO through exchanges of experts and in some cases the provision of computers for analyzing climate data and applying it to specific problems. This can be carried out at the regional level as well as the national level.

The WCRP is devoted to research on the physical basis of climate change and improving theoretical models of the climate system. It is not a new program, since it is in a very real sense a continuation of the climate-related part of the highly successful GARP, which has already been described. As under GARP, the WCRP will be jointly directed and coordinated by the WMO and the ICSU-- a unique arrangement between an intergovernmental agency and a nongovernmental body that has turned out to have a number of advantages, though it was originally opposed by certain countries on political grounds.

The last of the four subprograms, the WCIP, is the newest and least well formulated at the present time. It has four stated objectives, namely:

(a) Improvement of our knowledge of the impact of climatic variability and change in terms of the specific primary responses of natural and human systems (such as agriculture, water resources, energy, ocean resources and fisheries, transportation, human health, land use, ecology and environment, etc.);

(b) Development of our knowledge and awareness of the interactive relations between climatic variability and change and human socio-economic activities;

(c) Improvement of the methodology employed (e.g., case studies and models) so as to deepen the understanding and improve the simulation of the interactions among climatic, environmental and socio-economic factors;

(d) Determining the characteristics of human societies at different levels of development and in different natural environments which make them either especially vulnerable or especially resilient to climatic variability and change and which also permit them to take advantage of the opportunities posed by such changes.

In establishing the WCIP the WMO Congress invited the U.N. Environment Programme (UNEP) to assume responsibility for this component of the WCP, and UNEP's Governing Council has agreed to do so. The exact way in which WCIP will be organized, administered, funded, and reviewed is still being worked out between UNEP and WMO; and it has been UNEP's hope that certain international research organizations, such as IIASA, IFIAS, and SCOPE would be willing to undertake certain kinds of impact studies under UNEP sponsorship. Negotiations have already begun.

At present the WMO has rather vaguely assigned the overall responsibility for overseeing the scientific and technical progress of WCP to the WMO Scientific and Technical Advisory Committee (STAC), but the STAC has so many other responsibilities that it is likely that some more suitable apparatus will be needed for directing the WCP. Several alternatives are being studied by the WMO with the help of a series of interagency and intergovernmental meetings convened by the WMO. It is recognized that several other U.N. agencies besides UNEP have a stake in the WCP, the main ones being FAO, UNESCO, and WHO; and, as mentioned earlier, ICSU has an official shared responsibility for WCRP.

It is important to realize that, while WMO and the other U.N. agencies can help to arrange for international programs like the WCP, they cannot do the work. The financial support and scientific and technical talent to carry out the WCP and its four component programs must come from the governments who are members of WMO (or groups of governments like the EEC or ASEAN), with only a dribble of "seed money" from WMO and UNEP. Thus, while the WCP appears to have the support of most governments, as evidenced by the action of the WMO Congress, its success will depend on the continuing commitment of many governments to the program, together with their weather services, national academies of science, and interested individuals.

V. CONCLUSION

This brief survey has shown how meteorologists, climatologists, and oceanographers have had a long history of international collaboration. The first impulse for this came from sailing captains who needed climatic information, and then came the telegraph, the radio, and the airplane, all of which led to emphasis on current weather information and weather forecasts.

Now climate appears to be back in the middle of the international stage, and we have every reason to see a growing interest on the part of governments and the scientific community to work together in this area. This collaboration is being carried on by the intergovernmental bodies such as the WMO, UNEP, UNESCO, and so forth, together with the nongovernmental scientific bodies under ICSU.

Climatic change and variability are now seen as a common theme which can unite a number of other world efforts to preserve our forests, our arable soil, and our water resources. Climate is seen as but one of a set of global environmental problems, along with population growth and famine, which the world will have to face in the years ahead. It may very well turn out to be the most important and all-inclusive factor in the long run.

3
International Organizations and Climate Change

John S. Perry

Air flows quite freely over political boundaries, so it is almost inevitable that any concerns we might have about climate would have an international flavor. In today's world, this implies the involvement not only of the politicians and diplomats of individual nations, but also of the specialized international organizations whose number and mass have grown so mightily since the last great war. This paper presents some informal reflections on how these international organizations can contribute to the resolution of the issues raised by man's possible impact on climate.

I

First, I must disclaim any great authority in the complex arena in which international organizations work. Whatever experience and opinions I have gained have come from middle-level staff work in a few international programs dealing with but a small subset of the vast menagerie of international organizations. My insight might thus be likened to "a scribe's view of the Roman Empire," certainly not to Caesar's.

With that disclaimer aside, I would begin by asserting that the international organizations really do not <u>do</u> very much in concrete terms. There are exceptions, of course: Food and Agriculture Organization (FAO) and the World Health Organization (WHO), for example, have some operating budgets and actually manage a few active and highly useful projects. But by and large, it is people in individual nations, directed and funded by national programs, who do things. The international framework acts primarily as a means to motivate national efforts and to "lubricate" their interactions. As I will suggest later, this can be a very important function indeed. However, the main point is that we cannot reasonably expect the international organizations to solve any specific problem; at best they can only help the nations

33

acting in concert to reach a solution.

The international organizations have a difficult
time carrying out even this limited function. One fundamental reason is suggested above. The real entities in
the world that collect taxes, control trade and travel
across lines on the map, and make wars are the sovereign
nations that form the constituency of the international
organizations. Sovereignty, defined as "freedom from
external control," is an uncommonly powerful and durable
notion; sovereign nations defend their national interests
and viewpoints with great vigor and tenacity. Thus, the
international organizations are constituent organizations. In order to perform any useful work at all, and
indeed to remain in existence, they must seek a consensus
on the part of their constituents. This ceaseless striving for agreement and consensus, almost at any cost,
leads to a certain vagueness and blandness in their
actions and outputs. True, they can be driven away from
blandness by strong interests of key nations, by the
availability of financial or other support for one set of
actions over another, and even by the strength of will
and personality of certain key individuals. For example,
the effectiveness of the World Meteorological Organization (WMO) in the recent past was due in large measure to
the influence of the U.S. Permanent Representative,
Robert M. White. On the whole, however, a typical international organization resembles much more closely the
tenants' association of a condominium apartment house
than an army platoon.

Moreover, nations are in fact represented in each
international organization through specific individuals
who owe allegiance not only to their nations but also to
specific interest groups within their nations. Thus, the
Permanent Representatives to the WMO are the heads of
weather services, the delegates to FAO governing body are
Secretaries of Agriculture, doctors look after the World
Health Organization, and professors mostly worry about
ICSU. Hence, each international organization reflects to
some extent a global constituency that cuts across national boundaries. WMO often acts like the "International Union of Weather Forecasters," FAO like a "global
4-H," the International Council of Scientific Unions
(ICSU) like the "World's AAUP." These common interests
are in healthy competition with often divergent national
interests, sometimes permitting international organizations to do useful things despite deep conflicts between
their national constituents. WMO has been able to keep
the world's weather data collection system going through
periods in the turbulent post-war years when little else
worked. WHO has managed to wipe out smallpox, even on
the deeply divided Indian subcontinent.

On the other hand, these differences in constituency between organizations sometimes hamper their cooperation as badly as similar special interests impede the achievement of consensus within a single nation. This is particularly evident when conflicts between constituencies within nations become reflected in the international arena. For example, the Soviet Union is represented in the WMO through the State Committee for Hydrometeorology and Control of Natural Environment, which not only runs the meteorological and hydrological services, but also operates a network of related research institutions. The Soviet adhering body to ICSU, however, is the USSR Academy of Sciences, which also operates a number of research institutions dealing with meteorology and hydrology. Internally, these institutions and their parent bureaucracies compete vigorously, perhaps even acrimoniously, for personnel, missions, and funds. These internal conflicts cause continuing friction in cooperative WMO-ICSU projects which, by all reason and logic, should be marriages made in heaven. In the lengthy planning of the Global Atmospheric Research Program, for example, the USSR's predominantly exemplary and constructive participation was frequently interrupted by diatribes against joint WMO-ICSU efforts that could only be understood in the context of internal Soviet interagency rivalries. This externalization of internal conflicts is a topic that would merit a few doctoral dissertations.

Superimposed on the web of divergent national and technocratic interests is a patchwork quilt of national styles or personalities that may induce nations to pursue similar goals in widely dissimilar ways. For example, the Russians--individually the warmest, most open-hearted, most generous of people--are institutionally rigid, suspicious, formalistic, and bureaucratic. Involvement of the Soviets in any international undertaking guarantees great parties, lasting respect and affection for the Russians who happen to be allowed to participate, and endless difficulties in agreeing on the text of the final report. The Americans, on the other hand, tend to be impatient with bureaucracy and procedure, excessively pushy for instant results, and infuriatingly moralistic. We are impatient with process, and look for final solutions--often where a controlled process of piecemeal accommodation is in fact the only solution. Other nations have similarly individual styles that are reflected in the positions their delegations take in international forums, the way in which they adjust these positions to approach a consensus, and the way they must justify their actions to their masters at home. These differences in national styles slow and muddle the process of international discussion and planning. How-

ever, at their roots, the differences reflect real and
important differences in values between nations. A truly
useful international consensus demands that all parties
concerned are not only content with the conclusions
reached in terms of their individual value systems, but
also with the process by which they are expressed and
implemented. It takes time to evolve such a consensus.

The organizations also have their idiosyncratic
styles, virtues, and vices. Some -- WMO is the best example I know -- are blessed with superlatively efficient
machinery. The reports of WMO meetings of all kinds are
without exception completed and in delegates' hands in
the languages required on the last day of the meeting.
Others -- discretion bids me to withhold names -- can
take three months to turn out a one-page letter. In
part, these differences may arise from the charters of
the individual organizations and the degree of authority
granted to their Secretariats and Executives. But, as an
alumnus of Geneva, I suspect also that Swiss efficiency
tends to be a bit contageous.

The unfortunate incidents associated with the Tower
of Babel created a growth industry for language teachers,
translators, and interpreters; they also made the processes of international coordination a lot more difficult.
First, it is inherently difficult, and sometimes impossible, to translate exactly from one language into
another. Even when the same words exist in both languages, they convey different clouds of meanings: "coordination" means different things to an American, a
Frenchman, and a Russian. Secondly, the process of working through interpreters and translators of widely varying ability can be unspeakably frustrating and exhaust-
ing. In desparation, people turn to some common language
to get the work done. In the good old days, there was a
widespread common language, Latin, that was non-contro-
versial because it was safely dead. No doubt everyone
wrote it badly, and no one knew how the native Romans
spoke it. More recently, French served as the language
of diplomacy. This was probably a fine choice: no doubt
almost everyone spoke and wrote it equally badly except
for the French, and they aren't particularly interested
in communicating with anyone but themselves anyway.

Now, however, English has become de facto the universal language. While this is nice for us North Americans, it is not an unmixed blessing for the process of
international dialogue. I suspect that there may be some
inherent linguistic problems with English: its vocabulary
may be too big, with too many subtly shaded choices of
words for every nuance of meaning. Certainly its historical rather than its phonetic orthography and infinite
peculiarities of usage make it at best an imperfect in-
strument. (Try to explain in German how one can chop a

tree down and then chop it up.) More seriously, however,
the use of a very live and widely spoken language as a
vehicle for international discourse gives its native
speakers and a few foreign polyglots a significant, and
rather resented, advantage in international doings. The
English-speakers tend efficiently and cozily to sort
things out to their satisfaction with marginal participation by a few token English-speakers from heathen lands.
The results are then wrapped up as faits accomplis in the
necessary languages for minor tinkering by the rest of
humanity. I exaggerate, of course: with time and effort, major issues penetrate the linguistic barrier.
However, the day-to-day mechanics of international discourse are unfairly dominated by English and its native
speakers. A working language in which everyone is equally awkward would greatly improve the democracy of international dialogue. Esperanto was not a bad idea at all.

As the original owners of this continent knew well,
most of the work of the world is done by Indians, not by
their chiefs. The day-to-day work of international organizations is done by their secretariats and the international civil servants who assist them. Since these
people come from many nations and many disciplines, they
reflect the national and special-interest constituencies
noted above. Languages hinder or unfairly help them, as
the case may be. Moreover, these men and women find
themselves in a complex of conflicting motivations and
constraints. They cannot escape sympathy and indeed
loyalty to the constituencies from which they come. Yet
their day-to-day work in their organization and their
advancement within it depend largely upon their loyalty
to its institutional goals. On the one hand, the international civil servants are pampered, privileged, and
overpaid with a dazzling array of tax exemptions and diplomatic privileges. On the other hand, they live in
cultural islands in foreign countries, cut off from the
human exchanges of their own cultures, the processes that
keep us all sane. They struggle with the exasperating
logistics of getting anything done in a strange country,
they see their kids becoming Swiss or New Yorkers or
Viennese, they undertake gruelling trips through unspeak-
able countries to sit in meaningless meetings. It is a
life that breeds a certain kind of schizophrenic appara-
tchik who is more comfortable with form than substance,
who has but one little niche in the whole world in which
he can conceivably earn a living, and who will defend to
the death the tiniest shred of bureaucratic trivia that
may tend to buttress his job. The problems with which
the international organizations deal are inherently important, and good people are attracted to work on them.
But the grinding down process inexorably operates as
these people acquire experience and seniority. Thus,

energy and competence tend to be inversely related to
rank in the international organizations.

Despite these problems, the secretariats are where
the work is done, and where the decisions made by the
governing bodies are implemented or frustrated. It is
therefore important that the secretariats operate efficiently, intelligently, and objectively. To do this,
they need a balanced mix of good people from all the
nations that really care about international affairs.
Americans are at present under-represented in both
quality and quantity in the international organizations.
We are not really comfortable in other lands, speaking
other tongues. We have it pretty good at home, and find
little attraction in living in Nairobi for half a decade
or so. We tend to be at once impatient with foreigners
for their funny ways, and at the same time defensive and
fearful that these ways may be better than ours. These
factors deeply rooted in the national psychology of a
still nouveau-riche superpower are hard to eradicate,
and hamper the recruitment of the best qualified Americans for long-term service in the international organizations.

One barrier to work in international organizations,
however, could be easily eradicated. We are the only
major nation that insists on taxing income of its citizens received overseas and derived from the international
organizations to which we contribute.[1] Citizens of other
nations receive a net income free of tax. U.S. citizens
pay tax on their combined income from all sources, and
are then reimbursed by their organization for the portion
of tax attributable to service with the organization.
The organization then claims reimbursement from the U.S.
State Department for this refunded tax. This ludicrous
procedure has many effects, all bad. The organizations
expend significant resources in reviewing tax returns,
computing adjustments and reimbursements, and bookkeep-
ing. This costly process is paid for by the U.S. and
other nations: the money could be put to better use.
The individual's tax return becomes unbearably complicated: the instructions for the partial exemption form
used by overseas taxpayers are as lengthy as the entire
instructions for the domestic return. Moreover, the net
effect is that the individual is taxed in a high bracket
on allowances intended to equalize overseas and domestic
living costs, while his domestic investment income is
taxed at a still higher bracket on top of an artificially ballooned salary. If the United States wished to
take but one single step to increase its presence and
influence overseas, the best choice would be to eliminate taxation on income of U.S. citizens received from
international organizations.

II

So far, I have only presented a catalogue of the bad news about international organizations. There is good news also -- not as lengthy a catalogue, but perhaps more important. First, one can often enough do some things better in an international environment than at home. Consider an international scientific working group addressing some technical question. Participants have been carefully chosen, it is an honor to take part, and the best people from a dozen countries may partici- pate. Indeed, it is sometimes easier to assemble a really high-quality, balanced group internationally than domestically. Once they are safely assembled in some pleasant city, their phones ring much less frequently than at home. They have come a long way, and they do not mind staying long enough to do some useful work. The international context and the distance from home foster an objectivity and balance that is hard to achieve surrounded by domestic bureaucracy.

Multilateral activities in the context of the inter- national organizations also offer a path around the ob- stacles of conflict between individual nations. Count- ries that have severed all other ties with each other often still maintain common ties with a network of inter- national organizations and can cooperate usefully through these mechanisms. As mentioned earlier, the flow of weather data between East and West continued virtually unimpeded during even the chilliest phases of the cold war, and today U.S.-Soviet cooperation in climate re- search and environmental problems moves ahead quite nicely despite Afghanistan and Sakharov.

While the worlds of finance and trade, and indeed of peace and war, are mostly run by the great powers, the world of the international organizations tends to be dom- inated by the developing countries. There are more of them, each with a voice and a vote, and each with less to lose and more to gain by free exercise of voice and vote. On the one hand, this democracy run wild tends to para- lyze the organizations or push them into unrealistic and fruitless positions. But at the same time, the organiza- tions provide the less-advantaged majority of the human race with a means of participating in a dialogue with the globe's rich and often arrogant minority on something like an equal footing.

There is one more unique and surpassingly important job that international intergovernmental organizations can do, but I will defer its discussion for the moment. However, the remarks made so far suggest my personal assessment of their role and utility. It is difficult for them to carry out bold and sweeping solutions to problems, and we should not expect them to be more

effective in imposing solutions upon nations than the
nations are in imposing solutions upon their own internal
constituencies. However, where a consensus on some problem exists or is achievable, the international organizations can perform a limited but useful range of things to
foster coordinated national actions to address the problem. As long as the nations of the world continue to
encounter problems that extend beyond their borders, they
will need some degree of international organization expressed in a network of specialized institutions. Like
all other works of man, they do not work perfectly; but
they may work well enough to ease considerably the inevitable stresses of running one world with many sovereign managers.

III

The efficacy of international organizations is best
tested by considering some specific problem, and climate
change provides a convenient experimental subject. Specifically, let us consider the issue of man-made climate
change resulting from increasing atmospheric carbon dioxide. The outlines of the currently accepted scenario
are no doubt familiar enough.[2] Combustion of fossil
fuels for energy, conversion of woodlands to farm and
pasture, and degradation of the soil release carbon dioxide to the atmosphere. Some of it is absorbed in the
oceans or captured by plants, but about half remains
airborne. Since it is an important absorber of heat
radiation, it tends to increase the atmosphere's efficacy
as a blanket for the earth against the cold emptiness of
space. Calculations show that significant climate
changes can result -- marked warming at high latitudes,
changes in storm tracks, shifts in temperature and precipitation patterns throughout the world. Plausible pro-
jections indicate that these changes may become percep-
tible within this decade and troublesome in the early
years of the next century.

While one may quibble with or question the details
of this scenario, its scientific credibility is at least
sufficient to merit serious thought by the inhabitants of
the planet in which this great geophysical experiment is
being conducted. The social and economic implications
were considered in the spring of 1980 by a panel of the
National Research Council.[3] They highlighted three
characteristics relevant to our discussion of the efficacy of international organizations. First, they noted,
the issue is inherently international. All nations need
energy for maintenance of their present welfare and development of the basis for a better future. Thus all
nations will contribute to some degree to combustion of
fossil fuels supplying that energy. At the same time,

all countries are accustomed to the climate in which
their social and agricultural infrastructures have
evolved: climate change is inherently global and would
at least inconvenience everybody. Moreover, many nations
now depend on other people's climates: much of the world
relies on continued high productivity in a handful of
grain-producing areas for cheap and reliable food supplies, at least for emergency relief. The CO_2 scenario calls for changes in climate on a time scale that is
quite short in terms of the evolution of the infrastructure of human society. It is hard to see how rapid climate change could fail to discomfort a significant number
of the world's nations.

The panel also noted the problem's inescapable link-
age to other intensely controversial issues. Energy production is already in many countries the focus of heated
debate between pro- and anti-nuclear proponents, environmentalists and promoters of economic growth, and "soft"
versus "hard" energy advocates. Internationally, the
issue is linked to north-south conflicts -- rich coal-
burners versus poor tree-choppers, food-eaters versus
food-producers, industrialized users of energy versus
marginal subsistence economies, coal-holders versus re-
source-poor potential consumers. Climate changes would
certainly amplify the population- and poverty-driven
pressures for migration that are already proving difficult to handle.

Thus, although the CO_2 issue must be dealt with
globally, it divides the nations of the world and the internal constituencies within them. The uneven distribution of fossil fuels and of potential climate changes
implies that there will be losers and gainers. One could
speculate that the north might come out ahead. By and
large, the northern countries hold more coal resources,
depend less on agriculture as a mainstay of their GNP,
and have overly cool climates to start with. Developing
nations in tropical climes might suffer. While models
suggest that their climate changes might be quantitatively smaller, their traditional agricultural systems are
specialized to the present climatic regime, and they have
little capital to invest in major adaptations to their
infrastructure. As the Sahelian drought of the early
1970's demonstrated, poor societies find it hard to
adjust to climatic fluctuations under modern conditions.
On the other hand, the 1976 European drought caused only
minor and transient distress. Climate change may be perceived as damaging the poor because of profligate energy
consumption by the rich. Such a perception would appear
more likely to generate divisive claims and counter-
claims for damages and compensation than to foster uni-
fied management of a global problem.

Carbon dioxide is therefore not just a climate issue. Any scenario that postulates a large increase in airborne CO_2 and a changed global climate also implicitly postulates a radically different economic climate. Most of the known fossil fuel resource consists of coal, and most of that is concentrated in but three countries -- the United States, the Soviet Union, and China. The massive increases in carbon dioxide usually projected can be realized only if these three countries are induced by some means to dig vast amounts of coal out of the ground, transform it into some feasibly transportable energy-carrying medium, and ship it to the multitude postulated to want it and to use it for welfare and development. A few moments thought on the economic system that might motivate such enormous transfers of real wealth might lead us to conclude that climate change would be the least of our worries in this new world. Certainly, our present difficulties in inducing a handful of Arabs to distribute their wealth should give us pause.

The alternative is no more credible or manageable. Suppose that the holders of coal keep it for themselves, smugly congratulating themselves on saving their landscapes from acid rain and the world from climate change. While basking in these environmental blessings, the rest of the world scratches for energy, improvising helter-skelter nuclear developments, tearing up their landscapes for biomass energy, but mostly just remaining poor. Is this a more manageable, a happier world? I think not. I think that the CO_2-climate issue simply poses in sharply-defined terms a complex of problems that we will have to grapple with as a global community no matter how we get our energy, use our land, and care for our environment.

Discussion of the issue generally focuses on the implications of a doubling of atmospheric CO_2 in the course of a long transition period to a sustainable energy system over a period of fifty years or so.[4] Mesmerized by the notion of a doubling sometime in the next century, we tend to act as though we could leave serious concern about the problem to the inhabitants of that far-off world. Such a notion is both irresponsible and unrealistic. There is no magic threshold in the influence of CO_2 on climate. We have already increased airborne CO_2 by more than ten percent, and we will surely add more each year. It is virtually certain that we have changed and are changing ever faster the subtle workings of the global climate system. The changes may be masked by the vagaries of weather and the consequent fluctuations of our best estimates of current climate. There is no convincing evidence, in my view, that man-made climate changes have yet hurt or helped anyone. But our inability to detect changes quantitatively and unequivocally does not prove that they are not there. Indeed, a paper recently presented to the Australian and New Zealand Association for the Advancement of Science[5] relates recent climatic trends in Australia to increases in CO_2. It seems increasingly likely to me that climatic damages allegedly inflicted upon energy-poor developing nations by the world's rich energy-burners will become major international issues within this decade.

IV

As we have seen, international organizations are poorly equipped to provide quick and easy solutions to such inherently divisive and controversial problems. Yet it is inevitable that the CO_2 issue will occupy an increasingly prominent place on international agendas in the years to come. Its controversial, divisive aspects will work their way through the internal constituencies of the world's nations and in varying forms be expressed in the national constituency groupings within the international organizations. The issue is not precisely matched to the terms of reference of any single international organization. All are likely to become involved. Thus, consideration of the CO_2-climate issue by the international organizations will bring to the fore their worst attributes, not their best.

We are therefore fools if we look to the international organizations for salvation in this complex hornets' nest of CO_2/energy/climate problems. We are no less fools if we do not look to them. For the international organizations can indeed effectively help the sovereign nations to deal with global issues where real shared interests and consensus exist. Our impotence in the face of this problem is not due to institutional deficiencies, but to the lack of the foundation of consensus upon which institutions, however imperfect, can build.

The prime need is to build a global community of interest and a shared consensus on the scientific, physical, social, and economic factors that will shape our future. A long and tortuous process of consciousness-raising and consensus-formation will have to be structured and patiently carried out before actions that can never be imposed but must evolve jointly can be devised and implemented. The international organizations cannot mandate this consensus, but they can serve as effective vehicles for its development. They can carry out this delicate process not through sophisticated and delicate diplomacy, but through what they are best at -- pure bureaucracy. While all international organizations have lofty goals, what they actually do is to carry out a never-ending process of agenda-constructing, meeting-holding, report-writing, letter-sending, and memorandum-circulating.

Those who are impatient with the lack of visible, concrete results of this process fail to see that the process itself is the end product. The agenda for an international meeting causes a chain of bureaucratic busywork through the establishments of other international organizations and the individual nations. Position papers, speeches, letters must be written, the composition of delegations must be discussed, financial support for travel and preparation must be secured. All of these generate a flood of paperwork that flows upward and downward and laterally through the administrative and executive structures of nations and organizations. These internal chains of discussion and coordination entrain hordes of people, from clerks to the foreign minister in issues that the workings of their own national governments might never bring to their attention. Eventually, real live people hop on planes, sit in meetings, gossip at cocktail parties, and have implanted in their heads ideas that would never have taken root if the ground had not been tilled by the ponderous workings of international and national bureaucracy.

This subtle process of involvement and entrainment can be mightily effective. A possible apocryphal anecdote deals with a World War I program of the U.S. Department of Agriculture to induce American housewives to use more of the cheap and plentiful "variety meats," i.e., hearts and brains and kidneys. Panels of housewives proved mightily ineffective in devising promotional campaigns to sway their contemporaries. But someone observed with amusement and dawning understanding that the members of the panels were feeding their husbands all sorts of stuff that had never entered their kitchens before! Those of us who remember the 40's and lived through the 60's should be vividly aware of the effectiveness of consciousness-raising and consensus-formation. In 1945, an executive who searched for a qualified female or minority-group member for a senior position would have been considered a madman in most parts of this land of liberty. Today, one who failed to do so would be considered criminally obtuse. This change has not been wrought by laws alone. The same national dialogue that made the laws possible changed our values to make them inevitable. By involvement in a process dealing with problems and solutions, the knowledge of what is wrong and how to fix it becomes a natural part of one's equipment for dealing with the world, not an alien intrusion in an established order.

After beginning on a pessimistic note, I thus find myself ending with optimism. It will be difficult indeed for us to provide for the continued welfare of every-increasing numbers of our brothers and sisters on this

very nice but awkwardly small planet. Energy, carbon
dioxide, and climate pose an interlinked complex of
issues for us to resolve. While they cry out for coordinated study, their most natural and immediate implications are profoundly divisive. The international
structure evolved in this century cannot produce any
magical solutions. However, by gradually injecting the
issues into the international agendas, we can set in
motion a global process of involvement, entrainment,
consciousness-raising, and consensus-formation that will
lay the groundwork for whatever we must do for our global
condominium.

NOTES

    1. The new tax law is designed to bring about the
change suggested here. See, e.g. Wall St. J., Jan. 16,
1981, at 34, col. 5.
    2. Geophysics Study Committee, Energy and Climate
(National Academy of Sciences, Washington, D.C., 1977),
158 pp.; Climate Research Board, Carbon Dioxide and
Climate: A Scientific Assessment. (National Academy of
Sciences, Washington, D.C., 1979), 22 pp.
    3. Letter report of an Ad Hoc Panel on Social and
Economic Aspects of Carbon Dioxide Increase, Thomas C.
Schelling, Chairman (1980). Available from the Climate
Research Board, National Academy of Sciences, Washington,
D.C.
    4. International Institute for Applied System
Analysis, Energy in a Finite World (Laxenburg, Austria,
1981).
    5. Tucker, G. B., Global Climatic Response with
Emphasis on Regionality and Predictability (CSIRO Divi-
sion of Atmospheric Physics, Aspendale, Victoria 3195,
Australia, 1980).

4
Food and Climate: Basic Issues and Some Policy Implications

Stephen H. Schneider

I. INTRODUCTION

A. Climate: One Factor in the Food Situation

One principal way in which climatic changes affect human affairs is by their impact on food production. But the production, distribution, storage and consumption of food depends on many interconnected factors, of which climate is but one. These include land, labor, capital, energy, level of technology, "know-how", population size, social organization, economic power, and (not least) climate. This paper concentrates on the interactions between food and climate, recognizing, however, that such interactions have restricted meaning outside of the over-all context of food production, distribution, and consumption issues. Thus, anyone contemplating policy matters on food-climate issues will need to consider many of these interconnected factors.

B. The Mid-1970's Food Crises

The example of the mid-1970's illustrates this well. In 1972 a series of adverse weather events motivated the Soviets to purchase some 20 million metric tons of grain from the United States and Canada. This "wheat deal" marked the beginning of a five-year period of rising grain prices, shrinking grain reserves, and famine conditions in some countries. It was triggered, in large part, by the combination in 1972 of Soviet and Central African droughts, weakness in the Indian monsoon rains, floods in Pakistan, and near-collapse of the Peruvian anchovy catch due to heavy fishing pressure at a time of shifts in winds and ocean currents. However, the food reserves and trade policies of major exporting nations were as important as the weather in creating the food price spirals and shortages of the mid-1970's.

46

II. CASE STUDIES OF FOOD AND CLIMATE INTERACTIONS

A. Subsistence Crises in 1840's: The Irish and
   Dutch Potato Famines

A look at a historical example of a climate-related
food disaster can show how these many factors come into
play. In the late 1840's cool damp weather contributed
to the blight that reduced potato harvests in Ireland.
Death and migration claimed some 50 percent of the Irish
population in this notorious famine. The Irish were
heavily dependent on this single crop, and this dependence coupled with the size of their population pushed
food demands close to food supplies in good production
years. Thus the blight-induced production shortfall
triggered catastrophe. But at the same time that the
Irish were enduring their crisis, two other countries
were coping with a similar problem, and faring much
better. Potato blight also occurred in the Netherlands.
Although it led to increased deaths and decreased births,
these calamities were some 15 times less severe than in
Ireland. Moreover, disaster-related migration from
Holland was a trickle compared to the masses of people
leaving Ireland.
Holland's southern neighbor, Belgium, also endured
harvest failures at the same time. But it did so virtually unaccompanied by death rate increases anywhere near
those of even the Netherlands. According to economic
historian Joel Mokyr the differential vulnerability of
these countries can be attributed primarily to economic,
social and political infrastructural differences among
them, in particular their relative levels of industrialization and the diversification of their respective economies. Hence, economic development and diversification
are seen as the key to avoiding devastating subsistance
crises. Improving food processing methods, better preservation techniques, and cheaper storage facilities meant
that during the nineteenth century the cost of insuring
oneself against harvest failure had declined.
But resilience against harvest failure is even more
complicated than technological developments. Along with
industrialization comes agricultural commercialization
which results in a larger proportion of consumption.
This implies that fewer people would be living at subsistence levels, and also that the wherewithal would
become available to allow purchase of food from others in
times of local harvest failures, whether climatically-
caused or not. In order to trade food, infrastructure
needs to be developed for trade, storage and transport;
and indeed such an infrastructure evolved with industrial
and economic development.

B. Marginal Farming: Developments in Northwest Europe
   Over the Past 1000 Years

It has already been noted that vulnerability of
farming to climate is a complex mix of physical, biological, technical, economic and social factors. This can
be demonstrated by reconstructing agricultural settlement
and abandonment. By examining aerial photographs, historical records and on-site remains in the Upland region of
Southeast Scotland, geographer Martin Parry found evidence that in the 12th century (i.e., the medieval climatic optimum), much of the land that is now covered by
heather was farmland, and that between 1600 and 1800
(i.e, during the Little Ice Age) agriculture retreated
far down the hillsides. In mapping climatically-marginal
areas in Northwest Europe, however, it is necessary to
rely on highly generalized agrometeorological data, which
include the number of growing months with a mean temperature above 10°C and the amount of change in average annual precipitation deficits during the months of July
through September. But even in regions where climate can
be shown clearly to be a strongly limiting factor in crop
yields, the interpretation of the relative role of climate and other social and biological factors on the via-
bility of farming is difficult.

C. Perceptions of a Disaster: The 1970's Sahelian
   Drought

Although it is clear that climate is only one factor
in the food situation, even its supporting role can be an
issue of debate. There are conceptual frameworks by
which different analysts perceive food and climate problems. Their proposed solutions to such problems then
naturally follow from their perceptions of the causes of
the problems. The Sahelian drought of the early 1970's
highlights these varying perceptions, some of which are
often keyed to ideological biases.

One of the most noted recent climatic events was the
drought in the Sahelian region of north central Africa.
The drought decimated nomadic tribes and their livestock,
ruined the crops of sedentary farmers, contributed to
increased death rates and malnutrition, helped create
political turmoil, and led to massive international publicity and relief programs for the inhabitants of the
Sahel. The "causes" of these impacts are hotly debated.

1. One point of view (e.g., R. A. Bryson) is that
long-term climatic stress in the Sahel is a major contributor to the human misery that ensued, and that this
climatic stress is related to large-scale climatic
trends.

2. Others (e.g., H. E. Landsberg) have argued that droughts in the Sahel are a regular feature of the climate, and the 1970's case was not generically different from previous such extremes. The problem in the Sahel, they contend, was related to lack of foresight in anticipating and dealing with precedented bouts of bad weather, not an adverse climatic trend.

3. Still others (e.g., M. H. Glantz) contend that the impact of the drought on the inhabitants of the region is more a function of social and political factors than climate. Modern technology, they point out, if presented in a piecemeal fashion, can actually increase the impact of droughts.

4. Another group of analysts (e.g., F. M. Lappe and J. Collins) see the Sahelian crisis as even more deeply embedded in social factors. They argue that the colonial legacy of the Sahelian countries to produce cash crops has been continued by the elites who took over after independence. These officials encourage annual cropping, rather than long fallow periods typical of traditional practices. Thus, in order to maintain cotton exports for the French, farmers were forced to expand their cotton acreage by reducing the planting of millet and sorghum. Continual cultivation rapidly depleted the soil, necessitating still further expansion of export cropping at the expense of food crops and pasture land. This, these analysts say, is how modern technology, infrastructure and political influence increased vulnerability of subsistence farmers and nomads to climatic and other stresses in the Sahelian region. The Sahelian governments over-emphasized export crops to earn foreign exchange so that government bureaucrats and other better-off urban workers could live an imported lifestyle.

5. To oversimplify somewhat, the causes of the Sahelian disaster in the latter view could be called "social structural". In an alternative view (e.g., S. Wortman and R. Cummings) of this subsistence crisis, which could be called "technology-transfer, market-oriented", the implementation of more modern technology and supporting infrastructure -- adapted to special Least Developed Countries (LDC) conditions of high labor intensiveness -- is considered the best answer to prevent repeat disasters. The development of market economies which provide incentives for farmers to raise their productivity is the safest route to the elimination of subsistence crises. One objective of agricultural development, these analysts agree, must therefore be to allow individual families to produce a surplus for sale so that total output of a locality exceeds total local require-

ments and permits sales in urban centers, other rural
regions or in international markets. Imports required
for higher productivity must be purchased and markets for
products must be established. In short, traditional
farmers must be brought in to the market economy.

6. The important issue for our purposes emerging
from the Sahelian case is that different suggestions for
solutions to food and climate problems are often based on
implicit conceptual beliefs. Thus, care is needed to
make as explicit as possible the separation of factual
and value issues in policy analyses of food and climate
interactions.

D. The U.S. Plains: Making of a Food Giant

1. Increasing Yields Over the Past Century

The U.S. plains began food production amidst controversy as to whether this region of highly variable
weather could ever sustain high food productivity. After
the early success during the Homestead era of the late
1800's, drought in the 1890's created serious outmigra-
tion of farm settlers and began a pattern of "boom and
bust" farming, where good weather years and high production were followed by drought years bringing economic
ruin and serious episodes of soil erosion. The most
severe drought occurred in the 1930's, known to history
as the "dust bowl era". Average wheat and corn yields
dropped by 50-75% and much topsoil was lost. The dust
bowl deepened the great economic depression of the 1930's.
However, the lessons of the dust bowl led to the
establishment of the U.S. Soil Conservation Service,
whose extension agents help farmers to protect soil reserves. Moreover, the advent of new genetic crop strains
better adapted to the climate of the region and the increasing availability of fertilizer (and expansion of
credit institutions to allow financing of technological
farming) followed in the aftermath of the dust bowl.
Grain yields have increased from two to three hundred
percent since the 1930's. The productivity of the U.S.
plains has contributed to the present place of the United
States as (by far) the leading grain exporting nation.
Since the 1930's the average variability of crop
yields from year-to-year in the U.S. plains has decreased
relative (i.e., as a percent of mean crop yields) to long
term trends in crop yield. (Absolute variability in crop
yields, however, has increased, even though relative
variability has declined.)

2. Climatic Effects on Year-to-Year Crop Yield Variability: An Unresolved Controversy

This decrease in relative crop yield variability has led to a major controversy. On one side some agriculturalists contend that not only are increasing trends in crop yields due to technology, but decreasing relative yield variability as well. This belief helped to motivate the United States to begin to liquidate government held food reserves in the early 1970's, a policy which contributed to food price spirals in the mid-1970's.

Other agriculturalists disagree, arguing that it was the unusually good weather after 1957 that led to decreased relative crop yield variability and that a vigorous program of food reserves is needed to hedge against a return of conditions as bad as the 1930's or mid-1950's.

Recent work by geographer Richard Warrick seems to suggest that, if one accounts for relative decrease in the severity of the weather, then relative crop yield variability in the U.S. plains is roughly unchanged over the era of technological expansion. (Of course, absolute year-to-year crop yield variability still seems to have increased.)

The probability, for example, of one year of unfavorable weather (i.e., reduced yields by more than 10%) for the U.S. corn is 23%, and the probability of two such unfavorable years is 11%.

Although this important issue of whether technology lessens or increases vulnerability to climate is still not definitely resolved, in the 1970's the U.S. plains have become such a major component of the world grain export markets that the impacts of fluctuations in food productivity in this granary are now felt worldwide.

E. The World Food Situation in the Past 20 Years

1. World Total Grains

a. Recent global trends. With the sole exception of 1974, each year in the past fifteen saw an increase over the previous year in total world average utilization of grains. And, with the exception of the "bad weather" years 1972, 1974, 1977 and 1979, world total grains production and total grains yields increased annually, both at a rate of about 2-4% per year. The increase in grain utilization, also at a rate of about 3% per year, reflects both the almost 2% annual increase in world population size and a world average increase in absolute standards of eating -- particularly the indirect consumption of grains used as animal feed in Eastern Europe, Japan and other relatively affluent places. In the developed countries (DC's), per capita food consumption increased well ahead of population growth, whereas in the LDC's (as a whole) food production per capita has remained about the same level over the past ten years.

b. Per capita food production by region. It would be misleading, however, to conclude that all LDC's merely "stood still" with regard to per capita food production. Indeed, while some large regions, such as Latin America or South Asia, maintained fairly steady per capita standards, other regions, such as East Asia, made considerable gains whereas still other regions, in particular Africa, saw further erosion in already low per capita levels of food production. Furthermore, within these large regions some nations have experienced considerably different standards over the past ten years than the regional average; and even within single nations vast inequities in per capita food production and consumption levels continue to exist. To refer to a "world grain situation", then, cannot provide more than a gross overview of a heterogeneous distribution of local food situations: some bad, some good, some steady, some deteriorating and some improving. Thus, great care is needed before applying world average food statistics to a regional context.

c. World grain security. Earlier it was mentioned that world food production climbed at an average of about 3% annually. This increase is partly a result of an increase in harvested area in the mid-1970's, but primarily it reflects an increase in grain yield from a spread of modern methods worldwide. The interannual fluctuations in production, however, (which became larger in the 1970's than over the previous decade) are largely attributed to unfavorable weather fluctuations. 1972, for example, saw a 3% decrease in world grain production over 1971 and 1974 saw a 4% drop over 1973. The 1972 shortfall occurred as major grain exporting nations, in particular the U.S., were implementing policies of liquidation of government held grain stocks and reduction of direct food aid to LDC's in favor of a new role as grain exporter to countries willing (and able) to purchase tens of millions of metric tons of grain (in particular, the U.S.S.R.).

The effect of the combination of these policies and the weather-induced shortfalls in 1972 and 1974 cut grain stocks by about one third. If one measures "World Grain Security" as the yearly grains in stock divided by the total annual utilization of grains, then one sees that from 1970 to 1975 world grain security dropped from more than 15% to about 10%. This drop helped create steep price rises of two to four hundred percent in major grains and soy beans after 1972, and stages of plant development, growth can be highly sensitive to one or more climatic factors, a sensitivity which can alter greatly over the life cycle of that crop. Consider a specific example: the application of an additional inch of water to spring wheat grown in the northern Great Plains of North America. While this generally improves yields, especially if it is added at the very beginning or the middle of the growing cycle, it may, however, reduce yields if the water is added near harvest time. Since climatic anomalies, such as short-term excesses in rainfall (or drought), will, in general, occur at different stages of growth of different crops in different places, there can be considerable compensation of negative and positive effects. That is, yield decreases in one crop in one place from, say, less-than-normal rainfall, are likely to be compensated, to some extent at least, by yield increase from other crops. Furthermore, droughts in one place can be compensated by excess rain in others.

Although we might take some comfort from such compensatory effects of climatic anomalies, large-scale (i.e., over a major granary) negative yields can occur, as can simultaneous "bad years" in more than one major grain region. For example, for wheat in the United States and India over the past 65 years, the probability of a single "unfavorable" year (defined as yearly wheat yields reduced by 10% below long-term trend line) is 17%; two such consecutive unfavorable years occurred only 9% of the time between 1910 and 1975. In Canada, on the other hand, unfavorable wheat years are more probable, having percentages of 33% and 17%. In the U.S.S.R. the situation is complicated, since spring and winter wheat regions are geographically dispersed. Nevertheless, a general characteristic is that the U.S.S.R. is more likely than the United States or India to have a single unfavorable year, but less likely to have a long sequence of them (again based on data from the past 50 years). The probability, as noted earlier, of simultaneous unfavorable yields in the United States and the U.S.S.R. is about 7-8% for one year, but generally less than 1% for two or more consecutive years. Thus there is an uncomfortable probability of both strings of unfavorable years in one region and the possibility of simultaneous bad years in several major granaries. It is these "infrequent" events which require policy considerations to minimize severe impacts.

2. Food Reserves and Distribution Systems

Short-term climate-induced fluctuations in food production are likely to continue at the level of several

percent production variations from year to year on a
world-wide average, and many tens of percent variations
on a regional basis from year to year. These fluctuations in food production can be damped out primarily by
the mechanism of sufficient regional food stocks and distribution systems. Unfortunately, there is little world
effort at maintaining or managing food stocks as a hedge
against climate-induced regional shortfalls. This is
because of squabbles over who should contribute to the
stocks, pay for the contributions, and who should determine where they are stored, when they are released, and
at what levels they are to be maintained. Bickering over
such non-climatic issues merely increases the probability
that simultaneous negative fluctuations in food production in several grain-growing areas will once again set
off a worldwide spiral of good price instability and
contribute to increases in malnutrition and famine-
related deaths in poorer, food-insufficient nations.

3. Maintenance of Diversity

Modern agriculture has tended to substitute a
mono-culture of highly productive genetic crop strains
for the lesser productive, but more diverse, set of
species of traditional agriculture. The danger of such
loss of diversity is potential vulnerability to single
pests or a negative climatic fluctuation. Even without
abandoning high yield varieties, agricultural policy
makers can reduce their nation's vulnerability to climatic fluctuations by encouraging the planting of a
variety of different crops in different places, planted
at different times. Particularly in warmer climates
where more than one crop can be planted per year, multiple cropping not only can raise yields, but offers some
measure of natural pest resistance and minimizes vulnerability to a short-term climatic anomaly. The more
diversity added to cropping patterns, the less likely it
is that single stressful events would prove catastrophic.

4. Minimize Vulnerability by Using Existing Climatic Information

Techniques such as the development of widely
adapted crop strains or implementation of irrigation
systems can mitigate the negative effects of climatic
variations. Knowledge of the frequency and severity of
climatic extremes can help in planning the details of
these strategies. Also, cultivation practices should be
consistent with local climatic conditions, in order to
minimize long-term loss of the productive potential of
the land through soil erosion or other environmental
damage. For example, in places where intense, but inter-

mittent rainfall is common, special attention to farming
practices which minimize soil erosion needs to be considered. The application and dissemination of existing
climatic information in a local context is an important
job for extension services. Efforts to increase the
effectiveness of such services are now under way as a
priority concern of the World Climate Programme.

5. Long-term Climatic Trends

One final climatic issue is the outlook for long-
term climatic trends, particularly those which might
arise as an inadvertent consequence of industrial and
agricultural activities. There is extensive and often
contradictory literature on this subject. Perhaps the
strongest statement that could be made which reflects
the state-of-the-art knowledge (and its uncertainties) is
that there is a weak (but evolving) concensus that the
"greenhouse effect" from increases in atmospheric CO_2
(from the growing use of fossil fuels and expansion of
deforestation and some kinds of agriculture) is likely to
cause man-induced global climatic changes some time
around and after the turn of this century. Such changes
could be unprecedented in modern experience. Specific
regional climatic scenarios from a CO_2-induced overall
planetary warming are fragmentary and speculative, although preliminary investigations suggest that some
regions would be adversely affected, some improved and
others unaffected, depending on where one is and what
activities and infrastructure are in place in the future.
Sea level rises of several meters are possible, but again
the probability and timing remain speculative. Although
this evolving area of concern bears close watching in the
food-climate context, for the next decade or so, at
least, it is much more likely that minimizing our vulnerability to repeated bouts with precedented short-term
climatic anomalies will be the priority food and climate
problem.

B. More General Food Policy Considerations

1. Food Aid: A Question of Values and Ideologies

The volume of food aid from DC's to LDC's decreased steadily from the mid-1960's to mid-1970's, with
the EEC being the only significant exception. The U.S.
aid, for example, in the late 1960's averaged about 15
mmt annually, dropping to about 3.5 mmt by 1974. The
EEC, on the other hand, more than doubled its annual food
aid over the same period, but the total amount of aid in
1974 was only about 1.4 mmt.

Considerable controversy is generated over whether food aid is in or against the interests of either donor or recipient nations, and these controversies generally are rooted in differing ideological perspectives as to whether LDC's should opt for either independent or interdependent food relationships with DC's. Other points of controversy center around issues of population growth, with some analysts arguing that food (or other kinds of economic or medical) aid should only be given to those nations in dire need of emergency help who are, at the same time, striving to increase local food production so it has hope of coming into balance with long-term population growth levels. The policy called for is triage. These analysts (e.g., W. and P. Paddock) would deny food (or other development) aid to any country not actively working to bring down its rate of population growth.

Other analysts (e.g., G. Hardin) argue that food aid to LDC's only allows more people to live in misery over the long run and thus they advocate a no-aid policy they call "lifeboat ethics". It is severely criticized often on moral grounds.

Other analysts (e.g., those in nongovernmental organizations like the Ford Foundation) argue that world food and other economic aid, coupled with transfer of high technology and market-oriented economic infrastructure, is needed to solve LDC food problems.

Yet others (e.g., P. Ehrlich or E. Schumacher) contend that wholesale technology transfer from DC's to LDC's will create both environmental and economic catastrophes, and recommend the development of so-called "appropriate technologies" which match the local environmental, economic and social conditions of each region.

Other analysts (e.g., R. Garcia or F. M. Lappe) contend that until social reform or revolution wrests power from "elites" and turns control of food producing capacity over to local inhabitants, no food aid or technology transfer will help the vast majority of people in LDC's. They blame the "Green Revolution" techniques for increasing the wealth differences between rich and poor in LDC's.

Finally, other analysts (e.g., S. H. Schneider) suggest that aid is appropriate, but that the terms of its amount and duration should be negotiated between donors and recipients based on the principal of creating economically and environmentally sustainable levels of food (and other commodities) consumption. Such a "global survival compromise" is offered as a middle course between extreme views of environmental, social or economic advocates.

While these contrasting views are clearly based on value differences of the analysts, they all depend on

contributed to an increase in famine conditions in some
LDC's.

Fortunately, increased planted area and
reasonably favorable weather conditions worldwide in
major granaries in 1976-79 allowed some rebuilding of
grain stocks, and world grain security levels in 1980
are at about the 14% level-- slightly below where they
were before the food crisis of 1972 occurred. Although
grain prices have stabilized somewhat (at higher levels,
of course) since 1975, price instability -- and expanded
famine conditions -- are not at all unlikely in the next
few years should unfavorable weather in one or more
major granaries recur, unless an effective world food
reserves and distribution system is set up in the interim.

d. World grain trade. Whereas world grain production increased by about 35% (from about 1050 mmt to
1400 mmt) since the late 1960's, world grain trade
doubled (from about 90 mmt to 190 mmt). In 1979 wheat
accounted for about 80 mmt, coarse grains for 100 mmt and
rice the remaining 10 mmt of trade (mmt = millions of
metric tons). Canada (about 14 mmt), Australia (about
13.5 mmt) and the U.S. (about 36 mmt) accounted for some
three fourths of wheat exports, whereas the EEC (about
5 mmt), Eastern Europe (about 6 mmt), Japan (5.5 mmt),
China (7.5 mmt), U.S.S.R. (10.5 mmt) and Brazil (4.5 mmt)
made up for slightly more than half the wheat imports.

For coarse grains, the U.S. alone accounts
for about three fourths of all 1979 exports (about 70
mmt), whereas western Europe (about 24 mmt), Eastern
Europe (10.7 mmt), Japan (8.5 mmt), and the U.S.S.R.
(17.3 mmt) make up about 2/3 of the imports. These
coarse grain imports are largely used as animal feed.

Thus, in 1979 coarse grains comprised nearly
half (about 730 mmt) of total grains production (1400
mmt) and more than half of grain trade, whereas rice production (about 250 mmt - milled) was more than 20 times
larger than inter-regional rice trade. The reason for
this is that rice is a staple crop in LDC's, where most
grains are produced and consumed locally; whereas coarse
grains are the largest grain trade commodity, since they
are imported by economically advantage countries with
high meat intake in their diets.

e. Nutritional differences between DC's
and LDC's. Indeed, the principal differences in dietary standards between DC's and LDC's can be
related to animal consumption. In LDC's total calorie
intake is usually in the form of direct consumption of
grains or roots, whereas in DC's direct consumption per
capita is less than most LDC's, although total calorie
intake (direct plus indirect - i.e., grain inefficiently

converted to animal calories) per capita in DC's exceeds
that of LDC's. Moreover, protein intake per capita in
DC's is typically two to three times greater than in
LDC's with animal proteins in the DC diets accounting
largely for this difference.

III. CLIMATE AND ITS VARIATIONS

A. Basic Concepts and Definitions

1. Weather is the instantaneous, local state of the
atmosphere whereas climate is a time average (and other
higher order statistics) of weather variables taken over
a period greater than a month. This period should be
specified by the person using the term "climate", for
much confusion in the literature about climate and climatic change occur when one author implicitly defines
climate over a different time-averaging interval than
another author.

2. Climatic change is then a difference in the climatic statistics from one averaging period to the next.

3. The climatic system comprises the interactive
elements of the atmosphere, oceans, cryosphere (snow and
ice), biota and land surfaces which lead to the climatic
state. Over short time scales (a few months) the atmosphere, upper oceans (including sea ice) and some surface
features (e.g., snow cover) are significantly interactive, whereas on longer time scales deep oceans, glaciers, forests and even continental positions all can
effect climate. The composition of the atmosphere is
important in regulating the flows of radiation within the
climatic system and between the Earth and space. Both
natural and human (i.e., "anthropogenic") factors can
alter atmospheric composition.

4. The causes of climate and its variations are complex and not fully understood. These include factors
external to the climatic system, such as solar energy
input, human pollutants which alter land surfaces or atmospheric composition or volcanic eruptions which inject
dust veils into the upper atmosphere.
Internal factors, such as the redistribution of
heat among its principal reservoirs (e.g., oceans, atmosphere and glaciers), also contribute to climatic fluctuations on all time scales.
Separating climatic "signals" caused by external
factors (e.g., carbon dioxide input from fossil fuel
burning) out from internal or self-fluctuations of the
climate system (so-called "climatic noise") is a principal pursuit of climatic researchers.

5. Climatic models are one major means of studying both the mean distribution of climate and the causes of its variability. Because of the complexity of the climatic system -- and the fact that some anthropogenic perturbations are unprecedented and have no known historical analogue from which to estimate potential effects -- elaborate mathematical models of the climatic system are developed, tested and run on the latest computers available. A hierarchy of these models is used, ranging in complexity from simple "back-of-the-envelope" calculations up to giant, computer-intensive coupled ocean/ atmosphere general circulation models. These "GCM's" compute daily weather patterns from millions upon millions of computations, and climatic statistics are then directly taken.

As all models are not exact replicas of the actual climatic system, they are constantly being tested against observational data and refined. As data collection is a global, long-term effort, many more decades will probably be needed to provide reliable verifications of some model predictions. Unfortunately, decades is the time frame over which present models suggest that global climatic changes from human pollutants (most notably CO_2 increases) are likely to create a "signal" larger than natural climatic "noise". How reliable such estimates are and what they might mean for food productivity, water supplies, heating demands or even global sea levels are now intense topics of research in the United States, Western Europe and to a lesser extent in other places. The World Climate Programme of the World Meteorological Organization is helping to organize and coordinate such needed research.

Of course, whether to act now on the basis of present information is a value judgment that depends upon whether one is more concerned with averting the prospect of climatic impacts from materializing or with the costs of altering or abating those human activities (most notably fossil fuel burning) which most threaten to alter long-term climate.

B. Climatic Variability

Regardless of the resolution to present controversies over long-term climatic trends, interannual variability has (e.g., as seen in 1972) and is likely to continue to create year-to-year fluctuations in food production of some several percent globally, and up to 50% in some regions.

1. Predicting climatic anomalies (e.g., how one year's climate will be different from say a 30-year mean) is now a largely empirical exercise, drawing on analogues

of past anomalous years, anomalous ocean surface temperatures, sunspots and pattern recognitions of individual
analysts. Consequently, despite some entrepreneurs'
claim to the contrary, such forecasts remain at marginal
skill levels. Thus, the most reliable method to estimate
the likelihood of future climatic anomalies is to tabu-
late such anomalies of the past: so-called "actuarial
forecasting".

2. Actuarial forecasts, while not able to predict
the magnitude or timing of specific climatic anomalies,
do offer an idea of the level and frequency of climatic
events which can alter crop yields. For example, a
recent study showed that over the past 50 years the probability of unfavorable yields (i.e., yields less than 90%
of the long-term trend) simultaneously occurring in the
U.S. and the U.S.S.R. is about 8%. Such information can
help food policy analysts choose food reserves and distribution systems policies which minimize the likelihood
of a reoccurrence of the food crises of the mid-1970's.

Of course, a specific forecast for next year is
preferable to an actuarial analysis, but at present low-
skill levels (e.g., 60/40 for temperatures a season
ahead) specific season-ahead forecasts remain of marginal
use to agricultural planners.

3. Is climatic variability increasing? This controversial question has touched off often-bitter debate
among climatologists and agronomists, as mentioned earlier in § II.D.2. Because of a 15-year period of good
growing weather in the U.S. plains after the 1957 drought
year, several agro-climatologists in 1973 expressed concern that such good "unvariable" weather could not be
expected to continue. Indeed, in 1974-1978 U.S. crop
yields reversed a two decade upward trend as poorer
weather occurred.

However, as the debate progressed, many contradictory (and often incommensurate) pieces of evidence
have been cited to claim that climatic variability has or
has not been increasing recently. Often, one analyst
cites, say, five year running mean standard deviations of
surface temperature whereas another analyst supplies
interannual summer precipitation differences. These are
not directly comparable.

Thus, at this time there is no clear evidence
that climatic variations (across the spectrum of time and
space scales which can define climate) are increasing or
decreasing, although many fixed-time, local-space exceptions are often cited in both directions.

On a worldwide crop-yield basis, however, a plot
of the trend in world total grains yields does indeed
show a fairly smooth rise from the early 1960's up to

1972, after which a several percent interannual fluctuation in yield is evident. Thus increasing fluctuation in
grain productivity has been cited by some agronomists as
evidence that climatic variations important to food productivity have been increasing through the 1970's.

IV. FOOD PRODUCTION FACTORS

Climate, soils, nutrients, irrigation water, carefully chosen crop strains, pest control and appropriate
management practices all contribute to food productivity.
Intensification of farming has led to significant advances in crop yields, but often these advances have been
accompanied by undesirable side effects such as air and
water pollution, susceptibility of a few high-yielding
genetic varieties to an outbreak of pests, soil erosion,
water logging or alkalinization of soils, displacement of
subsistence farmers to urban slums and, in some cases,
increased vulnerability of food systems to climatic fluctuations.
Although considerable arable land remains undevelop-
ed, it is usually less economic or productive than presently cultivated lands. Cost estimates for land and
infrastructure development over the next decade merely to
maintain present per capita standards typically range
from tens to hundreds of billions of dollars.
If mankind continues to increase agricultural production to meet the rising food demands of a growing
world population, great care must be exercised to ensure
that irreversible environmental damage is avoided. Maintaining the productive potential of global agro-ecosys-
ems is one of the most critical environmental issues facing humanity.
The complexity of the interactions among physical,
biological, economic, social and political components of
food production suggests that modern agricultural development requires an integrated management approach,
where all of these important factors are viewed systemat-
ically -- and in the context of the local conditions of
the agricultural region being considered. Few general
statements about food-climate interactions are possible
outside of specific regional context.

V. POLICY CONSIDERATIONS

A. Some General Food-Climate Policy Considerations

1. Climatic Variability and Crop Yields

It is also difficult to generalize outside of a
local context how a specific climatic change might affect
world food productivity. The reason is that at different

a critical question: What is the "Carrying Capacity" of the Earth?

2. Carrying Capacity

Underlying the various views expressed in the preceding section is a belief that the Earth can sustain only a limited number of people at reasonable nutritional levels. Some environmentalists believe that soil erosion, toxic waste build-ups, and other damages to food production potential will render the long-term Earth's carrying capacity below even the present population of 4 billion, and that eventual catastrophe is inevitable if population growth continues. This belief leads to a view that any aid which allows for more people or pollution is immoral, for it only will increase the ultimate size of the inevitable collapse.

Opposed to this view are the "technological optimists", who calculate that modern methods of irrigation, fertilization, pesticide application, genetic engineering and market incentives for growers could provide a carrying capacity of up to 40 billion -- ten times the present population. To those who believe that the carrying capacity can be raised, raising such capacity is the most moral alternative. While they readily admit that the costs of such development are measured in many billions of dollars annually, they rarely admit (or even discuss) environmental or social constraints to such development.

Thus, whether the risks of development (e.g., high population growth rates and environmental degradation) are worth the benefits of improving standards of living depends both on one's values and opinion as to whether the Earth's carrying capacity will allow a given sustainable future population size. Unfortunately, there is no wholly "scientific" method to assess reliably what the future carrying capacity might be since it depends on uncertainties such as future technological breakthroughs, the long-term effects of toxic wastes, the causes of birth rate reductions, long-term climatic variations, etc.

VI. CONCLUDING REMARKS

Although no more than a few global generalizations seem possible in the area of food-climate interactions, it is already clear that "actuarial analyses" of past climate-induced food production fluctuations are needed to help minimize societal damage when such fluctuations inevitably recur. At the same time, developing the capacity to predict both future climatic variations and their societal impacts is needed. Minimizing the human impacts of climatic fluctuations through (1) food

reserves and distribution systems, (2) diversity in
cropping patterns and (3) maintaining the long-term productive potential of existing (or new) croplands through
farming practices consistent with local climatic and
other environmental factors, remain as urgent policy
imperatives. The latter (3) policy is growing in importance, particularly in view of the need to increase
food availability to presently undernourished people, let
along to provide more food for a growing world population.

5
Anthropogenic Climate Change: Assessing the Responsibility of Developed and Developing Countries

Robert Schware and Edward Friedman

If world fossil fuel use continues to increase the carbon dioxide loading of the atmosphere at current rates and the apparent concensus of the international climatological community is correct, mankind is likely to cause a significant average warming of the Earth's surface in the next fifty years. Inevitably, questions will arise concerning responsibility for the costs of the adverse impacts that might be suffered by regions or nations as a consequence of increased atmospheric carbon dioxide. In practice this means that measures would need to be developed to determine the proportional indemnity to be charged each region or country.

One measure that has been used to quantify the relative atmospheric contribution of carbon dioxide emissions from regions and countries,[1,2] including developed[3] and developing[4] nations, has emphasized emissions in single, specific years. In our view, consideration should be given to calculating a measure of responsibility in terms of total past and future emissions of carbon dioxide. This is a function not only of annual emission rates but also a measure of the cumulative emissions over time.

In order to compute the future atmospheric burden of carbon dioxide, based on scenarios of future fossil fuel use and past emissions, one must use a model of the carbon cycle that accurately reflects the transient response of the earth-atmosphere-ocean system to annual carbon dioxide inputs. The model of Siegenthaler and Oeschger[5] provides a calculation of the response of the system to a "pulse" input of carbon dioxide. Those authors make clear the limitations of their model in dealing with large inputs of carbon dioxide to the atmosphere, since the transient response is a function of changes induced in the chemistry or dynamics of the ocean. However, their model offers results that can be used to approximate the date at which the atmospheric

burden of carbon dioxide will have reached a specific
level (chosen here to be a doubling relative to the
assumed "preindustrial" value of 290 ppm). This model
can also be used to calculate the relative contribution
of developed and developing countries.

The first step in the application of Siegenthaler
and Oeschger's model is the determination of the fraction
of each year's emission of carbon that remains airborne
after being released. The complete calculation requires
a sum of the following kind:

$$\sum_{t=1860}^{T} f(T - t) \ E(t)$$

which gives the cumulative carbon burden, at time T,
that results from annual emissions characterized by a
rate E(t) if a fraction, f, remains of each year's
emissions after T - t years. Siegenthaler and Oeschger's
decay factor, f(t), can be paramterized as x/x+t, with
x = 40 which takes account of the slow absorption of
the additional carbon dioxide by the deep ocean water
and the biosphere. For example, the remaining fraction
of the 1970 emissions will be 50 percent in 2010; but
only 40 percent of the 1950 emissions will remain airborne in 2010.

The doubling date and the relative fraction of the
added carbon dioxide contributed by developed and developing countries were computed by using the historical
record of emissions for the period 1860-1976[6,7] and
various scenarios of future carbon dioxide release that
assume an exponential growth of E(t) after 1976. By
computing the sum above, estimates are obtained of the
growth in the atmospheric burden of carbon dioxide as
well as the date at which the doubling will occur.

Figure 1 illustrates the fraction of the doubled
airborne carbon dioxide contributed by developed and
developing nations, as well as the date when the doubling
will occur. The growth rates range from 0.01 to 0.04
(approximately 1 to 4 percent) per year for developed
nations and 0.01 to 0.08 (approximately 1 to 8 percent)
per year for developing nations.

It is clear from the diagram that for the developing
nations to exceed 50% of the contribution to doubled
airborne carbon dioxide in the first half of the next
century, they must maintain an average growth rate in
fossil fuel use that exceeds 0.06 if the developed
nations have only a 0.02 growth rate, or 0.04 if the
latter can hold growth rates down to 0.01. Although
developing nations have surpassed these levels in the
past, such growth rates may become increasingly difficult
to maintain, given the Third World's economic prospects

for 1980 and beyond. Nor is it certain that the developed nations can limit their growth rates of fossil
fuel use to less than 0.02.[8]

Indeed, as of this writing a growth rate well below
previous estimates[9] would seem more likely in the case
of the Third World. Direct and indirect financial subsidies from OPEC has enabled the 89 oil-importing
developing countries to better cope with world inflation,
increases in the price of oil, and the heavy burden of
meeting external debts owed to developed countries.[10]
Given the continued depletion of OPEC's oil supply, no
one can be certain how much longer this aid will be
available.

The oil importing developing countries face substantial energy problems even with their economic ties
with OPEC countries. There is also no guarantee that as
petroleum resources are depleted and coal becomes the
major fossil fuel resource, the developing nations will
have the wherewithal to buy it from the coal-rich nations
of China, the U.S.S.R., and the United States. At the
same time, very large investments in either oil or coal
imports will diminish developing countries' ability to
make needed capital investments in agricultural modernization and industrial development.

As Table 5.1 shows, the prospects for high average
rates of growth in developing countries are not very
good. Of course, these countries vary greatly in terms
of aggregate trends in production, trade, population,
and foreign assistance. The middle income and oil
exporting developing countries recorded higher growth
rates than the poor developing nations. Even with improved trade performance, continuing agricultural progress, and increased aid from developed countries, growth
in developing countries for at least the coming decade
could fall below that of the 1970s.[11] A marked slowdown
in these countries would mean that Third World contributions to the doubling of global carbon dioxide emissions
may be considerably less than previously suggested.

In conclusion, if the international community of
nations is ever to assess responsibility for carbon dioxide production and changed distributions of climate,
calculations must be extended backward and forward to
encompass a range of reasonable scenarios of fossil fuel
use and carbon dioxide emissions. Our preliminary calculations indicate that developed countries might have
to bear the brunt of responsibility for new climatic
regimes; they are the suppliers of fuel to the world, the
major consumers, and the major cumulative contributors
of carbon dioxide to the atmosphere.

NOTES

   *The authors would like to acknowledge the useful
comments on the manuscript by Jesse Ausubel, Donald
Borock, Michael Glantz, William Kellogg and Stephen
Schneider. The views expressed are solely the authors'.

   1. Rotty, R. M., 1979a: (Material presented before
Congress) in Carbon Dioxide Accumulation in the Atmosphere, Synthetic Fuels and Energy Policy - A Symposium,
Committee on Governmental Affairs, U.S. Senate, Washington, D.C., July,185-94. Rotty, R. M., 1979b: "Energy
Demand and Global Climate Change," Man's Impact on Climate, W. Bach, J. Pankrath and W. Kellogg (eds.),
Elsevier, New York, 259-83. An illustration (taken from
the above sources) of an estimate of recent and future
carbon dioxide emissions is provided below. Again, the
point of view expressed in this paper is that the cumulative quantity of carbon dioxide over the years is
what should be taken into account rather than emissions
now or at some time in the future when considering who
should bear the responsibility for climate change.

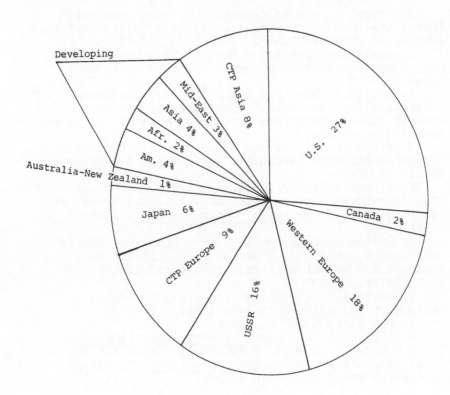

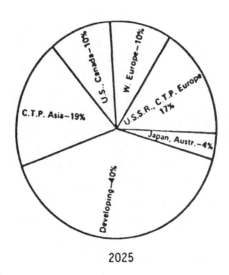

2025

Global carbon dioxide production by world segments.

2. Perry, H. and Landsberg, H., "Projected World Energy Consumption," Energy and Climate(1977). National Academy of Sciences, Washington, D.C., 35-50.

3. Australia, Canada, Japan, Israel, South Africa, United States, Western Europe, Eastern Europe, Soviet Union.

4. Africa (other than South Africa), Caribbean America, Middle East (including Turkey), Far East, Oceania, China, Democratic People's Republic of Korea, Mongolia, Viet Nam.

5. Siegenthaler, U. and Oeschger, H., "Predicting Future Atmospheric Carbon Dioxide Levels, 199 Science 388-95 (1978).

6. Zimen, K. E., P. Offermann and G. Hartmann, "Source Functions of CO_2 and the Future CO_2 Burden in the Atmosphere," 32a Zeits, Naturforschung, 1544-54 (1978).

7. United Nations, World Energy Supplies, Statistical papers, Series J, Department of International Economic and Social Affairs, Statistical Office, New York (1979).

8. Marshall, E., "Energy Forecasts: Sinking to New Lows," 208 Science 1353-56 (1980).

9. See notes 1 and 2, supra.

10. Attiga, A. A., Global Energy Transition and the Third World, Third World Foundation, London (1979).

11. World Bank, World Development Report, Oxford University Press, New York (1979).

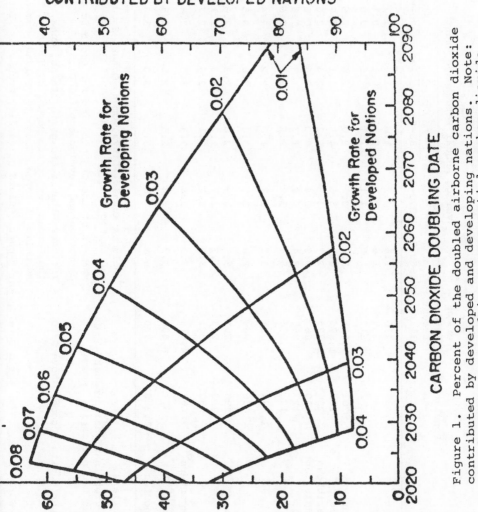

Figure 1. Percent of the doubled airborne carbon dioxide contributed by developed and developing nations. Note: Growth rates are used in an exponential carbon dioxide release model for dates after 1976.

Table 5.1 Growth of GNP per person by region, 1960-1990

Country Group	Population 1980 (millions)	GNP per Person 1980 (current dollars)	Average Annual Percentage Growth[a]		Low Case		High Case	
			1960-70	1970-80	1980-85	1985-90	1980-85	1985-90
Low-income oil importers[b]	1,133	216	1.6	0.9	1.0	1.3	1.7	2.4
Africa (Sub-Saharan)	141	239	1.6	0.2	-0.3	0.1	0.1	1.1
Asia	992	212	1.6	1.1	1.1	1.5	2.0	2.6
Middle-income oil importers[c]	701	1,635	3.6	3.1	2.0	2.4	2.6	3.5
East Asia and Pacific	162	1,175	4.9	5.6	4.1	4.1	4.7	5.2
Latin America and Caribbean	256	1,775	2.7	3.5	2.2	2.4	2.6	3.8
North Africa and Middle East	30	667	-0.2	0.4	0.0	0.6	0.6	0.8
Africa (Sub-Saharan)	125	867	2.4	0.9	1.3	1.3	1.6	1.4
Southern Europe	128	2,950	5.4	3.2	2.2	2.2	2.5	3.4
Oil importers	1,834	751	3.1	2.7	1.8	2.2	2.4	3.2
Oil exporters	456	968	2.8	3.5	3.0	3.0	3.5	3.4
All developing countries	2,290	791	3.1	2.9	2.0	2.3	2.6	3.3
All low-income	1,310	245	1.7	1.7	1.2	1.8	2.1	2.5
All middle-income	980	1,521	3.4	3.1	2.1	2.4	2.7	3.4
Capital-surplus oil exporters[d]	69	4,614	7.3	5.0	2.3	2.3	2.8	2.8
Industrialized countries[e]	671	9,684	3.9	2.4	2.5	2.5	2.8	3.5
Centrally planned economies[f]	1,386	1,720	n.a.	3.8	3.3	3.3	3.3	3.3

[a] Calculated in 1977 dollars.

[b] On the basis of 1977 gross national product (GNP), these countries had per capita incomes of $300 and below.

[c] These countries had per capita incomes above $300.

[d] Includes Kuwait, Libya, Oman, Qatar, Saudi Arabia, and United Arab Emirates.

[e] Members of the Organization for Economic Co-operation and Development (OECD).

[f] Includes Albania, Bulgaria, China, Cuba, Czechoslovakia, the German Democratic Republic, Hungary, the Democratic Republic of Korea, Mongolia, Poland, Romania, and the USSR.

Source: Adapted from World Bank, 1979; World Development Report, Oxford University Press, New York.

6
Global Climate, World Politics and National Security

Thomas W. Wilson, Jr.

The possibility of man-made change in the world's climate is only one of a range of credible dangers that should lead to a major reappraisal and expansion of our basic concepts of national security. For what is not generally realized is that <u>Planet Earth</u> is now threatened by a spectrum of non-military threats that call into question the very meaning of national defense.

A climate change that turned the Great Plains of North America into an arid zone would be analogous to a major military disaster. Damage to the ozone layer could cause an unacceptable rise in victims of skin cancers. We are less sure of the impact of continued destruction of tropical forests and coastal zones, or of the rising loss of genetic resources. And there are technical arguments about the loss of topsoil, the pressures on pastureland, the deterioration of fisheries and the loss of forest cover in general.

But this much is beyond question: we are talking about the basic strategic resources and systems that support life on this planet. And with these at risk, it is obvious that all nations, by definition, are insecure today, and survival -- the most elemental of human goals and the first duty of all governments -- is called into serious question.

It should not be necessary to labor the point that if Earth is threatened, so is each national subdivision of Earth; if the whole is insecure, so are its parts. There is simply no such thing as national security on an insecure planet -- nor can there be!

Yet the fact of the matter is that our present concepts, policies, and programs designed to support the security of the nation and people are focused almost exclusively on preparations for the military defense of geographical territory. Our debates are focused on geopolitical notions like "balance of power" and "vital national interests". Non-military threats to the integrity of vulnerable and irreplaceable planetary systems

71

simply do not enter into the official calculus of
security planning or strategy.

Nobody in his right mind would ignore the military
dangers of a world armed to the teeth, hag-ridden by
conflict, hatred, and fanaticism, and overhung by nuclear
arsenals that could wipe out the civilization of the
northern hemisphere. But nobody with his eyes open could
believe that military defense by itself can provide for
national security in the 1980's and 1990's.

The search for national security in the modern world
must somehow take account of this objective reality:
demographic, economic and environmental world trends have
combined in recent years to create a qualitatively distinct class of unavoidable world-level problems that are
virtually unknown to traditional diplomacy -- that are
beyond the reach of national governments, that cannot be
fitted into received traditions of interstate relations,
that cannot be wished away, that are coming increasingly
to dominate world affairs, and that are utterly indif-
ferent to military force.

As if this were not enough, the search for national
security must somehow take account of another political-
military reality of our times: the instruments and even
the nature of power are changing before our eyes. It
may be impossible to envision any workable society, above
the level of a small commune -- devoid of all forms of
power. But it is essential for any sustainable national
society to understand that effective power must be relevant to the contemporary political-social environment.
And that environment, of course, keeps changing. Indeed
it has changed so much in recent decades that some extraordinary things have come to pass with respect to the
uses and abuses of power. For example:

> In the last two wars we have fought, the United
> States has found no acceptable way to engage its
> most powerful military weapons.

> In Iran, the major weapon used to destroy a regime
> holding all the cards of conventional power was a
> general strike.

> For the past several years, the most economically
> and technologically powerful nations of the world
> have been staring down the barrel of something
> called an "oil weapon".

> Heads of desert sheikdoms with names hardly known
> a few years ago have the power today to make major
> nations sit up and take notice.

Kidnappers with only side arms have defied great power successfully, and bands of terrorists have shaken the foundations of state authority.

In the background of all this, we are becoming aware that extremely complex technologies in crucial fields like transport, communications and energy are vulnerable to sabotage by small groups and even unarmed individuals. And we have yet to recognize the potential power of minor states to disrupt international proceedings of crucial importance to traditional major powers.

The only answer to hostile military power remains military power. But it is of no avail as a counter to proliferating non-military forms and uses of power loose in the 1980's. This is another reality to be acknowledged, somehow, in a national strategy for security in modern times.

If the power environment is not what it used to be, neither is the diplomatic environment; for the mainstream of international politics has been moved. Until the middle of this century, the main business of the international relations game was the manipulation of power, based on military strength. The metaphor of diplomacy was the chessboard. The political-military tradition was relevant doctrine. Relations among nations were conducted mainly in bilateral channels. And the big issues were likely to be zero-sum in nature. At the heart of this international system was one factor that colored everything else: most of the world was run by a handful of military powers.

Today there are a hundred new players in the game and they make a new majority in a world in which nobody is in charge and no nation has the remotest possibility of taking charge. Furthermore, the new majority has injected a new set of issues into the mainstream of international politics, thus altering the content of international relations and changing the very nature of diplomacy as we have know it in the past.

During the decade of the 1970's there was an explosive expansion of the world agenda of problems that cannot be handled by any nation acting independently. Suddenly governments were seized at the international political level with an extraordinary range of pressing problems that they were accustomed to think of as domestic issues -- and, in any event, as matters for "experts" to cope with. What happened in the 1970's is that these issues were internationalized and politicized through a series of United Nations conferences to become part of a standing global agenda. It can now be seen that this agenda is made up of two extremely broad, fundamental, and inter-acting classes of problems:

<u>Issues bearing on the state of the planet</u>. During
the 1970's governments met at the plenipotentiary
level to consider manmade stresses on the global
environment, world water resources, pervasive
desert encroachment, and -- in seven long and
painful sessions -- management of the vast ocean
systems that cover most of the planet.

<u>Issues bearing upon the human condition</u>. During
the same decade of the 1970's, governments gathered
to see what they could agree to do about world
population growth, world hunger, the human habitat,
improving the roles of women, global employment,
basic health delivery systems, rural reforms, and
the use of science and technology to ease the
burdens of poverty.

These are not classical inter-state issues; they are
transnational and intrahuman issues. The dominant reality about them is not inherent conflict of national
interest; the dominant reality is a shared interest in
resolving or at least managing the problem. These are
not zero-sum but potentially positive-sum situations.
The relevant mode of behavior with respect to these
problems, therefore, is not competition but cooperation
and collaboration -- emphatically <u>not</u> because of inherent
good will and fellowship, but because when you get down
to the nuts and bolts of it, there is no other practical
way to cope with these real problems in this real world.
    Yet the connection between planetary politics and
national security is still obscured in the fog of in-
herited ideas and assumptions -- still lost in the maze
of governments subdivided into technical and sectoral
and geographic areas of specialization. Astonishing as
it may seem, nobody is in charge of the global agenda in
Washington today. Of course, people here and there work
on bits and pieces of it, usually from the technical
point of view, for some specific task or for some limited
period of time. But as a major political upheaval in the
world at large, of enormous vital interest to the United
States, the global agenda has made barely a ripple.
    Insensitive, then, to the realities of the global
predicament, the top echelon of the government has clung,
for all practical purposes, to a bipolar world view -- to
a one-dimensional vision of national security -- and to
bilateral maneuvering among traditional major powers who
are increasingly isolated from the major currents of the
new world politics.
    For the past decade-and-a-half, the United States
has lost, through neglect, its taste and its talents for
multilateral diplomacy, for innovation and initiative in
the politics that concern the new majority in the world

forum. We have become negative and defensive -- foot-
draggers and stonewallers -- as the developing nations
seek to engage us in a serious negotiation about reform-
ing an international economic system that they perceive
to be inadequate and inequitable. It is not too much to
say, I believe, that we have drifted into a sort of
siege psychology or, if you will, a latter-day Maginot
Line mentality. We have adopted, in the arena of new
world politics, the pitiful posture of "damage limitation."

And the danger of this can be illuminated in the
harsh light of pragmatism. The new global agenda that
emerged in the 1970's is not a figment of someone's
imagination, nor an ideological ploy of some kind. It is
the direct political fallout of two major political-
social phenomena of our times that cannot be ignored.

First, the historically unprecedented expansion of
total human activity, reinforced by explosive population
growth, that now burdens the carrying capacity of the
natural systems, creates the so-called problematique,
raises serious problems about the state of the planet's
capacity to sustain human society, and requires international action to defend and sustain planetary systems--
those most strategic of all strategic systems.

Second, there is the feverish spread around the
world of the drive for modernization of national societies. This once-western phenomenon was taken up by the
Japanese late in the last century. In this century it
raced through Latin America, the Caribbean, the Middle
East, Asia and Africa until it became a universal phenomenon when it was adopted as the centerpiece of Chinese
policy for the rest of this century by the successors of
Mao Tse-tung.

And everywhere, in all societies, regardless of
their state of development, the universal urge for social
progress through modernization, whatever that means in
any particular society, runs up against a universal need
for some measure of social and cultural continuity. To
some degree, this is a divisive and destabilizing factor
in all societies. Iran has shown just how violent the
collision can be between modernization and cultural
tradition, but for our purposes here the point is that
the now-universal urge to improve the conditions of life
throughout the planet has politicized the state of the
human condition and injected it into the mainstream of
world affairs.

The still-rising impact of technological societies
on natural systems and the dynamic spread of modernization to embrace all nations and peoples are stark realities of our world and our times. Together they have
created an agenda of problems relating to the state of
the planet and to the human condition. This is world-

level politics. This is the politics of the present
predicament.

It seems clear to me that, in a general but very
profound way, sustainable security for this country
rests crucially upon an active and creative participation
in the politics of the world predicament. Political
paralysis over global issues -- like paralysis over
lesser issues -- almost surely leads to political polarization, and polarization almost surely leads to violence
and chaos. How much evidence do we need? Belfast,
Beirut, Tehran, Pnom Penh, Kabul, San Salvador -- these
may or may not be models of things to come. What is
clear is that this nation has a greater stake in avoiding
political polarization and paralysis than any nation in
the world. And perhaps the greatest danger of all --
more credible than nuclear war or eco-disaster -- is that
the agenda of global issues identified in the 1970's
could become the abandoned agenda of the 1980's --
neglected through failure to perceive the connection between the state of the planet, the human condition and
national security.

Any concept of security relevant to the 1980's and
1990's would have to be broadened significantly beyond
preparations for military defense of geographic territory. Such a doctrine would have to include, at the
minimum:

A long-term international commitment to shore up
and enhance the basic biological systems of the
planet.

Improvement of international capabilities for managing other shared resources on a sustainable basis.

Avoidance of political polarization over transnational issues through positive participation
in the world-level political process.

Urgent improvement of the national capacity to
monitor long term global trends, plus a capacity
to assess their implications for U.S. interests
and to identify alternative policies for decision
making.

These are not very radical ideas. They have all
been formulated before. None is beyond technological
capability. But what has been missing is an awareness
that transnational issues bearing on the state of the
planet and upon the human condition are directly linked
to the national security of the United States. This
failure of perception has become part and parcel of the
contemporary security problem.

It is imperative that the security issue be viewed
in the context outlined here. Potential climatic changes
and their likely impacts demand that nation states
develop their scientific capabilities to learn more about
these phenomena and, even more important, that they adapt
their political thinking, especially their traditional
concepts about national security in light of the new
realities.

EXISTING AND ALTERNATIVE PUBLIC AND PRIVATE
INTERNATIONAL LAW AND INSTITUTIONS:
RESPONSES TO WEATHER AND CLIMATE PROBLEMS

7
International Strategies
and Institutions for
Coping with Climate Change

Robert Schware and William W. Kellogg

I. INTRODUCTION

If the present ever increasing use of fossil fuel
continues and there is a further buildup of atmospheric
carbon dioxide, the people of the world are likely to
face markedly different distributions of climate through
the next century. Even though there is some general
agreement among climatologists about the range of estimates of global average temperature rise for a hypothet-
ical doubling of carbon dioxide ($3°\pm1.5°C$), a level that
may be attained around the middle of the next century,[1]
important and nagging scientific and policy uncertainties remain.

One question has now been asked many times and in
many forums: What, if anything, should be done about this
potentially very serious situation? There is, of course,
no simple answer. It depends on how the leaders of the
world perceive both the advantages and disadvantages of
the predicted climate change, the financial and technological means at their disposal, and -- perhaps of most
importance -- the international mechanisms by which the
community of nations could decide what action if any (and
by whom) to take to avert the change or to mitigate its
impacts.

In the following sections we summarize some thoughts
on these complex issues that are expressed at greater
length in our book "Climate Change and Society".[2] First,
we briefly survey the international legal and political
mechanisms that have been brought to bear on related
issues. It seems that we lack powerful enough mechanisms
on the international level to be able to reach an agreement to limit the use of fossil fuels. Furthermore,
there will probably be little political or economic moti-
vation for taking such action.[3]

This apparently being the case, the next thing to
consider is what strategies we could adopt to reduce the

vulnerability of human settlements and activities regardless of whether carbon dioxide builds up and results in
a future climate change. These mitigating strategies
could be taken by groups of individuals, by industry and
agriculture, by national governments, and by international bodies. As will be shown, they turn out to be necessary and desirable steps to take in solving more immediate problems as well as helping to cope with a gradual
climate change taking place over many decades. It is
possible that the future shifts of temperature and precipitation patterns will spur the nations of the world to
take vigorous initiatives to cope with our variable and
changing environment. Until then, however, these strategies should be implemented in any event -- and some of
them have indeed already been implemented to a limited
extent.

II. EXISTING INTERNATIONAL INSTITUTIONS AND LEGAL MECHANISMS

A. Organizations for Environmental Cooperation

There has been a long tradition of meaningful scientific exchanges and international cooperation in the
field of climatology. The history of this cooperation
and the organizations that have been established to facilitate it are reviewed in Chapter 2 of this volume
(by William Kellogg), so it will not be repeated here.
The main points to keep in mind with regard to
international cooperation in climatology are, first, that
there is an active intergovernmental organization, the
World Meteorological Organization (WMO), that coordinates
the twice daily exchange of weather data through the
World Weather Watch (WWW) telecommunications and data
processing system. The WMO works in collaboration with
the International Council of Scientific Unions (ICSU) in
the realm of climate research.
In 1979 the WMO Congress approved the World Climate
Programme (WCP). The WCP has four component programs
devoted to climate data, to the applications of a knowledge of climate, to climate research, and to studies of
the impacts of climate variability and change. Responsibility for the last component program is shared by the
U.N. Environment Programme (UNEP); and responsibility for
the research component is shared with ICSU.
Though these various programs and operational systems are generally very effective and may be cited as
good examples of successful international cooperation,
they do not purport to set policy outside of their rather
narrow terms of reference. Thus, the national weather
services may be influenced by the actions and recommendations of the WMO or UNEP, but only rarely has the issue

of weather and climate been taken up in the broader
policy-making bodies of the United Nations. (An exception, described in Chapter 2, was the U.N. initiative
sparked by President Kennedy in 1961.)

While the scope and functions of those intergovernmental meteorological and environmental agencies have
been officially established, the nongovernmental Scientific Committee on Problems of the Environment (SCOPE),
a special ICSU committee, has broadened the institutional
framework. Founded in 1969, SCOPE currently represents
23 member countries. In addition to focusing on the environmental needs of developing countries, SCOPE has
launched a long term study of biogeochemical cycles of
carbon, nitrogen, phosphorous and sulfur; and it has
recently undertaken a review of methodologies for studying the impacts of climate variability and change on
society.

Since the end of the 1960's the growth of organizations and international meetings has accelerated, as have
the plans for scientific and political cooperation. In
1972 the International Institute for Applied Systems
Analysis (IIASA) was established as another nongovernmental organization. IIASA's membership consists of
scientific academies throughout the world; presently 17
countries are represented. Its principal areas of research include resources and environment, human settlements and services, management and technology, and "system and decision sciences", "a concern for society's
interaction with the climate pervades the Institute's
entire research activity, both actually and latently."[4]

We should also mention the regional organizations
gaining influence. It is notable that the Council of the
European Communities (CEC) has approved and funded a
European Climate Programme that has many similarities to
the U.S. National Climate Program.

B. International Legal Mechanisms

The existing institutions and norms of international
law are inadequate in resolving cases that deal with in-
juries or damages caused by carbon dioxide-induced atmospheric warming. In fact, there is currently no mechanism
by which to set carbon dioxide standards, establish uni-
versally applied control measures, and enforce the so-
called "global right to a clean atmosphere."

Obviously there is no policing body to control carbon dioxide production on a global scale, and there is
little chance that one could be established in the foreseeable future.[5]

It would make sense, however, to encourage international mechanisms that could:

° Examine the likely effects of a carbon dioxide-
  induced warming on national and international
  activities. Perhaps the Climate Impact Studies
  Programme under UNEP and WMO will be able to do
  this;
° Determine an equitable distribution of fossil fuel
  resources between countries;
° Recommend to governments practical measures to
  deter activities that enhance the atmospheric
  burden of carbon dioxide, such as "excessive" use
  of fossil fuel or large scale deforestation;
° Warn of impending climate related disasters, such
  as regional crop failures. One way to do this
  would be to continuously update forecasts of crop
  yields and inventories of food reserves;
° Exchange information on climate change and its
  impacts. Again, the Climate Impact Studies Programme may be in a position to do this.

Liability claims, sanctions, and indemnity awards
may be awkward ways to resolve carbon dioxide related
problems such as disruptions in trade, environmental
damages, and population relocations. By the time such
actions are brought to court, settled, and (if possible)
enforced by future international legal mechanism, the
potentially irreversible impacts will have probably
already occurred. The following section, however, outlines some mechanisms of international law that could
become applicable to carbon dioxide related issues in
the next few decades.

III. POTENTIALLY EFFECTIVE INTERNATIONAL MECHANISMS

A. International Agreements

So far no international legal agreements or regulations have been used to resolve problems associated with
increased atmospheric carbon dioxide. However, two recent international agreements may be moving in the right
direction. First, the Organization for Economic Cooperation and Development (OECD) Environmental Committee has
given some attention to the consequences of increased
carbon dioxide emissions from coal production. In 1979
the Council on Coal and the Environment specifically
recommended that: "Member Countries, in the light of
appropriate research results, seek to define acceptable
fuel qualities, emissions levels or ambient media qualities, as appropriate, for carbon dioxide".[6] Second, the
Economic Commission for Europe in 1979 signed a "Convention on Transboundary Air Pollution". The 34 member
states, including the United States and Canada, pledged
"to limit, and as far as possible, gradually reduce and

prevent air pollution. However, as Rosencrantz notes:

"The agreement does not compel abatement action.
It includes no mechanism for enforcement of its
terms, nor does it delineate the responsibility
of member states to abate pollution-causing
damage in another state or to award compensation
for such damage."[7]

There are other types of treaties and conventions
being negotiated that apply principles of international
law to established areas of transnational significance,
such as marine pollution, nuclear weapons tests, exploitation of the Antarctic, and the use of outer space.
Nations engaging in these agreements have taken preliminary steps toward clarifying the mechanisms and procedures through which regulation, control, and enforcement policies can be implemented.
     For example, the U.S. is proposing a treaty that
would require signatory governments to prepare an International Environmental Impact Statement on major projects, such as building a large power plant or seeding
clouds to enhance precipitation. Such projects could
have adverse environmental effects on neighboring countries. As spelled out in the U.S. Senate Resolution 49,[8]
the treaty would apply to potentially harmful activities
affecting land, water, and atmospheric resources.
     There seems to be a growing acceptance by nations of
regional organizations such as the European Economic Community, the OECD, the Association of South East Asian
Nations, the Organization of American States, and the
Organization of African Unity, among others. These
groups are set up to deal with specific supranational
problems. They may have a potentially valuable function
in organizing cooperative plans of action for carbon
dioxide control strategies, and for compensating member
countries for damages resulting from climate change.
     However, as we have already stressed, individual
nations or even regional organizations cannot by themselves effectively reduce the buildup of atmospheric
carbon dioxide. The problem is a global one so that all
countries of the world must work together to limit use of
fossil fuels and the resulting emissions.

B. International Commissions

     The findings and recommendations of international
commissions, ranging from "conciliation commissions" to
"arbitral tribunals" to "commissions of inquiry" can
sometimes influence international behavior. The International Joint Commission set up by the United States and
Canada was a particularly useful commission for investi-

gating atmospheric pollution, recommending control
measures, and supervising compliance with the provisions.
For carbon dioxide problems, such commissions may be
useful ad hoc devices to either arbitrate disputes or to
establish the opinion of experts on controversial legal,
political and scientific issues.

C. International Conferences

Conducting international relations through special
conferences is becoming an accepted practice among countries. The United Nations has encouraged this, convening
such conferences as the Conference on the Human Environment, the Law of the Sea, Desertification, Science and
Technology for Development, and Renewable Energy Resources.

The value of recommendations of international conferences is that they tend to clarify general principles
by calling attention to matters that should be dealt with
within the domestic jurisdiction of member states. For
instance, Recommendation 70 of the United Nations Conferences on the Human Environment (1972) states:

> that Governments be mindful of activities in which
> there is an appreciable risk of effects on climate
> and to this end: a) Carefully evaluate the like-
> lihood and magnitude of climatic effects and dis-
> seminate their findings to the maximum extent
> feasible before embarking on such activities;
> b) Consult fully other interested States when
> activities carrying a risk of such effects are
> being contemplated or implemented.[9]

To date, the World Climate Conference, organized by
the WMO and held in Geneva in 1979, has been the largest
international effort to foresee and investigate potential
human induced climatic changes.

We have only dealt with a few of the possible international legal mechanisms for handling the political and
economic consequences of a global carbon dioxide-induced
climatic change. Special mention should be made of diplomatic negotiations and the means of settlement of
disputes, including international arbitration, and the
International Court of Justice.[10]

Each of these institutional arrangements and procedures may be used to resolve possible carbon dioxide
related damage and compensation disputes. It seems unlikely, however, that they could be effective in achieving worldwide action to reduce fossil fuel use.

IV. STRATEGIES FOR MITIGATING THE EFFECTS

The uncertainties inherent in the carbon dioxide problem are often cited as justification for taking no action now. But whether carbon dioxide builds up or not, we know that weather and climate will continue to fluctuate greatly. Dealing with the carbon dioxide/ climate problem is one way of coping with climatic variability in general. Thus, we have strong incentives to: reduce the vulnerability of human settlements and activities to both climatic variability and change; begin actions to mitigate adverse carbon dioxide-induced impacts; and take advantage of the beneficial effects.

That most of the measures that will protect us from gradual carbon dioxide-induced changes will probably also benefit us in the short term has been reinforced by case studies in both developing and developed countries and in recent international meetings on carbon dioxide and global climatic change. In this section we highlight a few strategies that will help to increase our resilience and mitigate the effects of global climate change; they will likely be advantageous even if no climate change occurs. Moreover, some of these strategies may also slow the increase in atmospheric carbon dioxide.

Table 1. Strategies to mitigate the effects of increased atmospheric carbon dioxide, to help slow the advent of the climate change, or to encourage better choices of policy.

Strategies that:		
Increase resilience	Slow CO_2 increase	Improve choices
Protect arable soil	Energy conservation	Environmental monitoring and warning
Improve water management	Use of renewable energy resources	Provision of improved climate data and its application
Apply agrotechnology	Reforestation	
Coastal land use policies		Public information and education
Maintain global food reserves		Transfer appropriate technology
Disaster relief		

Table 1 lists the specific mitigating strategies that will be discussed. These seem to be the most important ones to pursue immediately; some of them have already been adopted in a limited way.

A. <u>Strategies That Increase Resilience to Climatic Change</u>

1. <u>Protect arable soil</u>. The loss of arable soil through erosion or salinization has been partly responsible for the decline of entire civilizations in the past.[11] Currently as much land globally is being lost to agriculture due to poor management practices as is being opened up.[12] To maintain or increase worldwide food production soil must be protected. This is especially important in marginal, semi-arid lands where overgrazing and poor agricultural practices have led to desertification.[13] The process has accelerated during periods of drought.

2. <u>Improve water management</u>. Building dams, aqueducts, reservoirs, and irrigation systems, and diverting rivers are all techniques that can provide an adequate and reliable water supply in times of drought and can protect against river flooding. These techniques are well developed; they must be applied with an intimate knowledge of the statistics of rainfall and runoff -- that is, the climate.[14]

3. <u>Apply agrotechnology</u>. The supply and adequate distribution of food will continue to be a major problem for the world. Agrotechnology, which led to the "Green Revolution," has permitted more food to be grown in many areas. But the monocultures that account for most of our food are generally more susceptible to both short and long term climate changes than are diversified crops. Thus, we will need to develop such agrotechnologies as more efficient irrigation systems, salt water crops, new forms of nitrogen fixing plants, and plants that will be adapted to changing climates expected in food growing regions. It may take special crops such as sorghum, millet, maize, and sesame to thrive in semi-arid areas. These are generally well adapted to the average climate of the tropical regions where they are grown, but they can be sensitive to climate variability there.[15] Agrotechnology can also exploit useful plants such as the versatile tree <u>leucaena leucocephala</u>, dubbed "the schmoo tree".[16]

4. <u>Improve coastal land use policies</u>. Floods, hurricanes, and typhoons cause environmental and property damage, and loss of human lives. This destruction has been extreme in coastal areas throughout the world.[17]

Much planning in coastal regions has been carried out without adequate application of climatic data. If coastal communities are to effectively mitigate adverse weather and climate events, this information must be used when proposing land use programs. A future sea level rise is one more factor that should be part of this planning even though its timing is still uncertain.

5. Maintain global food reserves. The growing world population will require a reliable food supply. Since any future temperature or precipitation shifts could adversely affect major food producing regions, it would be prudent to be prepared with adequate food reserves.[18]

6. Provide disaster relief. International relief organizations can help countries better cope with short term climatic variations and long term climatic changes. However, in recent years relief efforts have been viewed suspicously; some believe they have been conducted in pursuit of national interests.[19]

B. Strategies That Slow Worldwide Carbon Dioxide Emissions

1. Conserve energy. A low growth energy future would mean that carbon dioxide-induced environmental impacts could be delayed or even largely avoided. There are strong incentives to conserve, including reducing dependence on OPEC oil, and protecting the environment.[20] Conservation is one part of the "soft energy path" that can result in more energy efficiency. It should involve a more extensive use of renewable energy resources. However, in order to achieve a significant reduction in carbon dioxide emissions this strategy would have to be adopted by most countries of the world.

2. Use renewable energy resources. These include wood and other biomass substances; nuclear fission reactors that "breed" plutonium fuel; nuclear fusion reactors that use the virtually limitless hydrogen found in water; garbage; wind; and solar energy, which includes direct capture of sunlight, hydroelectric power, and ocean thermal sources. There are tradeoffs related to each of these energy forms: some are less risky and less polluting than others, and some produce more net energy for a given capital investment.

3. Reforest. To some extent all countries depend on wood for fuel and construction material. More than half of the mass of the entire biosphere is in the tropical forests of the world. Some reports indicate that these forests are being reduced by as much as one percent per

year, although this information is not very reliable.
Such widespread deforestation ruins a valuable economic
asset. But in India, Nepal, Sri Lanka, Brazil, and parts
of Africa, removal of the forest cover has also degraded
the soil and caused severe flooding and erosion. However, many countries have instituted reforestation projects, [21] and this is a hopeful sign. A regrowth of
trees takes up atmospheric carbon dioxide and converts it
to plant tissue through photosynthesis. Thus, reforestation is not only a strategy that makes sense in economic
terms, it also provides another sink for the carbon dioxide we are releasing.

C. Strategies That Lead to Improved Choices

1. Employ environmental monitoring and warning
systems. As noted above, acquisition of climate data
and global monitoring of the environment are functions of
the WMO and the UNEP (see Chapter 2). Thus, we are able
to keep track of the environment of our planet, despite
some gaps in the coverage, such as conditions below the
ocean surface, the size and shape of the ice sheets of
Greenland and the Antarctic, and the state of the tropical forests.

2. Provide and apply improved climate data. Climate
data have been gathered at many stations throughout the
world, but only a small part of it is available in readily usable forms, notably in some developing countries.
The data needs for applied climatology have been well
defined by the WMO's Commission for Special Applications
of Meteorology and Climatology. But expert help and
financial assistance are needed to locate and process it
onto punch cards and magnetic tapes for computer use.
This is the function of the newly established World Climate Applications Programme.[22] Together these new international programs should improve the availability and
application of climate data for planning and operations
in many countries that lack the expertise or the computers needed to use our knowledge of climate and its
influence on human activities. While the immediate
thrust of this effort is to cope with short term climate
variability, it will also help people prepare for long
term climate change.

3. Provide public information and education. Disseminating the results of carbon dioxide/climate studies to
reporters, environmentalists, and other interested groups
should raise the general level of public awareness about
the problem. Such information would encourage the design
of new products and facilities that could respond to new
climatic conditions as well as to climatic variations.

Furthermore, long term measures to cope with climate change will be more readily accepted if a well informed public understands the reasons for their adoption.

4. Transfer appropriate technology. Immediate investment in applied climatology and weather prediction techniques is highly desirable for most developing countries. These investments would fulfill needs in areas such as water supply, plant husbandry, energy resources, housing design, and land use planning.[23] The benefits would likely outweigh the costs. Technology transfer should be encouraged in a number of areas, such as renewable energy resources and agrotechnology.

D. Acceptance of These Strategies

Even if there is no global climate change, there are benefits to be gained by implementing these and similar strategies. Thus, there is no need to delay action and wait for firmer scientific evidence about the carbon dioxide threat.

The need for vigorous initiatives throughout the world to cope with our growing population and changing environment has been voiced recently by the Council on Environmental Quality.[24] It states:

> The available evidence leaves no doubt that the world--including this nation--faces enormous, urgent, and complex problems in the decades immediately ahead. Prompt and vigorous changes in public policy around the world are needed to avoid or minimize these problems before they become unmanageable. Long lead times are required for effective action. If decisions are delayed until the problem became worse, options for effective action will be severely reduced.

Whether societies will have the required resources to take effective actions or adapt to major climate changes is another question. This will be determined by several indices. The first is gross national product (GNP), or income per capita. GNP is a rough measure of aggregate economic activity and is an index of the economic resources to build new facilities or move people.

The second is the gross rate of investment, or ratio of investment to GNP. A high ratio means that many new facilities are being built and capital stock is turning over rapidly. Since new plants and equipment can be designed for the expected climatic conditions and can be built in the right places, rapid turnover means that most

of the capital stock can be tailored to a new economic
or climatic regime.

The third measure is the flexibility and diversity
of the capital stock. Some plants and equipment are so
highly specialized that they cannot accommodate changes
in raw materials, product design, or fuels. For example,
an electricity generator can be designed to burn any two
or all three of the fuels -- natural gas, oil, or coal.
This greater flexibility means there is less need to
replace the capital stock, making adjustment easier.
Diversity of the capital stock gives the economy the resilience to avoid disaster in the face of changing conditions such as climate. This is much like diversifying
crops, instead of depending on a monoculture. The mono-
culture can give greater yield under a narrow range of
conditions but can lead to crop failure if conditions
change. Hence, flexible, diverse capital stock may increase costs and lower output, but it offers insurance
against changing conditions.

A fourth characteristic is the ability to foresee
changing conditions and adapt to them quickly. A better
educated population and good planning in social institutions will help. An important aspect of this is the
ability and willingness of planners to recognize the
signals of coming change and interpret them for the population and for the social institutions that lack this
ability.

NOTES

1. NAS, Carbon Dioxide and Climate: A Scientific Assessment (Report of ad hoc Study Group on Carbon Dioxide
and Climate Woods Hole, Mass. Climate Research Board,
National Academy of Sciences, Washington, D.C. 1979);
WMO, Report of the Meeting of CAS Working Group on Atmospheric Carbon Dioxide (Boulder, Colo. 1979), WMO Proj.
on Rev. and Monitoring of CO_2 Dept. No. 2, World Meteorological Organization, Geneva (1979).
2. Kellogg, W.W. and R. Schware, Climate Change and
Society: Consequences of Increasing Atmospheric Carbon
Dioxide (Westview Press, Boulder, Colorado, 1981).
3. Meyer-Alrich, K. M.,"Socioeconomic Impacts of
CO_2-induced Climatic Changes and the Comparative Chances
of Alternative Political Responses: Prevention, Compensation, and Adaptation." Climatic Change, 2, 373-336
(1979).
4. Levien, R. E., Welcoming address. In Carbon
Dioxide, Climate and Society, J. Williams (ed.), (Pergamon Press, New York, 1979).

5. Note 3, supra; Kellogg, W. W. and M. Mead (eds.), The Atmosphere: Endangered and Endangering. Fogarty Intl. Cntr. Proc. No. 39, Nat'l Inst. of Health, Washington, D.C. (DHEW Publ. No. NIH) 77-1065,(1977).

6. Weiss, B. B., A Resource Management Approach to CO_2 During the Century of Transition. Chapter 12 infra.

7. Rosencrantz, A., "The Problem of Transboundary Pollution." Environment, 22, 5, 15-20 (1980).

8. Pell, C., Senate Resolution 49 relating to international environmental impact statements. Congressional Record, Washington, D.C., 123, 12 (January 24, 1977).

9. Recommendation 70 of the Central Nation Conference on the Human Environment, 1972 U.N. Stockholm Conference, adopted June 16, 1972, U.N. Doc. A/Conf. 48/14, reprinted in 11 Int'l Legal Mats. 1416, 1420 (1972).

10. Nanda, V. P., "The Establishment of International Standards for Transnational Environmental Injury." Iowa Law Review, 60, 5, 1089-1127; (1975), Weiss, B. B., "International Liability for Weather Modification." Climatic Change, 1, 3, 267-290 (1978); Jessup, P. C., "Revision of the International Legal Order," Denver J. Int'l Law and Policy 10, 1-10 (1980).

11. Carter, V. G., and T. Dale, Topsoil and Civilization (revised edition, University of Oklahoma Press, Norman, Okla., 1974).

12. Kouda, V. A., Land Aridization and Drought Control. (Westview Press, Boulder, Colorado, 1980).

13. Glantz, Desertification: Environmental Degradation in and around Arid Lands. M. H. Glantz (ed.) (Westview Press, Boulder, Colo. 1977). Oguntoyinbo, J. A. and R. S. Odingo, "Climatic Variability and Land Use: an African Perspective," Proceedings of the World Climate Conference (WMO No. 537, World Meteorological Organization, Geneva, 552-580, 1979).

14. Schaake, J. C., Jr. and F. Maczmarek, "Climate Variability and the Design and Operation of Water Resource Systems," Proc. World Climate Conference (WMO No. 537, World Meteorological Organization, Geneva, 290-312, 1979).

15. Mattei, F., "Climate Variability and Agricultures in the Semi-arid Tropics," Proc. World Climate Conference, (WMO No. 537, World Meteorological Organization, Geneva, 475-509, 1979).

16. "Schmoo Tree: It Gives Food and Fuel." Time Magazine, December 10, 1979, p. 95.

17. Kates, R. W., "Climate and Society: Lessons from Recent Events." Weather, 35, 1, 17-25, 1980.

18. Schneider, S. H. with L. E. Mesirow, The Genesis Strategy (Plenum, New York, 1976).

19. Garcia, R., Nature Pleads Not Guilty (Pergamon Press, New York, 1981).

20. C.E.Q., Environmental Quality. The tenth annual report of the Council on Environmental Quality (U.S. Gov't. Printing Office, 041-011-0047-5, Washington, D.C., 1979).

21. C.E.Q., The Global 2000 Report to the President, Vol. 1. Report by Council on Environmental Quality and the Department of State, 6-O. Barney (Study Dir.), Washington, D.C., 1980.

22. WMO, Outline Plan and Basis for the World Climate Programme 1980-83. WMO No. 540, World Meteorological Organization, Geneva, 1980.

23. Sach, R., Priorities of LOCs in Weather and Climate, unpublished paper, Economic Research Unit, University of Pennsylvania, 1979; Lele, U., The Design of Rural Development: Lessons from Africa. Johns Hopkins University Press, Baltimore, 1979.

24. Note 20, supra.

8
Global Management of the Environment: Regional and Multilateral Initiatives

Ved P. Nanda and Peter T. Moore

I. THE NATURE OF THE CHALLENGE

The current decade began with an ominous warning in a 1980 report, Global 2000 Report to the President,[1] a three-year inter-agency study conducted by the U.S. Government. The Report's message is clear:

> If present trends continue, the world in 2000 will be more crowded, more polluted, less stable ecologically, and more vulnerable to disruption than the world we live in now. Serious stresses involving population, resources, and environment are clearly visible ahead. Despite greater material output, the world's people will be poorer in many ways than they are today.
> For hundreds of millions of the desperately poor, the outlook for food and other necessities of life will be no better. For many it will be worse. Barring revolutionary advances in technology, life for most people on earth will be more precarious in 2000 than it is now--unless the nations of the world act decisively to alter current trends.[2]

Serious concern with global environment and its management is of recent origin. A growing global awareness of transnational environmental problems as reflected in the scientific and legal literature of the early 1970's[3] and the activities of "various bodies and organizations of the United Nations System,"[4] coincided with the Club of Rome's controversial study, The Limits to Growth,[5] which painted a grim picture of man's future.

Although man's concern for the environment is not new[6] and although it has been generally recognized that environmental degradation respects no political boundaries, efforts toward its management have been sporadic and ineffectual.[7] Given the horizontal structure of the world community, it should come as no surprise that, notwithstanding the need for international cooperative measures to control transbounday environmental damage caused by state activities in the course of industrialization and exploitation of natural resources, the concept of "global management" of the environment has gained significance only during the last few decades. Until the 1950's, transnational environmental efforts found expression either in a limited group of diplomatic and arbitral cases,[8] or in a number of weak international treaties in a selected area of conservation issues such as the protection of whales or the protection of migratory birds.[9]

To illustrate, the principle of state responsibility for transboundary environmental damage was explicitly recognized in the often-cited Trail Smelter Arbitration[10]. This 1935 arbitral case settled an air pollution dispute between the United States and Canada involving the operation of a smelter located in British Columbia which, because of its sulfur dioxide emission, allegedly caused substantial damage to a number of farms in the State of Washington.[11] The specially-created tribunal concluded in 1941 that:

> [U]nder the principles of international law, as well as of the law of the United States, no State has the right to use or permit the use of its territory in such a manner as to cause injury by fumes in or to the territory of another or the properties or persons therein, when the case is of serious consequence and the injury is established by clear and convincing evidence.[12]

The tribunal imposed a detailed regime of controls over the emissions of SO_2 fumes from the smelter. The case, however, is perhaps of questionable validity as a precedent since Canada had specifically assumed international liability for damage caused to the United States from activities within Canada and because it was agreed by both countries to establish a special binational tribunal to "arbitrate" the amount of damages.

But for the partly successful 1909 Boundary Waters Treaty between the United States and Canada,[13] pre-World War II treaties related to the environment can be characterized by the array of international conventions on the conservation of birds and migratory wildlife, or the unsuccessful League of Nations efforts during the 1920's and 1930's.[14] After the war, however, a number of noteworthy developments occurred. For example, in a 1949 decision, the Corfu Channel Case[15] the Internationl Court of Justice provided a useful antecedent for the principle subsequently incorporated into the 1972 Stockholm Declaration on the Human Environment that states are obligated "to ensure that activities within their jurisdiction or

control do not cause damage to the environment of other
States or of areas beyond the limits of national jurisdiction."[16] Subsequently, the principle of state responsibility for transboundary environmental damage also
found expression in a number of diplomatic cases, including the 1954 Japanese Fisherman Case (U.S. responsibility
for nuclear tests),[17] the 1957 Lake Lanoux Arbitration
(French-Spanish river pollution dispute),[18] the 1958
Pacific Tests Case (U.S. nuclear tests),[19] the 1961
Ciudad Juarez Case (U.S. responsibility for river pollution),[20] and the 1973 International Court of Justice
decision in Nuclear Tests Case (France's responsibility
for nuclear testing in the South Pacific).[21] The prece-
dential value of these cases, however, is uncertain, both
because of their limited context (nuclear testing or
river pollution), and because the results in each case may
be interpreted as a diplomatic modus vivendi rather than
a response to developing customary international law.[22]

The heightened awareness about the global environment and concern for "global management" of the environment can be attributed to several factors. These include: the accelerated exploitation of natural resources in much of the world; enhancement of the ecological concerns as a consequence of an awareness of the
havoc that the "second industrial revolution" was
wreaking on the environment; the recognition and understanding that national environmental protection remedies
alone were ill-equipped to cope with transnational pollution, further confirmed by a number of well-publicized
disasters such as the wrecks of the Torrey Canyon and the
Argo Merchant;[23] and the availability of several international organizations such as the United Nations and the
European Economic Community as suitable fora from which
to address the crucial international environmental concerns.

By the late 1960's, these factors catalyzed a pro-
liferation of bilateral, regional, and multilateral conventions on such diverse issues as oil pollution on the
high seas, nuclear transportation and waste disposal,
river pollution, protection of endangered species, acid
rain, weather modification, and transboundary air pollution.[24] To illustrate, by the early 1970's, there were
over twenty institutional arrangements and over 300 bilateral and multilateral conventions covering the rivers
of the world.[25] It is worth noting that although a large
proportion of the river basins thus covered are in
Europe, a growing percentage of basins in Asia, Africa and
South America are now coming under international control.[26] The second large area of international agreements
is in the management of oil pollution on the high seas.[27]
By 1974, there were over 30 multilateral conventions and
numerous protocols governing the transport of oil.[28]

Yet, despite these advances, it was clear by the early 1970's that environmental efforts were scattered, over-lapping and inadequate to meet the global environmental challenge.

In 1972, the United Nations responded to the need for coordination by sponsoring the U.N. Conference on the Human Environment, held in Stockholm.[29] The Stockholm conference was the most successful international meeting on the environment to date, and resulted in the formula-tion and approval of principles and recommendations to serve as guidelines for the future conduct of states in environmental and developmental matters, both nationally and internationally.[30] In addition to the adoption of a Declaration on the Human Environment[31] and of an Action Plan containing recommendations for environmental manage-ment,[32] the Conference established the framework for the creation of the United Nations Environment Programme (UNEP), an organization envisioned to coordinate the comprehensive goals of global environmental assessment and management.[33] Despite this grand plan toward consol-idation, however, ten years after UNEP's creation, the task of environmental management is still being attempted by a diverse group of universal, regional, bilateral and nongovernmental organizations.

This chapter will assess the institutional progress and direction of the present environmental "system" from the period of 1972 to 1981. Section one will analyze the activities of United Nations, including those of UNEP, the International Law Commission, the Economic Commission for Europe, the Economic and Social Commission for Asia and the Pacific, and the Third United Nations Conference on the Law of the Sea (UNCLOS III). The second section will assess, with a view toward understanding the emerging environmental institutions, the activities of (a) the United Nations specialized agencies; (b) the inter- and nongovernmental organizations; and (c) selected regional organizations. This will be followed by a concluding section which will attempt to assess the prospects of this complex system of international environmental management.

II. RECENT TRENDS IN THE ENVIRONMENTAL MANAGEMENT
     ACTIVITIES OF THE UNITED NATIONS

Although the United Nations Environment Programme is the primary U.N. body with competence in the area of environmental management, a number of other agencies and programs also play an important role in shaping the de-veloping environmental law regime. For example, the mandate of the International Law Commission (ILC), established in 1947 to make recommendations for the progressive developments and codifications of international law,[34] is so broad that some of its work is related to the environment. The Economic Commission for Europe (ECE), and the Economic and Social Commission for Asia and the Pacific (ESCAP), both of which were established by the Economic and Social Council in 1947,[35] were originally intended to be post-war agencies primarily responsible for the reconstruction and development of their respective regions. Now, after over thirty years of work on the economic front, these agencies are becoming increasingly concerned and involved with by-products of industrialization, including the issue of the integration of development and environment. Additionally, the proposed Convention on the Law of the Sea prescribes norms to prevent marine pollution and to regulate environmental aspects of activities in the oceans, including those on and under the seabed.[36] Yet, despite this diversification of functions, UNEP is still the focal point of the United Nations' environmental management activities. This section will assess the direction and progress of UNEP and the associated U.N. agencies and programs during the last decade.

A. United Nations Environment Programme

The term "environment programme" belies the complex task that faced UNEP upon its creation in 1972. As the Stockholm Conference on the Human Environment opened, the simmering conflict between developing countries, which desired a greater degree of resource exploitation, and developed nations, which urged a greater degree of environmental control, had already surfaced.[37] Due to a last-minute compromise, a balance was struck between the goals of economic development and environmental management. This balance found expression in the well-known principle 21 of the Declaration of the United Nations on the Human Environment:

> States have, in accordance with the Charter of the United Nations and the principles of international law, the sovereign right to exploit their own resources pursuant to their own environmental policies, and the responsibility to insure that activities within their jurisdiction or control do not cause damage to the environment of other States, or of areas beyond the limits of national jurisdiction.[38]

The functions and activities of UNEP reflect an effort to meet these auspicious goals. UNEP's Action Plan encompasses a three-part framework: environmental assessment, environmental management, and supporting measures.[39] This section will consider the progress of UNEP in these areas.

1. Environmental Assessment

The environmental assessment activities of UNEP, which include evaluation and review, research, monitoring, and information exchange, are primarily undertaken by the Earthwatch Program. The Program is defined as "a dynamic process of integrated environmental assessment by which environmental issues are identified and the necessary data gathered and evaluated to provide proper assessment statements forming the basis for (a) information to assist better understanding for effective environmental management; (b) future research; and (c) early warning of significant environmental changes."[40]
Earthwatch has several major components, including the Global Environmental Monitoring System (GEMS); the International Referral System for Sources of Environmental Information (INFOTERRA); the International Register of potentially toxic Chemicals; the assessment of basic human needs in relation to outer limits of the tolerance of the biosphere and assessment of the outer limits to climatic changes, weather modification, risk to the ozone layer, and social outer limits; research and assessment; and environmental data.[41] Only GEMS and INFOTERRA will be briefly described here.
In keeping with UNEP's dual mandate to coordinate environmental programs within the United Nations system and to play a catalytic role in initiating action where there are program gaps, GEMS encourages and coordinates the acquisition, analysis, storage and dissemination of data by governments and international organizations. GEMS has attempted long-term studies of trends in environmental changes and the relevant UNEP goal for 1982 calls for "an operational GEMS with results available, evaluated and published in the fields of health-related monitoring, climate-related monitoring, long-range transport of pollutants in Europe and resource monitoring."[42]
The INFOTERRA Program has performed the complimentary function of providing a referral network for the exchange of available environmental information. The INFOTERRA network has continued to expand -- by the end of 1980, 76 countries had registered information sources with the INFOTERRA Directory, the number of registered sources stood at 8,400, and the number of states participating in the Program had reached 112.[43] The 1982 goal for INFOTERRA calls for "an operation INFOTERRA with all interested countries having registered sources and making use of the service."[44] To accomplish its overall objective of ensuring that "the information needed for rational decision-making and for achieving environ-

mentally-sound development is available to those who need it,"[45] its future activities will be focused at gaining enhanced cooperation and linkages with governments, international organizations and appropriate information systems, and promoting the use of INFOTERRA.[46]

Under the GEMS Program, projects include those related to resource monitoring, climate-related monitoring, health-related monitoring which includes monitoring air quality, global water-quality, and food, and assessment of human exposure to air pollution; long-range transport of pollutants; ocean monitoring; and research and publications.[47]

2. Environmental Management

a. Overview

Environmental management has to be seen as a broad approach in resolving the problems of sustainable development, were it to be defined as aiming at "the management, in a sustainable fashion, of natural resources, of the development processes which have environmental impacts, and, in some cases, of the social and economic conditions which influence the form which development takes."[47a] UNEP's activities related to environmental management have included the development of frameworks for the preparation of environmental impact assessment statements and for the application of cost-benefit analysis to environmental protection measures.[48] A significant recent development was the signature by nine multilateral development financing institutions in February 1980 at the United Nations Development Program headquarters in New York of a Declaration of Principles for incorporating environmental considerations into development policies, programs and projects.[49]

Major areas of UNEP activities include: environmental aspects of human settlements planning and health of people and the environment; terresterial ecosystems, which include arid and semi-arid ecosystems and desertification, tropical woodlands and forest ecosystems, mountain, island, coastal and other ecosystems, soils, water, genetic resources, wildlife and protected areas; environment and development, which includes integrated approach and environmentally sound and appropriate technology, industry and environment; oceans which include marine pollution, living marine resources, regional seas program; energy; natural disasters; and the development of environmental law.[50]

b. Environmental Law

Although UNEP has no formal mandate for the development of international environmental law, it constitutes

an important component of environmental management.
Also, because UNEP has the primary responsibility for
implementing the principles incorporated in the Stockholm
Declaration on the Human Environment, it may be argued
that UNEP is obligated to formulate such rules. The
pertinent principles in the Declaration, Principle 22,
is unambiguous: "States shall co-operate to develop
further the international law regarding liability and
compensation for victims of pollution and other environmental damage caused by activities within the jurisdiction or control of such states to areas beyond their
jurisdiction."[51]
    It should be noted that UNEP has not shirked its
responsibility. For example, in response to the United
Nations General Assembly resolution 3129 of 1973, UNEP
established a working group of experts to prepare draft
principles for the guidance of states in the conservation
and harmonious exploitation of natural resources which
they share in common.[52] A set of draft principles was
presented by the group in 1978. Subsequently, the General Assembly at its 34th session requested all states to
use the principles as guidelines in the formulation of
bilateral or multilateral conventions regarding natural
resources shared by two or more states.[53] More recently,
a team of experts in environmental law which met under
UNEP auspices in Montevideo from October 28 to November
6, 1981, concluded that UNEP should give priority to
three areas in developing guidelines, principles or
agreements. These three areas are: (1) marine pollution
from land-based services; (2) protection of the stratospheric ozone layer, and (3) transport, handling and disposal of toxic and dangerous wastes.[54]
    The experts also selected several other areas in
which they would recommend that the UNEP take action.
These areas include international cooperation in environmental emergencies; coastal zone management; soil conservation; transboundary air pollution; international trade
in potentially harmful chemicals; protection of rivers
and other inland waters against pollution; legal and administrative mechanisms for the prevention and redress
of pollution damage; and environmental impact assessment.[55] They also recommended that periodic review of
environmental law be undertaken by UNEP,[56] and that in
the process of the "codification, progressive development
and implementation of environmental law," special attention be given to the developing countries' need for technical cooperation and other assistance in the field of
"institution building, education, training and information regarding environmental law."[57]
    The revised goals for UNEP for 1982, set earlier in
1976 and 1978, include: "Wide acceptance by Governments
and application of international conventions and proto-

cols in the field of the environment [both those now existing and those being developed]," and "Agreement on the principles which should guide States in their relations with each other in respect of shared natural resources, the problems of liability and compensation for pollution and environmental damage, weather modification and risks to the ozone layer."[58] Although at the ninth session of the governing council of the UNEP in May 1981 there were some delegates who objected to the UNEP's initiatives in the development of environmental law,[59] it is anticipated that UNEP will continue its initiatives in the formulation of environmental law.

In addition to the UNEP's activities in selecting and disseminating full texts of important international conventions and protocols in the area of environment,[59a] which should help fill a critical information gap, UNEP is also concerned with a major problem of administration faced by developing countries which lack a sufficient number of lawyers who are trained in environmental law. In response to this problem, UNEP has adopted specific goals and strategies to encourage the growth of environmental law administration skills in the developing country. A brief sketch of the four-pronged approach follows:

(i) The Promotion of National Environmental Law

A pre-condition to acceptance of international environmental management principles is the development of a national appreciation of ecology. Through a number of organizations, agencies and individual experts, UNEP assists developing countries to develop and implement national environmental legislation. Although work to achieve this objective began only in 1977, UNEP's medium-term plans for 1981-83 for the promotion and development of national environmental law are ambitious. During this period, the focus will be on Latin-America and the Caribbean.[60] A survey will be taken during this time to identify the sectors of the environment in Latin America which lack adequate laws, so as to make it possible for programs to be developed to promote existing legislation and to formulate new laws. This survey will also be used to determine the strategy for harmonization of regional laws and the promotion of regional cooperation.[61] An intergovernmental meeting will be held to review the results of the survey, to establish guidelines for developing compatible environmental legislation and machinery, and to provide avenues for cooperation among the concerned governments, FAO, the Caribbean Conservation Association, the Economic Commission for Latin America, and the International Union for the Conservation of Nature and Natural Resources (IUCN).[62]

(ii) The Stimulation of Environmental Law
Education and Research

Since 1977, UNEP has conducted surveys on existing
environmental law teaching and research programs to establish a network of selected institutions with which to
cooperate.[63] Phase two of this program to be completed
in 1982 calls for the preparation of a model curriculum
capable of being adapted for teaching environmental law
and practice in universities and institutions in different regions.[64] The final phase to be completed in 1983
calls for arranging seminars to discuss the prepared
materials and to adopt model syllabi and other teaching
materials so that environmental law education programs
may be coordinated throughout the world.[65]

(iii) Promotion of Wider Acceptance and Implementation of International Environmental
Agreements

UNEP's medium term objectives for 1982-83 include
ascertaining the difficulties governments face when they
wish to become parties to conventions or when they attempt to implement conventions, promoting the development
of laws related to environmental provisions of UNCLOS III,
and promoting the development of legal instruments for the
follow-up of the World Conservation Strategy.[66]

(iv) Technical Cooperation Among Developing
Countries to Develop Environmental
Legislation

Efforts for 1982-83 will focus on (1) training programs for environmental lawyers; (2) technical assistance
on environmental legislation; (3) the revision of the
Manual on Environmental Legislation; and (4) the publication of the Handbook on Environmental Legislation.[67]

3. Supporting Measures

Supporting measures include environmental education
and training, the communication of environmental information to decision-makers and to the public at large, and
technical assistance.[68]

a. Environmental Education and Training

UNEP and UNESCO have jointly sponsored ecological
training programs which have resulted in enhancing
awareness of environmental matters in many countries.[69]
At the ninth session of the UNEP governing council held
in Nairobi in May 1981, the representative of UNESCO said
that it was essential to provide further support for the
training of specialists in integrated management of

environmental resources,[70] and that environmental education and training programs should be carried out in full
cooperation with the relevant specialized agencies.[71]

Current objectives include developing, refining, and
establishing the principles, theory and application of
environmental education;[72] the integration of environmental education into existing educational systems;[73]
the promotion and support of research, experimentation
and appropriate evaluation procedures in environmental
education;[74] the promotion of training programs in environmental matters so as to provide decison makers
involved in the environmental field with appropriate
understanding and competence in such matters;[75] the preparation of resource materials for the support of training
programs in environmental fields;[76] and the provision for
effective international coordination, harmonization and
development of environmental training programs.[77]

b. Information Dissemination

In the dissemination of information, six UNEP
Regional Information Officers now share the primary responsibility for communicating environmental information
to the various audiences.[78] The major objective is to
develop and strengthen established procedures with a view
to communicating more effectively with governments and
the public for the dissemination of environmental information.[79] Ever since its first session, the UNEP Governing
Council has considered public information a priority
activity.[80]

c. Technical Assistance

The overall objective of the technical assistance
program is to provide assistance to developing countries
in identifying their national and regional environmental
priorities, especially in environmental legislation and
machinery, and to enhance their capability to participate
in substantive environmental programs.[81] Technical assistance is usually provided in the form of technical
advice to governments on law through UNEP's various
regional advisory services, and also through consultants.[82]

B. Recent Activities of other U.N. Bodies Related to the Environment

1. International Law Commission

The International Law Commission, which was established in 1947, has the primary responsibility to make
recommendations for the progressive development and
codification of international law. During the 1970's,
the ILC's activities in the area of environmental law

centered around two subjects: (1) the law of non-navigational uses of international water courses; and (2)inter-
national liability for injurious consequences arising out
of acts not prohibited by international law.[83]

With respect to the first topic, the ILC, seeking to
compile state practice on the subject, submitted a questionnaire to member states. A report analyzing the governmental replies to this questionnaire was submitted to
the International Law Commission at its 31st session in
1979. In considering this report, the Commission noted
that the demand for water will continue to grow with the
inter-related surges "in world population, the spread of
industrialization and urbanization, the expansion of
agriculture, and increasing needs for power."[84]

In discussing the report, members were in general
agreement that the problems of fresh water are among the
most serious problems mankind faces and could be effectively managed only if adequate norms, procedures, and
institutions were developed.[85] Members of the Commission
however, were not in accord on the most desirable approaches to take in drafting principles governing the use
of international water courses. While some members
favored initial drafting of principles focusing on such
specific uses as irrigation or power production, others
preferred the formulation of general principles of law
regarding the non-navigational uses of international
water courses.[86]

On the second topic, international liability for
injurious consequences arising out of acts not prohibited by international law, the Commission established
a working group in 1978.[87] The Working Group recognized the need for urgent development of legal norms and
the Commission appointed a special rapporteur who submitted his first preliminary report to the Commission in
1980.[88] The Commission is pursuing both the topics.

2. Economic Commission for Europe (ECE)

ECE has worked closely with UNEP and several other
United Nations specialized agencies such as the Food
and Agriculture Organization (FAO) and the International
Labor Organization (ILO) regarding environmental issues.
The major accomplishment of the ECE regarding the development of international environmental law is the work it
undertook in the development of the Convention on Long-
range Transboundary Air Pollution (the Convention).[89]
The Convention entered into force in November 1979 and
has been signed by 35 countries including the United
States, Canada and most of the East and West European
states. Subsequently, it adopted a Declaration of Policy
on Prevention and Control of Water Pollution in April
1980.[90]

The Convention obligates contracting parties to consult on request on activities affecting or posing a "significant risk" of long-range transboundary air pollution. It also contains provisions for information exchange, continued monitoring of pollutants, and collaborative research toward the objective of mitigating sulfur dioxide (SO_2) emissions. ECE's main activities include its work toward the implementation of the Convention and its contribution toward the development of international environmental law in the ECE region in the area of water pollution. On the latter subject, the ECE Committee on Water Problems continues to work for building on the revised Declaration on Water Pollution.[91] Also, ECE has been active in arranging seminars on environmental pollution and on environmental impact assessment and has been devoting considerable attention to the problem of disposal of toxic wastes.[92]

It is noteworthy that many of the ECE agreements and declarations not only influence development of environmental law in the region since those principles and guidelines are used by European governments in fashioning national regulations, but also might set the pattern for regulation in other regions as well.

3. Economic and Social Commission for Asia and the Pacific (ESCAP)

In 1974, ESCAP took over the activities of its predecessor organization, the Economic Commission for Asia and the Far East.[93] ESCAP's activities are primarily conducted by legislative committees, which include those working in the areas of development planning, natural resources, population, trade and shipping, and transport and communications.[94] The Commission has recently engaged in a number of activities related to the development of environmental legislation at the regional level. To illustrate, it has completed a detailed study of marine pollution legislation in numerous countries of the region, with specific focus on the relationship between international conventions and national legislation and the formulation of a draft regional convention for combating marine pollution in the region.[95] It is expected that similar studies will be undertaken in the areas of land use planning and forest development. Other ESCAP activities include those related to environmental impact analysis and regional cooperative environmental policies.[96]

4. Third United Nations Conference on the Law of the Sea (UNCLOS III)

As of April 1982 negotiations on the drafting of an umbrella treaty are still continuing. UNCLOS III, however, has reached accord on the provisions concerning the marine environment. If a comprehensive treaty comes into force, this would be a significant accomplishment because the state parties would have accepted a general obligation to protect and preserve the marine environment as a whole. The Draft Convention on the Law of the Sea[97] incorporates the principles enunciated in the Stockholm Declaration on the Human Environment[98] and perhaps builds upon those principles.

The Draft Convention defines pollution of the marine environment as "the introduction by man, directly or indirectly, of substances or energy into the marine environment . . . which results or is likely to result in such deleterious effects as harm to living resources and marine life, hazards to human health, hindrance to marine activities, including fishing and other legitimate uses of the sea, impairment of quality for use of sea water and reduction of amenities."[99] States are obligated to protect and preserve the marine environment;[100] specifically, they are to take all measures "that are necessary to prevent, reduce and control pollution of the marine environment from any source, using for this purpose the best practical means at their disposal and in accordance with their capabilities, . . . and they shall endeavor to harmonize their policies in this connection."[101] Further, they are obligated to take all the necessary measures to "ensure that activities under their jurisdiction or control are so conducted as not to cause damage by pollution to other States and their environment, and that pollution arising from incidents or activities under their jurisdiction or control does not spread beyond the areas where they exercise sovereign rights in accordance with this Convention."[102]

For the protection and preservation of the marine environment, states are required to "cooperate on a global basis and, as appropriate, on a regional basis directly or through competent international organizations, in formulating and elaborating international rules, standards and recommended practices and procedures" consistent with the Draft Convention.[103] Also, states are to notify other states as well as the competent international organizations of imminent or actual damage by pollution,[104] they are to develop and promote contingency plans against pollution,[105] and are to cooperate on conducting studies, research programs and exchange of information and data and on the establishment of appropriate scientific criteria for the formulation

and elaboration of rules, standards and procedures for
the prevention, reduction and control of marine pollution.[106] Additionally, under the general provisions of
the Convention, states are required to monitor risks or
effects of pollution,[107] and to make assessment of potential effects of their activities on the marine environment.[108]

The Draft Convention addresses several major areas
of marine pollution. They include pollution from
(1) land-based sources, (2) seabed activities, (3) vessels, (4) activities in the International Area, and
(5) from or through the atmosphere. The Convention also
provides for enforcement measures,[109] and safeguards,[110]
and especially provides for ice-covered areas.[111]

Specifically regarding land-based pollution, states
are obligated to adopt laws and regulations to control
it.[112] The Draft Convention seeks to promote national
measures as well as regional and international approaches
to combat land-based pollution. States are required to
"endeavor to harmonize their national policies at the
appropriate regional level,"[113] and to "endeavor to
establish global and regional rules, . . . taking into
account characteristic regional features, the economic
capacity of developing States and their need for economic development."[114] These provisions are designed to
prevent, reduce and control marine pollution in the
coastal states' exclusive economic zone by blending
regional and international measures with national policies.

In controlling marine pollution from seabed activities, coastal states are required to adopt laws and
regulations which "shall be no less effective than international rules, standards, and recommended practices and
procedures."[115] States are required to establish global
and regional rules, standards and procedures and are to
harmonize their national policies at the appropriate
regional level.[116] Similarly, states are required to
adopt the necessary measures to prevent marine pollution
from activities in the International Area "undertaken
by vessels, installations, structures and other devices
flying their flag or of their registry or operating
under their authority. . . ."[117] Also, international
rules, regulations and procedures are required to be
established to control marine pollution activities
within the International Area.[118] Similar provisions
exist to prevent pollution from dumping.[119] Efforts to
control vessel-source pollution focus on the establishment of international rules and standards "through the
competent international organization or general diplomatic conference."[120] The international organization is
intended to be the Intergovernmental Maritime Consultative
Organization (IMCO).[121]

It is noteworthy that competing interest of the
world community in the freedom of navigation and of
coastal and flag states to minimize pollution are seemingly well-balanced in the Convention. For example:
flag states are required to adopt appropriate laws and
regulations to minimize pollution, and these must have
at least the same effect as that of generally accepted
international rules and standards;[122] states which have
established particular pollution requirements of condition of entry of foreign vessels into their ports or
into internal waters are required to give due publicity
to such requirements and communications are encouraged
between IMCO and states which have adopted reciprocal
requirements in respect of pollution;[123] coastal states,
in the exercise of sovereignty within their territorial
seas, may adopt pollution regulations related to innocent
passage, provided that these do not hamper such passage;[124] and coastal states may adopt laws and regulations
regarding pollution from vessels in the EEZ of their
coasts, conforming to and giving effect to generally
accepted international rules and standards.[125]

The Draft Convention explicitly provides that when
the pertinent international rules and standards are
inadequate to meet special circumstances and when a particular coastal state has reasonable grounds for believ-
ing that a particular area needs special protection, that
state after appropriate consultation with the competent
international organization, i.e., IMCO, and with the
other states concerned, may, with the approval of the
international organization, adopt special regulations
applicable to that area.[126]

The Draft Convention binds the states to adopt laws
and regulations and to take measures necessary to implement international rules and standards for the protection
of the marine environment from land-based pollution,
pollution from seabed activities, and pollution from off-
shore structures within their jurisdiction.[127] It also
contains a number of safeguards against improper treatment of vessels accused of causing pollution or violating
local laws implementing international standards.[128] To
control pollution from vessels in ice-covered area within
the limits of the exclusive economic zone, where such
pollution could cause major harm to or irreversible dis-
turbance of the ecological balance, coastal states are
allowed to adopt and enforce laws and regulations which
are non-discriminatory.[129]

Critics have suggested that UNCLOS III has not made
a significant advance toward the control of marine pollution[130] and that coastal state are likely to be unduly
hampered in their efforts to prevent pollution of the
marine environment. It is, however, submitted that
UNCLOS III is a desirable first step toward the pre-

vention of marine environment from pollution. Many of
the prescriptions will need detailed work before they
could be specific enough for the purposes of implementation; in their present form many norms are abstract, in
need of elaboration on both the regional and global level
in order to have detailed obligations upon nation states
and to have precise international standards and implementation measures. Nontheless, the accomplishments of
UNCLOS III are substantial insofar as states parties to
the proposed treaty would assume responsibility for the
prevention and control of marine pollution and would
undertake the necessary cooperative measures for the protection and preservation of the marine environment.

C. Activities of the U.N. Specialized Agencies

1. The International Labor Organization (ILO)

As reflected in the preamble of the ILO Constitution
of 1919, one of the primary functions of the ILO is to
promote the improvement of the working conditions and
working environment of workers.[131] ILO considers the
working environment as an integral part of the human
environment. Its contribution to the development of
environmental law lies primarily in the setting of
standards in the form of conventions, recommendations and
guidelines. However, not all the instruments of the ILO
have the force of law, as for example, the guidelines are
intended to assist ILO member states to develop their own
standards for implementation of environmental law.
Since 1929, ILO has adopted 153 conventions and 161
recommendations in the field of occupational safety and
health,[132] several of which are related primarily to the
working environment. To illustrate, ILO has addressed
such topics as protection of workers from radiation, air
pollution, noise and vibration in the working environment, and has adopted recommendations relating to workers' compensation arising from occupational diseases in
the work place.[133] In 1976, ILO launched the International Programme for the Improvement of Working Conditions and Environment.[134] A Draft Convention and a
draft recommendation on the subject are on ILO's
agenda.[135]
Perhaps the most important contribution of the ILO
is in two areas: (1) dissemination of information on all
aspects of occupational safety and health, including
legislation and standards, occupational hazards and basic
prevention data, and (2) its international cooperative
efforts with other international organizations, including
UNEP.[136] The dissemination of information is done
through the International Occupational Safety and Health
Center.[137]

2. Food and Agriculture Organization (FAO)

A primary function of the Food and Agriculture Organization, as reflected in Article 1 of its Constitution of 1945, is to recommend national and international action with respect to the conservation of natural resources and adoption of improved methods of agricultural production.[138] This mandate was interpreted by the 59th FAO Council to include the monitoring and conservation of the productive capacities of natural resources "for agriculture, forestry and fisheries and the mutual interactions of these activities and the environment, including the related problems of wastes, pollution and food contamination."[139] One of the current objectives, approved by the FAO Conference at its 20th session, is the promotion of measures "to halt degradation and depletion of natural resources, to restore them and to increase and sustain their productive capacity including these related problems of waste pollution and food contamination."[140]

FAO is primarily concerned with the development of environmental laws in specific problem areas such as desertification, arid grasslands, salinization or waterlogging of irrigated areas, endangered genetic resources, degradation of watersheds, water pollution in agriculture, forests, marine pollution effecting fisheries, and flood control.[141] As related to environmental law, ILO's areas of special concern include: (1) collection and dissemination of legislative information; (2) legal studies and guidelines on critical areas of food, agriculture and the environment; (3) technical assistance to member governments; and (4) training.[142] It has developed the necessary institutional framework for providing legislative services and technical assistance programs.

In the field of legislative information dissemination, FAO maintains a central legislative catalog, which contains approximately 120,000 legislative texts, indexed by subject and country, many of which subjects are relevant to environmental concern.[143] In the area of legal and technical assistance, FAO has provided advice and assistance recently to many countries including Colombia, Honduras, Indonesia, Trinidad and Tobago, Morocco, Tunisia, Sudan, and Central African Republic.[144] At the international level, FAO has been closely associated with several of the UNEP programs including its work on natural resources, environmental impact assessment, and the formulation of regional seas programs.[145]

3. World Health Organization (WHO)

WHO is primarily involved in information transfer and technical cooperation in health and environmental

legislation. Under WHO's Constitution member states are
required to communicate promptly to the organization
important laws and regulations pertaining to health
which have been published in the state concerned.[146] Its
quarterly journal, the "International Digest of Health
Legislation," regularly publishes the national legal
texts as well as texts of summaries of legal instruments
adopted by or under the auspices of international organizations within as well as outside the United Nations
system.[147] To cite an example of the WHO activities
toward the promotion of environmental health, WHO has
recently called for collaboration "with countries as
required in formulating policies and legislation and in
setting up infrastructure for the surveillance of wastes
disposal networks and of drinking water quality, and
particularly for the detection of a number of deleterious
substances. It will encourage the simultaneous development of adequate administrative and legal structures.[148]

4. World Meteorological Organization (WMO)

WMO's activities which are pertinent for the development of environmental law include research and monitoring of atmospheric carbon dioxide, long-range transport
of pollutants, global ozone research and monitoring, and
weather modification.[149] It coordinates the monitoring
and research activities of member states, actively
cooperates with UNEP, and assists developing countries
with their participation in the World Weather Watch
Program.[150]

5. The Intergovernmental Maritime Consultative Organization (IMCO)

As a specialized agency of the United Nations, IMCO
is exclusively involved in the maritime field. IMCO's
activities in the field of marine environmental protection
are centered around: (1) the development and adoption
of the highest practical standards for the prevention and
control of deliberate and accidental pollution from ships
and other equipment operating in the marine environment;
(2) the encouragement of governments in the effective
implementation and enforcement of internationally accepted standards; (3) the promotion of cooperation among
governments, particularly at the regional level, for
combating pollution in cases of emergency; and (4) assistance to developing countries regarding the implementation and enforcement of internationally accepted
standards and regional cooperative arrangements among
governments for combating pollution in emergencies.[151]
IMCO's major accomplishments include the promotion
and adoption of numerous conventions in a wide-range of

subjects,[152] and its cooperative efforts with UNEP in
regional seas program,[153] and technical assistance to
developing countries on measures to prevent, control, and
combat pollution from ships.[154]

6. International Atomic Energy Agency

Among other organizations, the International Atomic
Energy Agency's activities include ensuring the safe use
of atomic energy and improving the protection of workers,
the general public and the environment against harmful
effects of ionizing radiation arising from peaceful
nuclear applications.[155]

III. ACTIVITIES OF THE INTERNATIONAL INTER- AND NON-
GOVERNMENTAL ORGANIZATIONS OUTSIDE THE
UNITED NATIONS SYSTEM

Among the intergovernmental organizations active in
the field of international environmental law, the following should be noted: the European Economic Community,[156]
the Organization for Economic Cooperation and Development,[157] the Council for Mutual Economic Assistance,[158]
and the Asian-African Legal Consultative Committee.[159]
Among non-governmental organizations, those actively
involved in environmental matters include the International Union for the Conservation of Nature and Natural
Resources,[160] International Juridical Organization,[161]
and the International Institute for Environment and
Development.[162]

IV. ASSESSMENT OF REGIONAL ARRANGEMENTS

In the recent past, several new regional arrangements
have been instituted or the existing regional organizations used for the prevention, regulation, and control of
environmental degradation. Among the more successful
attempts are the initiatives undertaken by the European
Economic Community (EEC) and UNEP's regional seas program. On the other hand, attempts in the developing
regions of the world in Africa, Asia and Latin America
have had limited success in only a number of specific
fields such as international water basins.

The accomplishments of the EEC in environmental
matters are at least partly attributable to special
features which distinguish the EEC from other regional
groupings. Such features include EEC's legislative
competence insofar as it can adopt legislation in the
field of the environment, which is binding on its member
states; and the competence of the community law to confer
rights directly on individuals which are justiciable in
the members' courts. Additionally, the Community has a

network of institutions which formulate, implement and enforce community policies.

The EEC's environmental policy has a dual objective: proper management of natural resources and the introduction of concern for the quality of life into the issues of economic and social development.[163] The tasks designed to accomplish these objectives fall into three categories: (1) the prevention and reduction of pollution which harms natural resources, the biosphere and the quality of life; (2) the protection of natural resources and the improvement of the quality of life by measures including new preventive instruments of economic and land-use planning; and (3) the search for international solutions to the problems posed by environmental protection and improvement.[164] The principles which guide this policy include: (1) the "polluter pays" principle, which means that the polluter assumes financial responsibility for making good any environmental damage caused by the polluter; (2) the principle of giving priority to prevention over cure; and (3) the principle of finding a most appropriate geographical basis -- local, regional, national or community -- for every action.[165]

Since 1973, the Community has adopted more than fifty instruments defining the characteristics of products with the objective of imposing limits on the pollution which they cause.[166] To illustrate, the Community has established standards regarding the permissible discharge by industry into the environment of dangerous substances, motor vehicle exhaust, and permissible levels of industrial noise.[167] The Community action on environmental issues has included the study and promotion of new tools for land-use and economic planning; the coordination of research designed to improve the environment; education and public awareness activities; and the creation of new institutions, such as the European Foundation for the Improvement of Living and Working Conditions, which was established in Dublin in 1975.[168]

Following the U.N. General Assembly's directive to the Governing Council of UNEP to explore the possibilities for regional programs,[169] the first major accomplishment was the Convention for the Protection of the Mediterranean Sea Against Pollution (Barcelona Convention).[170] In 1975, the Mediterranean littoral states adopted the Mediterranean Action Plan.[171] A year later, the Barcelona Convention and its two related protocols on dumping and emergencies were signed by representatives of 15 Mediterranean states.[172] Subsequently, at a diplomatic conference of the Mediterranean States held in Athens in May 1980, an additional protocol on land-based pollution was adopted and signed by twelve Mediterranean States and the EEC.[173]

Following the successful Mediterranean effort, UNEP has initiated several other regional plans. For example, it has supported the Arab League Educational, Cultural and Scientific Organization as the coordinator of a regional convention on the Red Sea.[174] In January 1976, the coastal states of the region adopted an Action Plan and have already considered preliminary drafts of a regional convention.[175] Similarly, in April 1978, UNEP convened the Kuwait Regional Conference of Plenipotentaries on the Protection and Development of the Marine Environment and the Coastal Areas. The participants, eight coastal states of the region, adopted an Action Plan at the Conference and signed the Kuwait Regional Convention for Cooperation on the Protection of the Marine Environment from Pollution and a protocol concerning regional cooperation in combating pollution by oil and other harmful substances in cases of emergency.[177] Both the Convention and protocol entered into force in June 1979, and by March 1981 had been ratified by 7 coastal states.[178] Also, UNEP convened a Conference on West and Central African Regions in Abidjan in March 1981.[179] The Conference adopted an Action Plan for the region[180] and also adopted two legal instruments: the Convention for Cooperation in the Protection and Development of the Marine and Coastal Environment of the West and Central African Regions; and a protocol concerning cooperation in combating pollution in cases of emergency.[181] Ten coastal states of the region signed these instruments.[182] Also, UNEP has been pursuing similar plans for the protection of the Caribbean region, East Asian seas, and Southeast Pacific.[183]

Other regional organizations which have assumed responsibilities for the protection of the environment and the improvement of environmental quality include the Organization for Economic Co-operation and Development (OECD),[184] the Council for Mutual Economic Assistance (CMEA),[185] and the Asian-African Legal Consultative Committee.[186] The OECD has been active in planning impact studies and coordinating and harmonizing member states' policies, and has formulated a set of principles which can be incorporated in domestic laws and regulations for environmental protection and in international agreements. Similarly, CMEA is concerned with environmental protection[188] and is active in harmonizing member states' environmental laws[189] and has undertaken studies on problems related to the protection and enhancement of the environment[190] as well as the rational use of natural resources.[191]

The Asian-African Legal Consultative Committee, an intergovernmental organization,[192] is concerned with assisting its member governments in their efforts in connection with the adoption of appropriate legislative and administrative frameworks for the protection of the

environment and in combating pollution.[193] Special areas
of concern include the fields of human settlement, land
use, mountain ecology, industrialization and marine pollution, and with the establishment of an enforcement
machinery suited to their needs.[194] Also, the effort is
to promote regional cooperation,[195] especially in the
area of marine pollution and trans-frontier pollution
regarding international waterways.[196]

During the last decade there has been considerable
progress on regional arrangements among countries in a
geographical area for the prevention and control of
transnational marine pollution.[197] In addition to the
UNEP's efforts already mentioned,[198] the pollution problems
in the North Sea and the Baltic Sea Area led to conferences and conventions in these regions. In 1974, a
conference was held in Paris on the Prevention of Marine
Pollution from Land-Based Sources and a convention adopted for the prevention of marine pollution from land-
based sources which entered into force on May 6, 1978.[199]
Also, in 1974 another conference was held in Helsinki
which resulted in the adoption of the Convention on the
Protection of the Marine Environment of the Baltic Sea
Area,[200] which entered into force on May 3, 1980.

Among several factors which have affected the promotion of regional arrangements to prevent and control
marine environmental pollution, perhaps the most significant consideration is that efforts thus far to establish a single international regime for this purpose have
been futile primarily because of the complexity of land-
based pollution control and the divergent interests of
developed and developing states.[201] Furthermore, while it
seems unlikely that a comprehensive global agreement on
transnational marine pollution is a likely prospect in
the near future, regional mechanisms and organizations
seem capable of resolving and managing environmental
problems, many of which are especially amenable to
regional solutions. That seems to be one important reason why the UNCLOS III has also supported the regional
approach.[202]

It is important to note that usefulness of the
regional approach is not confined just to the marine
environment, as has been unambiguously demonstrated by
the experiences of both the EEC[203] and OECD.[204] However, the difficulties in establishing and implementing
comprehensive regional environmental plans in the developing areas of the world in Africa, Asia, the Caribbean,
South America, and the South Pacific stem primarily from
two sources: (1) the perception shared by many governments in these regions until recently that the goals of
economic development and environmental protection are
often competing and that the former has to be given
priority in their developmental planning processes, and

(2) the lack of adequate understanding as well as the necessary wherewithal including resources to prevent and combat environmental degradation. The recent progress, as evidenced by the work of UNEP[205]and the Asian-African Legal Consultative Committee is encouraging.

V. APPRAISAL AND RECOMMENDATION

The developments in the recent past have been encouraging. The efforts toward devising norms, institutions, and procedures have produced tangible results. For example, mechanisms have been created for the gathering and evaluation of the essential data for environmental assessment.[206] UNEP has assumed the primary responsibility for coordinating activities of governments and international organizations in the acquisition, analysis, storage and dissemination of data.[207] Similarly, environmental management no longer is an abstract concept -- it has gained acceptance as a useful tool for the management not only of natural resources and developmental processes with environmental impact, but also of the economic and social conditions which influence the form of development.[208] Environmental law, both on national and international levels, is being slowly developed.[209] A number of new conventions, both regional and universal, are being negotiated and in the recent past many have come in force.

These encouraging signs notwithstanding, the task ahead is immense. The pace of the developments noted earlier has been agonizingly slow. Some nations are only reluctantly willing to cooperate in these regional and international measures.[210] A candid appraisal of the past trends and the state of affairs at present will show that (1) there are wide gaps in our knowledge of environmental affairs which are compounded by a lack of effective mechanisms for coordinating environmental research activities; (2) as yet there is no real consensus in the international arena to establish workable and enforceable norms and institutions to prevent and remedy international environmental degradation because of resistance by some states and a consistent lack of the necessary political will and vision on the part of many; and there are unresolved questions regarding the balancing of the sensitive issues of environment and development. Additionally, the developing world is in need of more technical assistance and support in the formulation of national environmental policies and the implementation of regional and universal environmental policies and prescriptions.

It seems imperative that more attention be paid simultaneously on several fronts, such as: environmental education; environmental research and training; the dedelopment of both preventive and remedial policies,

norms, and institutions; experimentation with both regional and universal mechanisms; and improved and
strengthened measures of coordination. The nascent international environmental law is in dire need of effective means of implementation.

NOTES

1. Council on Environmental Quality, The Global
2000 Report to the President: Entering the Twenty-First
Century, Summary Report (1980).
2. Id. at 1.
3. See, e.g., David Davies Memorial Institute of
Int'l Studies, Water Pollution as a World Problem (1971);
R. Falk, This Endangered Planet (1971); Global Effects
of Environmental Pollution (S. Singer ed. 1970); E.
Goldsmith, R. Allen, M. Allaby, J. Davoll & S. Lawrence,
A Blueprint for Survival (1972); Institute of Ecology,
Man in the Living Environment (1972); Law, Institutions
& The Global Environment (J. Hargrove ed. 1972); Man's
Impact on the Global Environment (1970)(reporting find
ings, conclusions, and recommendations of the Massachusetts Institute of Technology sponsored Study of Critical Environmental Problems); Symposia dealing with
international environmental problems were published in a
number of law journals. See 13 Nat. Res. J. 177 (1973);
12 id. 131 (1972); 11 id. 221 (1971); 7 Tex. Int'l L. J.
1 (1971); 6 U.B.C.L. Rev. 111 (1971); 2 U. Toronto L. J.
173 (1971). Legal periodicals such as Ecology Law
Quarterly, Environmental Affairs, Environmental Law, and
the Environmental Law Review were devoted entirely to
environmental law. For more complete listings of the
relevant literature see Henning, A Selected Bibliography
on Public Environmental Policy and Administration, 11
Nat. Res. J. 205 (1971); U.N. Doc. A/CONF.48/13/Rev. 1
(1972) (bibliography of documents collected for use by
the participants at the Stockholm Conference on the
Human Environment).
4. For a summary of the work of these agencies, see
The U.N. System and the Human Environment, U.N. Doc.
A/CONF.48/12, Annex I (1971). See also id., U.N. Doc.
A/CONF. 48/12 at 53-58 (discussion of U.N. efforts to
promote and coordinate unilateral, bilateral and regional pollution control measures).
5. D. Meadows, D. Meadows, J. Randers and W. Behrens
The Limits to Growth (Report to the Club of Rome, 1972).
6. For example, as early as 1273 a statute against
air pollution was enacted in England, which was followed
by a 1307 Royal Proclamation banning the use of coal in
village furnaces. UNEP, Environmental Law: An In-Depth
Review 5 (UNEP Rep. No. 2, 1981) [hereinafter cited as

UNEP Rep. No. 2]. See generally Utton,"International Environmental Law and Consultation Methods," 12 Colum. J. Transnat'l L. 56, 57-59 (1973).

7. See generally UNEP Rep. No. 2, at 5-6.

8. See, e.g., id. at 5; notes 10-15 infra.

9. UNEP Rep. No. 2, at 5.

10. See 3 R. Int'l Arb. Awards 1911 (1938).

11. Id. at 1920.

12. Id. at 1965 (1941).

13. Treaty with Great Britain Relating to Boundary Waters Between the United States and Canada, Jan. 11, 1909, 36 Stat. 2448, T.S. No. 548. See generally Nanda, "The Establishment of International Standards for Transnational Environmental Injury," 60 Iowa L. Rev. 1089, 1106-1108 (1979) and the authorities cited there for a discussion of the United States-Canadian experience regarding the utilization of the treaties and of the regulatory machinery created under the treaty for environmental purposes.

14. See UNEP Rep. No. 2, at 5. For a listing of conventions, see Register of International Conventions and Protocols in the Field of the Environment, UNEP/GC./ INFO./5 (1977), and accompanying supplements for 1978-1981.

15. The Corfu Channel Case (Albania v. United Kingdom), [1949] I.C.J. 4.

16. Principle 21 of the Declaration. See Report of the United Nations Conference on the Human Environment (Stockholm, 5-16 June 1972), 1 U.N. GAOR (21st plen. mtg.), U.N. Doc.A/CONF. 48/14/Rev. 1 (1972).

17. For a report, see N.Y. Times, Jan. 5, 1955, at 6, col. 1. For discussion of the incident see Arnold, "Effects of the Recent Bomb Tests on Human Beings," 10 Bull. Atomic Scientists 347 (1954); Margolis, "The Hydrogen Bomb Experiments and International Law," 64 Yale L. J. 629, 637-39 (1955).

18. See generally 53 Am. J. Int'l L. 156 (1959). For the text of the award, see 62 Revue Générale de Droit International Public 79 (1958).

19. See 4 M. Whiteman, Digest of International Law 578-96 (1965).

20. See 6 M. Whiteman, Digest of International Law 256-59 (1968).

21. See [1973] I.C.J. 99, 135; [1974] id. at 252, 257.

22. See, however, Nanda, supra note 13, at 1100-1101.

23. See generally Nanda, "The 'Torrey Canyon' Disaster: Some Legal Aspects," 44 Den. L. J. 400 (1967); Herman, "Flags of Convenience -- New Dimensions to an Old Problem," 24 McGill L. J. 1, 2 (1978); Dempsey & Helling, "Oil Pollution by Ocean Vessels -- An Environmental Tragedy," 10 Den. J. Int'l L. & Pol'y 37 (1980).

24. See generally U.N. Doc. UNEP/GC./Info./5 and Supp. 1-4.

25. See Developments in the Field of Natural Resources -- Water, Energy and Minerals -- Technical Aspects of International River Basin Development, U.N. Doc. E/C.7/35, at 13 (1972).

26. See id., Annex VI, at 21.

27. See generally Mensah, "International Environmental Law: International Conventions Concerning Oil Pollution at Sea," 8 Case W. Res. J. Int'l L. 110 (1976).

28. Id.

29. See generally Report of the United Nations Conference on the Human Environment, U.N. Doc. A/CONF.48/14/Rev. 1 (1972) [hereinafter cited as Stockholm Report].

30. For comments on the use of these principles by states and international organizations, see generally Weiss, A Resource Management Approach to Carbon Dioxide During the Century of Transition, ch. 11 infra. ns. 24-25 and accompanying text.

31. See generally Stockholm Report, supra note 29, at 3-5.

32. Id. at 6-28.

33. See G.A.Res. 2997, 27 U.N. GAOR Supp. 30, at 43, U.N. Doc. A/8730 (1972). See generally Joyner and Joyner, "Global Eco-management and International Organization: The Stockholm Conference and the Problems of Cooperation," 14 Nat. Res. J. 533 (1974).

34. See G.A.Res. 174 (II) (1947).

35. See E.S.C.Res. 36, 37 (IV) (1947).

36. See Draft Convention on the Law of the Sea, U.N. Conference on the Law of the Sea resumed Tenth Session, Geneva, August 3-28, 1981, U.N. Doc. A/CONF. 62/L. 78 (August 28, 1981) [hereinafter cited as Draft Convention]. Part XII of the proposed convention, articles 192-237, prescribe such norms.

37. See generally Almeida, Beckerman, Sachs and Corea, "Environment and Development -- The Founex Report," Int'l Concil., Jan. 1972. See An Action Plan for the Human Environment, Rep. by the Secretary-General, U.N. Conf. on the Human Environment 1, at 27, U.N. Doc. A/CONF. 48/5 (1972).

38. See note 16 supra.

39. See U.N. Doc. A/CONF. 48/5 (1972).

40. UNEP, The Environment Programme: Medium-Term Plan 1982-1983, UNEP/GC.9/6, March 1981, at 11 [hereinafter cited as UNEP/GC.9/6].

41. See id. at 11-54.

42. Id. at 12.

43. UNEP, The Environment Programme: Programme Performance Report -- Report of the Executive Director, UNEP/GC. 9/5, February 25, 1981, at 13 [hereinafter ited as UNEP/GC.9/5].

44. UNEP/GC. 9/6, at 22.

45. Id.
46. See id. at 22-28.
47. See Id. at 14-21. See also UNEP, Report of the
Governing Council of the United Nations Environment Programme on the Work of Its Ninth Session, Nairobi, 13-26
May 1981, UNEP/GC. 9/15, 5 June 1981, at 48-49 [herein-
after cited as UNEP/GC.9/15]; UNEP/GC. 9/5, at 8-12.
47a. UNEP, Environmental Management -- An Overview,
UNEP Report No. 3 (1981), at 8 [hereinafter cited as
UNEP Report No. 3].
48. See id. at 12-16.
49. See Id. at 17.
50. See Id. at 53-67.
51. See note 16 supra.
52. See UNEP Report No. 2, at 28; see also G.A.
Res. 3129, 28 U.N. GAOR, Supp. (No. 30) 49, U.N. Doc.
A/9030 (1973).
53. See UNEP Report No. 2, at 28.
54. See UNEP, Programme Performance Report --
Addendum, UNEP/GC. 10/5 Add. 2, 7 December 1981, at 2
[hereinafter cited as UNEP/GC.10/5/Add 2].
55. Id. at 2-3.
56. See id. at 4.
57. Id.
58. See UNEP Report No. 2, at 15.
59. See UNEP/GC. 9/15, at 66.
59a. UNEP Rep. No. 2, at 195.
60. See id. at 197.
61. Id.
62. Id.
63. Id. at 198.
64. Id.
65. Id.
66. See id. at 195-96.
67. See Id. at 197-98.
68. See UNEP/GC.9/5, at 41-45; UNEP/GC. 9/15, at
68-70.
69. See UNEP/GC.9/15, at 68.
70. Id. at 69.
71. See id. at 75.
72. See UNEP/GC. 9/6, at 192.
73. Id.
74. Id. at 196.
75. Id. at 199.
76. Id. at 201.
77. Id.
78. See UNEP/GC. 9/5, at 42-43.
79. See UNEP/GC. 9/6, at 203.
80. Id.
81. See id. at 211.
82. See UNEP Report No. 2, at 32.
83. See generally id. at 38-41.
84. Id. at 40.

85. Id. at 41.
86. Id.
87. Id.
88. Id. at 40.
89. The Convention was Done Nov. 13, 1979, 1 U.N. ECE, Annex 1, U.N. Doc. E/ECE/HLM. 1/2 (1979), reprinted in 18 Int'l Legal Mat. 1442 (1979).
90. See UNEP Rep. No. 2, at 45.
91. See id.
92. See id. at 46.
93. See id. at 47.
94. Id.
95. See id. at 47-48.
96. See id. at 48.
97. See Draft Convention on the Law of the Sea, U.N. Doc. A/CONF. 62/L.78, 28 Aug. 1981 [hereinafter cited as Draft Convention].
98. See note 16 supra.
99. Draft Convention, art. 1, para. 4.
100. Id., art. 192.
101. Id., art. 194, para. 1.
102. Id., art. 194, para. 2.
103. Id., art. 197.
104. Id., art. 198.
105. Id., art. 199.
106. Id., arts. 200-201.
107. Id., art. 204.
108. Id., art. 206.
109. Id., arts. 213-222.
110. Id., arts. 223-233.
111. Id., art. 234.
112. Id., art. 207(1).
113. Id., art. 207(3).
114. Id., art. 206(4).
115. Id., art. 208(3).
116. Id., art. 208(4),(5).
117. Id., art. 209(2).
118. Id., art. 209(1).
119. Id., art. 210.
120. Id., art. 211(1)
121. See generally H. Burmester, Vessel Source Pollution: The Integration of International and Domestic Responses in the Search for an Effective Legal Framework (Center for Ocean Law and Policy, University of Virginia June 1978).
122. Draft Convention, art. 211(2).
123. Id., art. 211(3).
124. Id., art. 211(6).
125. Id., art. 211(5).
126. Id., art. 211(6).
127. Id., arts. 213-222.
128. Id., arts. 223-233.

129. Id., art. 234.

130. See, e.g., Schneider, "Something Old, Something New: Some Thoughts on Grotius and the Marine Environment," 18 Va. J. Int'l L. 147, 158-64 (1977).

131. See UNEP Report No. 2, at 53.

132. See id. at 58-59.

133. See id. at 58-60.

134. See id. at 58.

135. See id. at 61.

136. See id. at 65.

137. See id. at 63-64.

138. See id. at 65.

139. Id.

140. Id. at 66.

141. Report of the FAO Conference, 17th Session (73/REP), Para. 295, cited id. at 68.

142. See id. at 71.

143. See id. at 71.

144. See id. at 72.

145. See id. at 72-73.

146. Art. 63 of the Constitution, cited id. at 79.

147. See id.

148. Id. at 78.

149. See id. at 83.

150. See id. at 83-85.

151. See id. at 87.

152. See id. at 128 for several conventions adopted under IMCO's auspices relating to prevention and control of marine pollution from ships.

153. See id. at 90-91.

154. See id. at 91-93.

155. See id. at 104-122.

156. For a short report, see id. at 142-48.

157. See id. at 148-60.

158. See id. at 161-64.

159. See id. at 164-67.

160. See id. at 167-76.

161. See id. at 177-80.

162. See id. at 180-82.

163. See id. at 103.

164. See id. at 143-44.

165. See id. at 144.

166. See id. at 145.

167. See id.

168. See id. at 146.

169. G.A.Res. 2997, 27 U.N. GAOR, Supp. (No. 30) 43, U.N.Doc. A/8730 (1972).

170. The Convention is reprinted in 15 Int'l Legal Materials 290 (1976), in force February 12, 1978. See generally Robinson, Convention for the Protection of the Mediterranean Sea Against Pollution, 2 Earth L. J. 289 (1976); Note, "Mediterranean Protocol on Land-Based

Sources: Regional Response to a Pressing Transnational
Problem," 13 Cornell Int'l L. J. 329 (1980).
171. Reprinted in 14 Int'l Legal Materials 475 (1975).
172. See UNEP Report No. 2, at 26.
173. Id.
174. See id.
175. Id.
176. See id. at 27.
177. See id.
178. Id.
179. Id.
180. Id.
181. Id.
182. Id.
183. Id.
184. See note 157 supra.
185. See note 158 supra.
186. See note 159 supra.
187. See UNEP Report No. 2, at 148-49.
188. See id. at 161-64.
189. See id. at 162.
190. See id. at 161-64.
191. See id. at 163.
192. See id. at 164.
193. See id. at 165.
194. See id. at 166.
195. See id. at 167.
196. See id.
197. See generally Alexander, "Regional Arrangements
in the Oceans," 71 Am. J. Int'l L. 84 (1977); Okidi,
"Toward Regional Arrangements for Regulation of Marine
Pollution: An Appraisal of Options," 4 Ocean Develop.
& Int'l L. J. 1 (1977).
198. See notes 169-183 supra and accompanying text.
199. The text of the Convention is reprinted in 13
Int'l Legal Materials 352 (1974).
200. See generally Johnson, "The Baltic Conventions," 25 International and Comparative Law Quarterly,
1 (1976). The text is reprinted in 13 Int'l Legal
Materials 546 (1974).
201. See, e.g., Okidi, supra note 197, at 13-20.
202. Draft Convention, art. 276.
203. See notes 163-168 supra and accompanying text.
204. See note 157 supra.
205. See § II A supra.
206. See, e.g., note 40 supra.
207. See generally notes 40-47 supra and accompanying text.
208. See notes 47a-50 supra and accompanying text;
Weiss, ch. 12.
209. See, e.g., notes 51-62 supra and accompanying
text.
210. See, e.g., Rosencranz, ch. 12.

9
Unilateral Actions to Control Planned and Inadvertent Climate Modification: Options and Obstacles

George William Sherk

> Man has already modified weather inadvertently
> on an important scale and, by conscious effect
> on a smaller scale he will also, in time, have
> at least some capacity to "control" weather on
> a regional, national, continental or conceivably
> on even an international scale.[1]

I. INTRODUCTION

The global atmosphere is a universal common property resource. It cannot, in its entirety, be divided into parcels each of which would be subject to nation state sovereignty.[2] Because of this, direct impacts of both planned and inadvertent climate modification on the atmosphere of one nation state may be the indirect result of the political, economic and environmental policies of a number of nation states.

The extent to which inadvertent climate modification results in direct adverse impacts on nation states not contributing to the causes of such climate modification is becoming increasingly apparent. As the causes of inadvertent climate modification, as well as the extent of its impacts, become better understood, the need of alternating institutional structure to control such impacts becomes increasingly obvious.

Continuing research and development activities have made deliberate climate modification programs operational on a small scale. The future of planned weather modification activities is not limited by whether such activities will occur, for they surely will. The critical issue concerning future planned climate modification programs is the geographic size of the Earth's surface to be affected. The adequacy of existing institutional climate modification is open to question.

This analysis examines the role of the nation state in controlling both planned and inadvertent weather modification. Historic trends affecting the capability and willingness of a nation state to regulate such activities are noted. Existing regulatory inadequacies are examined. Finally, unilateral alternatives which could result in the control of transnational climate modification are considered.

II. NATURE OF THE PROBLEM

Every human activity has an impact on climate. Fortunately, the cumulative impact of <u>almost</u> every human activity is <u>de minimis</u>. Those activities having an effect on climate, however, can have a devastating effect. The adequacy of existing unilateral programs to control both planned and inadvertent climate modification is subject to serious criticism. Neither public institutions (a nation state or its political subdivisions) nor such private institutions as multinational corporations (MNCs) and nongovernmental organizations (NGOs) has demonstrated a capability to control climate modification.

In fact, public and private activities are a primary cause of both planned and inadvertent climate modification. Existing laws and policies result both directly and indirectly in climate modification. In the United States, for example, the recently created Synthetic Fuels Corporation[3] and the Powerplant and Industrial Fuel Use Act portion of the National Energy Act[4] could lead to increases in acid precipitation, as well as other inadvertent climatic changes, because of an increase in hydrocarbon and carbon dioxide (CO_2) emissions. The United States policy of selling high sulfur coal to the European countries could further aggravate Sweden's acid precipitation problems. The relaxation of vehicular emission standards, which has been proposed to bolster automobile production in the U.S., could further intensify the problems associated with such emissions. In the United States, both state and federal budget provisions will determine the extent of weather modification research and operational weather modification programs.

These are but some of the direct causes of planned and inadvertent climate modification. Essential research in atmospheric science will further define the cause/ effect relationships that result in climate modification. In evaluating the adequacy of unilateral approaches to the control of planned and inadvertent climate modification, the following issues must be given special attention.

A. Inadvertent Climate Modification

The byproducts of industrial, agricultural, and transportation systems are being dispersed into the atmosphere in ever increasing quantities. While it is

not possible to consider every activity resulting in
inadvertent climate modifications,[5] it is essential to
consider several activities which have foreseeable transnational impacts.

1. Acid precipitation. Beginning with the Industrial Revolution, the use of coal as an energy source increased as did the concentration of coal burning facilities in urban areas. Acid precipitation problems have
increased, and may intensify, with increased use of
fossil fuels. There are several causes of acid precipitation including the release of sulfur dioxide, nitrogen
oxides and, in some instances, hydrogen chlorides from
power plants, smelters, and automobile exhausts. Taller
smoke stacks have made what once was a local problem into
a regional problem with international complications where
a number of countries are clustered together (e.g.,
Europe) or if occurring along national boundaries (e.g.,
U.S./Canadian).[6]

2. Carbon dioxide (CO_2) buildup with resultant
potential for "greenhouse" effects. The amount of CO_2 in
the atmosphere is likely to increase in direct proportion
to an increased use of fossil fuels. As the use of fossil fuels increases and expands, the CO_2 concentration in
the atmosphere should also increase.[7] If the use of
fossil fuels increases at the rate of four percent per
year, the amount of CO_2 in the atmosphere would double
within approximately seventy years.[8] Climatological
models currently in use suggest that this would result in
a global temperature increase of between 1.5 and 4.5
degrees Celsius (2.7 to 8 degrees Farenheit).[9] Any increase in atmospheric temperature might be delayed, but
not halted, by the thermal inertia of the oceans.[10] Unfortunately, when this thermal intertia is overcome, the
atmosphere could heat more rapidly than anticipated with
a resultant intensification of temperature-related
damages. The impacts of a 1.5 to 4.5 degrees Celsius
temperature increase, be it a gradual or rapid increase,
could be devastating.[11]

3. Particulate accumulation in the atmosphere.
Particulates from a number of different sources could
accumulate in the atmosphere with resultant increases in
precipitation[12] and the potential for a global "cooling"
effect.[13] Increases in the use of fossil fuels could
result in increased release of particulates into the
atmosphere.

4. Ozone depletion. While there are a number of
factors which affect the ozone layer, both the halocarbons from aerosol propellants[14] and the water vapor

and nitric oxide emissions from aircraft engines (especially in supersonic flight) appear to have a damaging impact. Reduction in the ozone layer could result in increases in ultraviolet light.[15]

B. Planned Climate Modification

Deliberate weather modification activities include a number of different programs: seeding storm systems to increase the efficiency of the system (e.g., seeding wintertime orographic systems to increase precipitation), hail suppression procedures, fog dispersal procedures, proposed procedures to reduce the damaging effects of or to increase precipitation from convective systems and proposed procedures to alter the course and intensity of hurricanes. At present, most weather modification procedures are in the research and development stage. Those procedures which are operational, however, raise issues of the impacts of weather modification activities beyond the target area of the activity. International legal consequences arise when there are adverse downwind impacts from either weather modification research and development or of operational weather modification programs that transcend national boundaries.[16]

III. HISTORICAL PERSPECTIVE

The tragedy of the commons as a food basket is averted by private property, or something formally like it. But the air and waters surrounding us cannot readily be fenced, and so the tragedy of the commons as a cesspool must be prevented by different means, by coercive laws or taxing devices that make it cheaper for the polluter to treat his pollutants than to discharge them untreated. We have not progressed as far with the solution to this problem as we have with the first.[17]

The conflicts over law and policy intended to control planned and inadvertent climate modification illustrate the complex interaction of different historic trends. For countless generations, the atmosphere has been treated as a "common" resource. Available to anyone, it was controlled by no one. As the problems of atmospheric pollution and climate modification have become more acute, the historic approach of no regulation is being increasingly challenged by those seeking the protection and preservation of the "commons." Many of these conflicts can also be seen in the debates and working papers of the United Nations Conference on the Law of the Sea.

The only truly historic trend is the sovereignty of the nation state. A laissez-faire approach to international law and policy, this approach stresses the freedom of a nation state to act according to the dictates of its own political, economic and environmental needs. There is little or no state responsibility for the actions of the citizens of the state. The state allows the "invisible hand" of the marketplace or the needs of the state to control policy decisions. There is little, if any regulation, no economically justifiable policies, and no voluntary internalization of externalities.[18]

A second trend is that reflected in the approach of many developing countries in opposing regulations relative to planned and inadvertent climate modification. Such countries fear that restrictions on the use of the atmospheric commons will make it impossible for them to develop to the same level as developed countries. Many of the developing countries view atmospheric pollution as the price of progress.[19] In essence, many developing countries desire such development at almost any price. There is little likelihood that they will place any real restrictions or limitations on their own development.

An emerging trend reflecting the Dai Dong concept stresses the need to conserve and protect the atmospheric commons. "The common heritage of mankind," a concept frequently used in connection with oceans' reources, can also be applied to the atmospheric commons. The common law concept of sic utere tuto ut alienum non laedas with both injunctive and compensatory relief for nuisance is reflected in this trend. Those arguing that the natural law requires environmental protection are also associated with this trend.[20] This trend is also reflected in Principal 21 of the Declaration on the Human Environment (the Stockholm Conference).[21]

Any unilateral approach to the control of either planned or inadvertent climate modification will reflect the political strength of the adherents to these three approaches. In any nation state, each approach will have its own constituents. Given pluralist constitutent groups, the need for compromise may result in law and policy which, while politically justifiable, may not be ecologically appropriate. Competing interests may produce inconsistent policies on different structural levels (e.g., unilateral policies conflicting with multilateral goals). Existing inconsistencies in unilateral policies exemplify the inadequacies of unilateral responses to planned and inadvertent climate modification.

The principle of nation state liability for actions over which it has control which adversely impact other countries continues to be accepted into the body of international law. This is, in essence Principle 21 of the Stockholm Conference.[22] What has yet to be accepted is nation state liability for actions by entities over which it has jurisdiction which occur outside the nation state (in space, on the high seas, on the seabed, or in other countries). It is well argued, however, that "interdependence, and the increased mobility, communications and trade among States have created pressures on States -- particularly those with extensive overseas 'interests' -- to project their law beyond their territory."[23]

IV. UNILATERAL APPROACHES

A number of authors have considered unilateral approaches to pollution control in different states.[24] It is apparent from an anlysis of existing approaches that there are areas of inadequacy. It is equally apparent, however, that there exists substantial potential for unilateral control of both planned and inadvertent climate modification.

A. Obstacles to Effect Unilateral Control

The most obvious area of inadequacy is that the development of a unilateral approach to climate modification control requires a national commitment to develop such controls. Absent such a commitment, any unilateral approach is unworkable. If the United Kingdom, for example, does not find it to be in its best interests to regulate the burning of high sulfur coal, then the problem of acid precipitation in countries downwind from the United Kingdom will continue. Also, on a unilateral level, there is very little that a country affected by the U.K. decision could do. In this case, Sweden's acid precipitation problem would be aggravated. The willingness to commit national resources to reduce the possibility of inadvertent climate modification is missing in many of the developing countries.[25]

Second, unilateral actions by definition are limited in scope. At present, such actions have little, if any, extraterritorial effect. Furthermore, any extraterritorial effect which might exist is difficult both to monitor and to enforce. The difficulty of extraterritorial enforcement is especially true with regard to multinational corporations. It has been suggested, for example, that the National Environmental Policy Act (NEPA)[26] should control federal actions regardless of their location. The potential extraterritorial effect of NEPA was severely restricted by Executive Order 12114 by which President Carter restricted the NEPA definition of "environment" and prohibited recourse to the courts to enforce the Order.[27] Because of these restrictions, any extraterritorial control of NEPA has been eliminated. On the other hand, however, the unilateral position of the United States regarding SST landing rights may have been a factor in preserving the ozone layer.[28]

Third, given the number of countries and the range of individual interests represented, a unilateral approach results in a piecemeal policy. Furthermore, policy may be an ad hoc response to a specific problem. Specific standards may be either lacking or in conflict with standards established by another country. The conflicting standards (or lack thereof) for motor vehicle emissions has resulted in the need for manufacturers to develop different automobile models tailored for the requirements of specific countries.[29]

Fourth, unilateral policy may be dictated by non-ecological considerations. The need for political accountability in one state may produce policies which either do not control planned and inadvertent climate modification or, as can be seen in current efforts to increase energy supplies through the increased use of fossil fuels, actually result in climate modification. Furthermore, the possibility of trade retaliation may encourage the establishment of unilateral standards favoring a specific country. Finally, unilateral policies are more likely to be the product of political and economic considerations.[30]

Fifth, unilateral policies reflecting the interests of individual countries maintain the north/south, rich nation/poor nation dichotomy. This dichotomy has resulted in an inequitable distribution of resources between wealthy and poor countries. It also may have encouraged the despoilation of the environment in poorer countries whose economic situation does not allow for the consideration of environmental safeguards.[31]

Sixth, given existing international markets, any country implementing strong national environmental protection policies may be economically disadvantaged, for it could be argued that "a State that proceeds with a vast environmental program at great cost to growth, technology, and its natural and human resources, will be at a disadvantage with respect to its adversaries."[32]

Finally, much of the discussion among scholars and politicians regarding nation state liability for environmental degradation thus far has focused on liability (fault) and the payment of damages.[33] In considering the long term impacts of both planned and inadvertent climate modification, however, this approach is inadequate. Carbon dioxide may be released into the atmosphere from innumerable sources in many different countries. Defining liability for specific releases would be nearly impossible. The resulting harm could, however, be devastating.[34] The emphasis, therefore, must focus on prevention, not compensation. Unfortunately, unilateral approaches lack the uniformity and consistency needed for effective preventive measures.

B. Options for Effective Unilateral Control

It is questionable whether the obstacles to unilateral control of planned and inadvertent climate modification can be overcome. Assuming, however, that it would be possible, there are a number of options available to individual nation states the implementation of which could assist in controlling planned and inadvertent climate modification. All of these options would be effective only if a specific nation state was willing to commit national resources to their implementation.

First, new national laws and regulations or amendments to existing laws and regulations are possible. This option is also available to the political subdivisions of a nation state if the subdivision has authority to exercise a "police power". Actions to regulate both planned and inadvertent climate modification are clearly within the authority of existing nation states. In the United States, for example, weather modification is controlled (if at all) by different state laws. Legislation has been introduced in Congress to establish a national weather modification program to control planned climate modification.

Such unilateral actions as the Clean Air Act are examples of the exercise of national authority to control inadvertent climate modification. Furthermore, it has been suggested that the United States develop an energy policy based on a reduction in the use of fossil fuels. Since the U.S. is the largest single consumer of energy, such a policy could become a model for other nation states.[35]

Second, a nation state may impose countervailing duties. Article XVI of the General Agreement on Trade and Tariffs (GATT) calls for the abolition of export subsidies. Article XI of GATT permits the imposition of countervailing duties by an importing country on goods which are subsidized by an exporting country.[36] Nonexistent or lax environmental laws in an exporting state could be considered subsidization of industries producing in the state and, as such, warrant the imposition by an importing state of countervailing duties.[37]

Despite the difficulty GATT members have had in defining that which constitutes a subsidy,[38] nonexistent or lax environmental safeguards must be so considered since they allow a manufacturer to escape payment of the full costs of a manufacturing process. If the internationalization of environmental costs is not manifested, the result is a production subsidy (an indirect subsidy) which can influence trade levels and patterns.[39]

It has been suggested that the best approach to transnational environmental protection in the absence of a multinational entity would be for a nation state having control over the cause of the degredation to bear the "full cost" of compensation.[40] The nation state would pay both compensation and control costs, apparently after taxing the operation causing the environmental degradation. Whether there are principles of international law to make this approach enforceable is open to question.[41] It can be argued, however, that avoidance of both compensation and control costs must be considered a subsidy under GATT. As such, the potential imposition of countervailing duties could force a nation state to adopt the "full cost" approach.

Subsidies applying only to exports are prima facie reprehensible. A general subsidy of all manufacturing processes may be acceptable.[42] While lax or nonexistent environmental regulations could amount to a general subsidy of all manufacturing processes, the real effect of such subsidy is only felt in the competition of exports with both the export and domestic production of countries imposing strict environmental controls. As such, the primary effect of a general subsidy is to bolster the marketability of exports. While not prima facie reprehensible, such effects could warrant the imposition of countervailing duties.[43] Although the United States, unlike other GATT members, "is not subject to the GATT limitation . . . that the imposition of countervailing duties requires prior demonstration of injury, or threat of injury, to a domestic industry,"[44] it would not be difficult to document such injury.[45]

It is obvious that political and economic factors must be considered. The possibility of trade retaliation is quite real. The imposition of countervailing duties is, however, one unilateral alternative which could help control inadvertent climate modification.[46]

Finally, Article XX of GATT (General Exceptions) allows an importing state to impose regulations "(6) necessary to protect human, animal or plant life or health, . . . (g) relating to the conservation of exhaustible resources if such measures are made in conjunction with restrictions on domestic production or consumption; . . . ."[47] While of a secondary nature, such authority has the potential to authorize import regulations which could encourage the adoption of environmental safeguards by exporting countries.[48]

A third option available to a nation state is conditional assistance. A number of authorities have suggested the possibility of the conditioning for foreign aid granted to specific countries on conformity with environmental safeguards by a receiving country.[49] These mandatory safeguards could be quite specific (applying

only to the project for which the aid was requested),
quite general (applying nationwide), or almost any
variation thereof (applying to other environmental problems in a receiving state). The goal of such conditional
foreign aid would be to encourage conformity with acceptable standards of environmental protection. The establishment and enforcement of operational environmental
protection regulations could result from conditional
grants. Such grants could also be used to remedy specific pollution problems.[50] In the U.S. federal aid to local
units of government is frequently made conditional on
conformity with environmental protection policies.

A related option would be the use of financial incentives by one nation state to encourage another nation
state to conform to certain environmental standards. In
the United States, for example, "most favored nation"
trade status decisions could turn, in part, on the willingness of a nation state seeking the status to conduct
environmental protection programs.[51] In addition, tax
credits in one nation state could be allowed for expenditures by MNCs for pollution abatement expenses in a
second nation state.[52] In general, financial incentives
could encourage conformity to environmental protection
standards.[53]

A fifth option would be expanded extraterritorial
jurisdiction. Those activities occurring in the atmospheric commons which affect a specific nation state could
justify an expansion of the jurisdiction of that state to
control or regulate the activity. Currently the best
example of this option is the establishment by Canada of
an Arctic Anti-pollution Zone. This zone, which extends
into the oceanic commons, places restrictions on activities which could affect Canadian interests in environmental protection. The Canadian approach could be a
workable short-term alternative until such time as
operational international principles and procedures are
developed.[54]

An "enterprise liability" approach would present a
nation state with a sixth option. It has been suggested
that unilateral regulation of multinational corporations
(MNCs) chartered in a specific state could lead to improved environmental protection procedures. Under this
concept, MNC activities regardless of location could be
regulated by the state in which the MNC is chartered.[55]
This is another means by which specific states can expand
the extraterritorial effects of environmental protection
policies. There are obvious problems under this option
of monitoring and enforcement. To be effective, a state
in regulating an MNC would be required to grant some form
of standing or recognition to environmental nongovernmental organizations (NGOs) to monitor the operations of
the MNC. These difficulties, however, are not insur-

mountable. The problem of states refusing to impose any form of enterprise liability on MNCs chartered within the state, and hence becoming a pollution haven having a "sky of convenience," argues strongly in favor of the establishment of standards on other than a unilateral level.[56]

Seventh, expanded research and development activities should be considered. It would appear that few nation states are aware of either the real costs of environmental degradation or the real value of their natural resources. Both nation states and NGOs could expand informational activities to better inform themselves and others of the real benefits and costs associated with planned and inadvertent climate modification. Toward this end, existing unilateral monitoring and atmospheric research activities could be expanded.[57]

An eighth option would be the establishment of institutional structures on a unilateral level to provide the financial resources needed to provide compensation should environmental safeguards fail. Canada, for example, required Dome Petroleum to post a bond before it allowed drilling activities in the Beaufort Sea.[58] Presumably, the bond would be returned with appropriate interest if there was no environmental degradation. A nation state may also wish to establish an insurance fund or pool to compensate the victims of environmental degradation. Such a pool would be funded through taxes on those entities engaging in activities resulting in environmental degradation.

A final unilateral option is the ratification and enforcement of standards and conventions proposed by different NGOs and governmental entities. The existing delays between the opening of a convention for signature and the final ratification of the convention may soon become environmentally unacceptable. Ratification and enforcement of existing proposals could regulate pollution sources the output of which currently results in inadvertent climate modification.[59] Furthermore, an alternative related to the first option is the passage of domestic legislation needed to bring existing conventions and treaties into full force and effect within a given country.[60]

V. CONCLUSIONS

This analysis has been based on two essential assumptions. First, it was assumed that the harm caused by inadvertent climate modification described here was of such a nature as to warrant its prevention or control. The second assumption was that the potential adverse impacts from planned climate modification activities also required regulation of those engaged in such activities.

These assumptions are, of course, open to question. There are those who would argue that the benefits from a fossil fuel based energy system to a nation state development outweigh the costs of acid precipitation, "greenhouse effects," etc. There are also those who see increasing water supplies through weather modification as a goal which can only be accomplished if such activities occur without any regulatory "burden".

Notwithstanding these questions, if one assumes that the potential harm from inadvertent climate modification and from uncontrolled deliberate climate modification requires strong controls, then the obstacles and options affecting unilateral action deserve serious consideration. While unilateral action alone cannot control all aspects of planned and inadvertent climate modification, multilateral decisions will have little effect unless supported by nation states. It is the responsibility of international law and institutions to encourage the development of unilateral and multilateral mechanisms to control both planned and inadvertent climate modification.

NOTES

The author would like to express his sincere gratitude to Ms. Ellen E. Fox, a student at Colorado College, Colorado Springs, Colorado, and to Mr. Richard W. Stodt, meteorologist, Water and Power Resources Service, U.S. Department of the Interior, Denver, Colorado, for their assistance in the preparation of this analysis.

1. Taubenfeld, "International Environmental Law: Air and Outer Space," 13 Natural Resources Journal 315, 322 (1973).
2. d'Arge and Kneese, "State Liability for International Environmental Degradation: An Economic Perspective," Natural Resources Journal 427, 433 (1980).
3. United States Synthetic Fuels Corporation Act of 1980, Pub. L. No. 96-294 (1980). The Synthetic Fuels Corporation price and loan guarantee program could "impact heavily on the CO_2 problem since it is estimated that during the production and combustion of synthetic fuels about 50 percent more carbon dioxide is emitted than from burning coal (on an energy-equivalent basis)." Becker, "Does A CO_2 Catastrophe Impend?" 38 Public Power 24, 26 (1980).
4. Powerplant and Industrial Fuel Use Act, Pub. L. No. 95-620, 92 Stat. 3289 (1978).

5. An ever increasing number of human activities have been determined to result in inadvertent climate modification. Urbanization and changing land use patterns result in climatic alterations as does the destruction of wetlands. The surface albedo of the earth has been changed through both deforestation and overgrazing. Increasing or decreasing acreage under irrigation had such impacts as does the damming of rivers to create new reservoirs. The release of energy in the form of heat appears to result in climatic alterations. Soil erosion can be both a cause and an effect of climate modification. Contrails produced by jet engines and ice nuclei resulting from rocket engine propellants also may have an altering effect on climate. Finally, as seen from the U.S. experience in Vietnam, war and the tools of war can have a pronounced impact on climate. See generally Inadvertent Climate Modification: Report of the Study of Man's Impact on Climate (SMIC) (1971); Sessions 1 and 2 of the Seventh Conference on Inadvertent and Planned Weather Modification (1979)(American Meteorological Society, Banff, Alberta, Canada, October 8-12, 1979); Coppoc,"The Environment: No Respecter of National Boundaries," 43 Albany Law Review 520, 524 (1979)(effects of lead in gasoline); Dickstein, "National Environmental Hazards and International Law," 23 International and Comparative Law Quarterly 426 (1979); Coppoc, "The Environment: No Respecter of National Boundaries," 43 Albany Law Review 520, 524 (1979) (effects of lead in gasoline); Dickstein, "National Environmental Hazards and International Law," 23 International and Comparative Law Quarterly 426 (1979)(effects of ionising radiation in the atmosphere); Jackson, "The Dimensions of International Pollution," 50 Oregon Law Review 223 (1971); Joyner and Joyner, "Global Eco-Management and International Organizations: The Stockholm Conference and Problems of Cooperation," 14 Natural Resources Journal 533, 535 (1974) (description of "chemical overload of the earth's ecosystem"); Muir "Legal and Ecological Aspects of the International Energy Situation," 8 International Lawyer 1, 5 (1974) (role of synthetic fuels as a solution to air pollution); Taubenfeld, supra note 1 at 322 (reversed flow of rivers and deforestation).

6. Several articles have considered the causes and effects of acid precipitation. See generally Babich, Davis & Stotzky, "Acid Precipitation: Causes and Consequences," 22 Environment 6 (May 1980); Coppoc, supra note 5 at 521; Ferenbaugh, "Acid Rain: Biological Effects and Implications," 4 Environmental Affairs 745 (1975); Graves, "Rain of Troubles," 209 Science 80 75 (July/August 1980) (includes Rosencranz, "International Forecast: More Acid Rain," at 79); Likens, Wright, Galloway & Butler, "Acid Rain," 241 Scientific American 43 (October

1979).

7. The potential impacts of CO_2 buildup in the atmosphere have been considered by a number of different authors. See Inadvertent Climate Modifications, supra note 5 at 84; Bleicher, "An Overview of International Environmental Regulation," 2 Ecology Law Quarterly 1, 64 (1972); Joyner & Joyner, supra note 5 at 535.

8. Becker, supra note 3 at 25. See generally Council on Environmental Quality, Global Energy Futures and the Carbon Dioxide Problem (1981).

9. Note 8, id., W. W. Kellogg & R. W. Schware, Climate Change and Society: Consequences of Increasing Atmospheric Carbon Dioxide (Westview Press, Boulder, CO., 1981). The validity and accuracy of existing climatological models is, of course, open to question. See "Carbon Dioxide and Climate", 210 Science 6 (1980) (letters of Schneider, Kellogg and Ramanathan and of Leovy; reply of Idso).

10. Madden and Ramanathan, "Detecting Climate Change Due to Increasing Carbon Dioxide," 209 Science 763, 765 (1980).

11. See generally Council on Environmental Quality, note 8 supra.

12. Sources and effects of particulates in the atmosphere are considered in Inadvertent Climate Modification, supra note 5 at 186. See also Borys, Rilling and Walsh, "Potential Effects of Coal-Fired Power Plant Emissions on Winter Orographic Clouds," Seventh Conference on Inadvertent and Planned Weather Modification, supra note 5 at 9 (suggesting no impact from a pollutant source within the immediate area of the source).

13. "[P]articles change the radiation field by scattering sunlight, some of it back to space, or by absorbing sunlight. The sunlight absorbed and backscattered does not reach the surface and cannot be absorbed and or rescattered there, as it would be in the absence of particles." Inadvertent Climate Modification, supra note 5 at 188. See also, Bleicher, supra note 7 at 64; Joyner supra note 5 at 535.

14. A fascinating depiction of the "accidental scientific method" leading to an understanding of the impacts of halocarbons on the ozone layer can be found in Sagan, Broca's Brain: Reflections on the Romance of Science 34 (1979).

15. The range of impacts resulting in modification of the stratosphere, including the impacts of aircraft engine emissions, is considered in Chapter 9 of Inadvertent Climate Modification, supra note 5 at 264. One analysis of the impacts on the ozone of a supersonic transport aircraft (SST) can be found in Falk, "The Global Environment and International Law: Challenge and Response," 23 Kansas Law Review 385, 402 (1975).

16. A number of authors have considered the potential of weather modification to enhance human control of climate and the legal problems which could result. Many authors have suggested the need for an international organization (the World Meteorological Organization is frequently suggested) to monitor or control weather modification activities. See generally Breuer, Weather Modification: Prospects and Problems (1976), first English language edition published by Cambridge University Press, 1979); Davis, "Weather Modification, Stream Flow Augmentation, and the Law," 24 Mineral Law Institute 833 (1978); Note, "Weather Genesis and Weather Neutralization: A New Approach to Weather Modification," 6 California Western International Law Journal 412 (1976); Samuels, "Prospective International Control of Weather Modification Activities," 21 University of Toronto Law Journal 222 (1971); Sigel, "International Control of Weather Modification in a Regime of Long-Range Weather Forecasting," 19 Harvard International Law Journal 535 (1978); Taubenfeld, "Weather Modification and Control: Some International Legal Implications," 55 California Law Review 493 (1967); Thomas (ed.), Legal and Scientific Uncertainties of Weather Modification (1977); Wood, "The Status of Weather Modification Activities Under United States and International Law," 10 Natural Resources Lawyer 367 (1977). The need for operational standards and the capability of existing institutions to develop such standards has also been considered. See Bleicher, supra note 7 at 47; Frenzen, "Weather Modification: Law and Policy," 12 Boston College Industrial and Commercial Law Review 503, 525 (1971); Hassett, "Weather Modification and Control: International Organizational Prospects," 7 Texas International Law Journal 89, 114 (1971); Samuels, "International Control of Weather Modification Activities: Peril or Policy?" 13 Natural Resources Journal 327, 336 (1973). Finally, it has been suggested that planned localized climate modification may, over time, result in inadvertent climate modification on a larger geographic scale. Inadvertent Climate Modification, supra note 5 at 68.

17. Hardin, "The Tragedy of the Commons" in Enthoven and Freeman, Pollution, Resources, and the Environment 1, 7 (1973). See also d'Arge and Kneese, note 2 supra.

18. See generally Lee, "International Legal Aspects of Pollution of the Atmosphere," 21 University of Toronto Law Journal 203 (1971); McDougal & Schneider, "The Protection of the Environment and World Public Order: Some Recent Developments," 45 Mississippi Law Journal 1085 (1974). See also, American Society of International Law, "Post Stockholm: Influencing National Environmental Law and Practice Through International Law and Policy," Proceedings of the Sixth-Sixth Annual Meeting 1, 9 (1972)

(comments of Mr. Hargrove); Holdman, "Pollution: International Complications," 2 Environmental Affairs 1 (1972);
Joyner & Joyner, supra note 5 at 540, 552; Vasek, "International Environmental Damage Control: Some Proposals
for the Second Best of All Possible Worlds," 59 Kentucky
Law Journal 673, 681 (1971).

   19. See generally, Lee, note 18, supra; McDougal &
Schneider, note 18, at 5; Joyner & Joyner, supra note 5
at 540, 542 (citing Development and Environment: Report
and Working Papers by a Panel of Experts Convened by the
Secretary-General of the U.N. Conference on Human Environment at Founex, Switzerland, June 4-12, 1971); Vasek,
supra note 18, at 676.

   20. The Dai Dong concept stems from the ancient
Chinese concept that: "For a world in which not only a
man's family is his family, not only his children are his
children, but all the world is his family and all children are his." See generally Brown, "International Environmental Law and the Natural Law," 18 Loyola Law Review 679 (1971-72); Lee, note 18 supra; McDougal &
Schneider, note 18 supra. See also, Bleicher, supra note
7 at 7, 11, 14 Grieves, "International Law and the
Environmental Issue," 1 Environmental Affairs 826, 830
(1972); Note, "New Perspectives on International Environmental Law," 82 The Yale Law Journal 1659, 1661 (1973);
Smith, "Toward an International Standard of Environment,"
2 Pepperdine Law Review 28, 39 (1974); Utton, "International Environmental Law and Consultation Mechanisms,"
12 Columbia Journal of Transnational Law 56, 59 (1973).
The sic utere principle states: "Use your property in
such a manner as not to injure that of another." The
usefulness of this principle has been questioned. It has
been pointed out, however, that it forms the basis for
the decisions in the Corfu Channel case, the Trail Smelter Arbitration, and the Lake Lanoux Arbitration. These
three cases comprise the essential precedents for international law dealing with planned and inadvertent climate
modification. Bleicher, supra note 7 at 28; Nanda, "The
Establishment of International Law Standards for Transnational Environmental Injury," 60 Iowa L. R. 1089 (1975).

   21. Principle 21 of the Declaration on the Human
Environment, 1972 U.N. Stockholm Conference, adopted
June 16, 1972, UN Doc. A/CONF. 48/14 at 7, reprinted in
11 Int'l Legal Mats. 1416, 1420 (1972).

   22. d'Arge and Kneese, supra note 2 at 427; Handl,
"State Liability for Accidental Transnational Environ-
mental Damage by Private Persons," 74 American Journal of
International Law 527-8, 535 (1980).

   23. Almond, "The Extraterritorial Reach of United
States Regulatory Authority Over the Environmental Impacts of Its Activities," 44 Albany Law Review 739-40,
(1980).

24. It is beyond the scope of this analysis to con-
sider all of the authorities who have reviewed the environmental laws and regulations of the United States.
See generally Zalob, "Approaches to Enforcement of Environmental Law: An International Perspective," 3 Hastings
International and Comparative Law Review 299 (1980).
With regard to other countries, the following sources are
offered as examples: Australia: Note, "The Impact of
Pollution Abatement Laws on the International Economy:
An Overview of the Hydra," 7 Law & Policy in Internation-
al Business 203, 217 (1975) (hereinafter cited as Inter-
national Business). Belgium: International Business at
227. Canada: International Business at 213. Denmark:
Wharam, "The Environment and the Law: Scandinavia II,
Norway and Denmark," 122 New Law Journal 1043, 1044
(1972). France: International Business at 229; Marty-
Lavauzelle, "Environmental Protection in France," 27 The
Business Lawyer 841 (1972); Wharam, "The Environment and
the Law: France," 122 New Law Journal 1151 (1972).
Italy: International Business at 234; Wharam, "Environment and the Law: Italy," 123 New Law Journal 77 (1973).
Japan: International Business at 210. The Netherlands:
International Business at 236, Briet, "Environmental Pro-
tection in the Netherlands," 27 The Business Lawyer 827
(1972). Norway: Wharam, "The Environment and the Law:
Scandinavia II. Norway and Denmark," 122 New Law Journal
1043 (1972). Switzerland: Freimuller, "Environmental
Protection in Switzerland," 27 The Business Lawyer 837
(1972). The United Kingdom: International Business at
237; Sanders, "Environmental Protection in the United
Kingdom," 27 The Business Lawyer 845 (1972). Union of
Soviet Socialist Republics: International Business at
221. West Germany (Federal Republic of Germany): International Business at 231; Ditzen, "Environmental Pro-
tection in West Germany," 27 The Business Lawyer 833
(1972); Wharam, "The Environment and the Law: West
Germany," 122 New Law Journal 921 (1972). Private recourse for environmental harm in Australia, Austria,
Canada, England, The Federal Republic of Germany, France,
Hong Kong, New Zealand, South Africa, Sweden, the United
States and the Union of Soviet Socialist Republics is
considered in McCaffrey and Lutz (eds.), Environmental
Pollution and Individual Rights: An International
Symposium (1978).

25. See generally Joyner & Joyner, supra note 5 at
552.

26. National Environmental Policy Act of 1969, Pub.
L. No. 91-190, 83 Stat. 852 (1970).

27. Executive Order 12114, "Environmental Effects
Abroad of Major Federal Actions," 44 Federal Register
1957 (1979). See Almond, supra note 23 at 744; Whitney,
"Regulation of Federal Decision Making affecting the

Environment Outside the United States, Its Territories and Possessions," 3 George Mason University Law Review 68 (1980).

28. It has been pointed out, for example, that foreign development done by the United States or by U.S. corporations is done under environmental standards which would be unacceptable if applied to domestic development within the U.S. American Society of International Law, supra note 18 at 8 (comments of Mr. Baldwin). See also Falk, supra note 15 at 402;d'Arge and Kneese, supra note 2 at 441, n.17; Whitney, supra note 27, at 73, 75-76.

29. American Society of International Law, supra note 18 at 6 (comments of Mr. Landsberg): Bleicher, supra note 7 at 2, 79; Busterud, "International Environmental Relations," 7 Natural Resources Lawyer 325, 326 (1974); Joyner & Joyner, supra note 5 at 553.

30. With regard to the effects of political and economic pressure on unilateral actions, see Lee, supra note 18 at 204, 207. In the United States it should be noted, for example, that amendments to the "Oil Blackout Bill" which would have limited emissions from coal burning power plants were defeated "after intense industry lobbying." "Acid Rain Agreement," 209 Science 890 (1980).

31. Falk, supra note 15 at 387; "New Perspectives on International Environmental Law," supra note 20 at 1669; McDougal & Schneider, supra note 18 at 1090.

32. Almond, supra note 23 at 779.

33. d'Arge and Kneese, note 2 supra; Handl, note 22 supra.

34. See text accompanying notes 7-11.

35. Council on Environmental Quality, note 8 supra.

36. On subsidies and countervailing duties under GATT, see British-North American Committee, The Gatt Negotiations 1973-79: The Closing Stage by Sidney Golt and A Policy Statement by the British-North American Committee 22 (1978) [hereinafter referred to as GATT Negotiations]; Bleicher, supra note 7 at 86; Kostecki, East-West Trade and the Gatt System 56 (1978); "New Perspectives on International Environmental Law," supra note 20 at 1680.

37. A number of authors have reached the conclusion that lax environmental laws constitute subsidies. A major difficulty arises in measuring the subsidy as any countervailing duty cannot, under GATT, exceed the amount of the subsidy. As has been noted, "it is very difficult to calculate accurately the extent to which differences in prices are the result of inadequate environmental regulation as opposed to other cost advantages such as cheaper raw materials, labor, production and sales techniques, financing, etc." Bleicher, supra note 7 at 86, 87. See also Goldman, supra note 18 at 14; Vasek, supra note 18 at 689. It has been noted, however, that the

price system is "essentially a regressive way" of dis-
tributing environmental control costs. American Society
of International Law, supra note 18 at 14 (comments of
Mr. Chayes). Authority to impose countervailing duties
on subsidied goods exists at 19 U.S.C. 1671 (1980). The
definition of "subsidy" (19 U.S.C. 1677 (5)) includes
nation state assumption of the costs of manufacture.
This is precisely what occurs when lax or nonexistent
environmental laws allow a manufacturer to escape the
true costs of production.

38. Subsidies have been narrowly defined by the
European Free Trade Association as "direct subsidies, tax
rebates, governmental price discounts, and currency control devised." Bleicher, supra note 7 at 87. See also
GATT Negotiations, supra note 36 at 23; Goldman, supra
note 18 at 14; Kostecki, supra note 36 at 57.

39. The differences between direct and indirect subsidies is considered by Kostecki, supra note 36 at 56.
At present, the United States has not imposed countervailing duties in response to production subsidies.
Bleicher, supra note 7 at 87.

40. d'Arge and Kneese, supra note 2 at 441.

41. Id.

42. GATT Negotiations, supra note 36 at 23.

43. "Proponents of such a tariff . . . might classi-
fy exports from countries without pollution control as
just another form of dumping, which, although difficult
to measure, is unfair and which fully justifies the
imposition of a surcharge." Goldman, supra note 18 at
14. See also "New Perspective on International Environmental Law," supra note 20 at 1680; Vasek, supra note 18
at 689.

44. GATT Negotiations, supra note 36 at 23.

45. For example, "The cost of thorough pollution
control for American firms could in many instances add
10% or more to the prices of American steelmakers compared to Japanese steel." Goldman, supra note 18 at 3.

46. Bleicher, supra note 7 at 88.

47. Bleicher, supra note 7 at 76, quoting Article XX
of the General Agreement on Trade and Tariffs.

48. Bleicher, supra note 7 at 77; Smith, supra note
20 at 35.

49. American Society of International Law, supra
note 18 at 8 (comments of Mr. Kaniaru); "New Perspectives
on International Environmental Law," supra note 20 at
1669.

50. For example, the International Bank for Reconstruction and Development (IBRD) now takes the environmental impacts of funding programs into consideration in
making program decisions. Utton, supra note 20 at 71.
See also "New Perspectives on International Environmental
Law," supra note 20 at 1669. Furthermore, the Export-

Import Bank of the United States has voluntarily con-
formed to NEPA in preparing an environmental impact
statement to assess the environmental consequences of its
funding decisions. Whitney, supra note 27 at 79.

51. See 19 U.S.C. § 1881 (1980). Under such an approach, equal treatment under existing trade agreements
would continue unless a party to the agreement failed to
enforce minimum environmental safeguards.

52. Accelerated amortization for pollution control
facilities built in the United States is allowed under
Internal Revenue Code of 1954, § 169 (April 2, 1980
edition). In addition, investment tax credits are provided for under Internal Revenue Code of 1954, § 46(c)(5)
(April 2, 1980 edition). Similar incentives for expenditures occuring outside the United States could serve to
encourage such expenditures.

53. Zalob, supra note 24 at 311.

54. Brown, supra note 20 at 689; Falk, supra note 15
at 418; "New Perspectives on International Environmental
Law," supra note 20 at 1678; McDougal & Schneider, supra
note 18 at 1112; Utton, supra note 20 at 61; Yates, "Unilateral and Multilateral Approaches to Environmental
Problems," 21 University of Toronto Law Journal 182, 188.
Such extraterritorial impacts may be unintended, as per
the prior consideration of extraterritorial application
of NEPA. A former member of the Council on Environmental
Quality has stated that "[W]e at the Council read NEPA
itself as applying to U.S. actions in the international
areas." Busterud, supra note 29 at 334. Whether such
extraterritorial applicability was intended by Congress
is open to question. Such applicability has, however,
been negated by Executive Order 12114. See text accompanying notes 26-28, supra.

55. It would be less expensive, for example, for an
MNC to design new facilities to conform to environmental
safeguards than to retrofit the same facility. If the
nation state in which the facility was to be constructed
did not require such safeguards, only the nation state in
which the MNC was chartered could require them. d'Arge
and Kneese, supra note 2 at 446. See also Almond, supra
note 23 at 739-40, 759.

56. Grieves, supra note 20 at 833; McDougal &
Schneider, supra note 18 at 1105, 1111, 1123; Yates,
supra note 54 at 191. The issue of standing raises a
number of fascinating issues:

> But who has standing to assert a claim on behalf
> of the future or the total ecosystem? The capacity
> of men to think of the future when the present
> is making such pressing demands for short-term
> benefits will be sorely tested in the coming
> attempts to establish international control
> over the use of the shared resources of the globe.

144

Bleicher, supra note 7 at 53.

57. McDougal & Schneider, supra note 18 at 1107.

58. Handl, supra note 22 at 547-48.

59. American Society of International Law, supra note 18 at 10 (comments of Mr. Hargrove); Brown, supra note 20 at 686.

60. A number of conventions and regulations have been proposed by different authors and environmentally oriented NGO's.

10
The Atmosphere: Change, Politics and World Law

Howard J. Taubenfeld

It may have been true a century ago that "everyone talked about the weather, but no one did anything about it." In recent years, however, while humans have been talking ever more about weather and climate, they are also doing something about it. In general, human activities have affected or may affect weather and climate in at least three ways: (1) conscious efforts to change weather and climate; (2) conscious national projects with unintended environmental shifts; and (3) major inadvertent environmental and climatic change. These effects, intended or not, create political issues, some of which are potentially issues of national and human survival. It is far from premature to focus attention on these areas. In many instances, the nature of the problems is already discernible and action is already necessary, for the effects of a failure to act immediately may not be felt for decades, and when these effects are felt, they may have become irreversible.

I. CONSCIOUS EFFORTS TO CHANGE WEATHER AND CLIMATE

Throughout recorded history, and perhaps for as long as humans have been able to formulate the thought, men have sought to change or at least influence the "gods of weather." They have danced, sung, sacrificed, prayed, fired cannons, and exploded dynamite taken aloft by kites. Only since the mid-1940's has science been involved in earnest. Just after the Second World War, Langmuir and Schaefer demonstrated that it was both theoretically and practically possible to affect water in the atmosphere by the introduction into a cloud of tiny particles of matter.[1] Dry ice was used initially; silver iodide has been used in most efforts since. Given a precipitation-pregnant situation in the atmosphere, the introduction of additional nuclei to which water vapor may cling appears to produce more precipitation than would otherwise have occurred. An excess introduction of particles might inhibit the creation of large hailstorms or, indeed, might lessen precipitation if it was so desired.

The efforts of the past thirty-five years to deliberately modify weather appear to have produced modest results. They have, however, created substantial domestic and even international controversy.[2] At present, there is no real evidence that large-scale climatic effects can be intentionally produced. We know that we can remove supercooled fog from airports for limited periods; that individual cumulus clouds can be made to grow and often to produce rain; that orographic clouds (those already rising as they are carried from west to east over the United States' western mountains, for example) can be induced to precipitate more than we would expect in nature.[3] With regard to increasing rain production from other large storm systems, to decreasing hail or hail damage, to modifying hurricanes to reduce their wind speed and hence damage due to wind and storm surge, the evidence is promising but unproven.

What are the risks at the international level from this promising if partially unproven technology? First, there is the possibility that an experiment or operation in one country will cause direct, demonstrable harm in another.[4] It is conceivable, for example, that augmenting the flow of an international river might cause damage to a lower riparian state. Where the cause-effect relationship is clear, there are precedents in the developing law of international rivers to make responsibility clear. The mechanisms for recouping losses are not as well developed.

Second, there is the possibility, demonstrated repeatedly in the United States, that a state or its citizens may feel that weather modification activites in another nation are causing harm to them even though no cause-effect relation can be shown. There is also the human perception that can be summarized as the "rob Peter to pay Paul" principle. There is an ingrained human feeling that an increase of rain in one place must correspondingly decrease it somewhere else. Most scientists feel this is not true, that there is so much water in the air that cloud seeding may increase precipitation outside a target area, or not affect the area at all. Yet even if scientifically demonstrable, many people will find this hard to believe. Disputes of this type have arisen, however, with respect to a perceived harm when in fact no weather modification activities have taken place. Since perceptions are as strong as reality, perhaps in such cases some form of impartial fact-finding will ameliorate the problem.

Third, there is the problem of risk-sharing between nations. Hurricanes (called typhoons in the Pacific) produce wind damage, storm surge damage, and

flooding rainstorms. Many nations, however, depend on
these storms for much of their needed rainfall. If it
becomes possible to diminish the wind but spread the
storm, or to dissipate much of the storm, who would
make the decision? If, to avoid great damage to Texas,
we could turn a hurricane toward Cuba, is this a permissible act of self-defense against a devastating natural phenomenon? While much of this is fanciful at present, it is important to consider the appropriate international approaches to channeling these capabilities for
weather modification into internationally acceptable
patterns.[5]

One further issue cannot be avoided although the
threat may have been laid to rest for the present.
Weather has always been of importance in military
operations.[6] As a Navy scientist stated to the Congress
many years ago: "We regard the weather as a weapon.
Anything one can use to get his way is a weapon and the
weather is as good a one as any."[7] The modest efforts
of American forces to enhance rainfall to interdict
enemy forces in some stages of the war in Vietnam do not
seem to have produced any long-lasting physical effects.
The general feeling that it is somehow wrong to tamper
with "Mother Nature," however, combined with more
realistic fears of the potentially untoward and unpredictable effects of attempting large-scale climatic
shifts have led to a treaty, accepted by the world's
major powers, renouncing the use of such environmental
modification as a weapon.[8] It is unclear whether humans
could do these things to each other and to the environment. It is well that they have agreed not to try.

II. CONSCIOUS NATIONAL PROJECTS WITH UNINTENDED ENVIRONMENTAL SHIFTS

Of potentially far greater importance to a politically stable world than intentional weather modification
are those human activities which have or may have inadvertent impacts on weather and climate.[9] Two major
examples may be cited.

First, scientists and engineers in the Soviet
Union have from time to time announced major engineering
plans to reverse the flow of major Siberian rivers.[10]
River flows can be altered. In the United States, the
flow of the river at Chicago was reversed in this century. Russia has already reportedly shifted the flow of
a river in Central Russia. Plans to shift the flow of
the Jordan River some decades ago were denounced by
both Israel and Jordan as a causus belli if the other
did it.[11]

The Soviet plans for Siberian rivers are not, however, "hostile." They are designed to serve several

national purposes. The changes would provide increased flows of water for irrigation over wide areas and would help replenish the waters in Russia's inland seas. Moreover, since fresh water freezes more rapidly than salt water, the diminished flow of fresh water into the Arctic Sea from the rivers which would now, in major part, flow south rather than north, would serve to help keep Russian Arctic ports ice-free for somewhat longer periods. Irrigation, more reserve water, and ice-free ports are all important for domestic purposes. Why is there a potential problem?

In analyzing this situation, scientists have pointed out that an irreversible chain reaction may be started. As the areas around the river mouths remain ice-free longer, more "black" water is available to absorb solar heat. Ice, in contrast, reflects more heat upward. As more heat is absorbed by the water, more ice will melt. As more ice melts, more open water is available to absorb heat until, at some point, the relatively thin ice cover on the Arctic Sea may disappear completely. We know that the Arctic has been ice-free many times in geological history. We do not know, however, what the short or long-term effects would be on regional and world climate if the Arctic ice disappeared rather precipitously in the next decades.[12]

Second, we are now witnessing a rather remarkable assault on many of the world's major forests. Brazil and other countries are making major inroads on the great forests which cover substantial portions of their territory. Brazil, for example, has been engaged in a large-scale effort to replace its forest with farm land. The dramatic increases in the price of wood and forest products in recent decades have further accelerated demand for the removal of the trees.

Again, it is reasonable to ask why a country's domestic policies can be suggested as an important area of international concern and scrutiny and, again, the answer is the same. The forests, as tremendous green areas (especially those in the equatorial belt), are the "source" of much of the world's climate. A dramatic change in these forests is certain to produce changes elsewhere, but no one is sure what these changes will be.

Furthermore, as will be discussed in more detail later, the world is already facing a number of potential problems due to the vast increase of carbon dioxide (CO_2) resulting from human activities. One major natural "sink" for carbon dioxide is the green areas of the globe. As forests are eliminated, the cutting and clearing apparently releases CO_2, as does the burning of wood, and the replacement of a forest with an open

or an urban area means that there is less green surface
available to absorb CO_2. These "domestic" practices
and policies may have extremely widespread, if completely unintended, effects.[13] At present, the international legal system has but the most embryonic techniques for dealing with such national activities. Even
raising the question may be considered an unwarranted
interference with domestic concerns. Still, the awesome
possibilities of unwanted and irreversible change do
exist.

III. MAJOR INADVERTENT ENVIRONMENTAL AND CLIMATIC
     CHANGE

In a broad sense, every human activity affects the
climate, at least on a tiny microscale. When humans
replace farm or pasture land, or a forest, with a city,
the local weather changes. A city is a "heat island."
Air is warmed and rises as it moves over the city.
Industry, specifically the burning of fossil fuels,
places large numbers of particles in the air. This un-
intentional cloud seeding has an effect similar to that
sought by intentional weather modification. Extensive
studies in and around St. Louis and its "downwind"
areas, for example, show that, as contrasted with some
decades ago, the downwind areas are subjected annually
to a substantially greater number of serious storms and
to an increased amount of hail.[14]

In a different way, some scientists have suggested
that desertification is, in part and in some areas, due
to patterns of animal husbandry. Cattle will eat
growing greens but leave a stubble; sheep will eat to
the earth; goats will dig the roots as well. Where
goats graze on the margins of a desert, they permanently
destroy the grass and the desert widens. As the desert
widens, some argue, more dust and nuclei are released
to the heavens. The result is that clouds are over-
seeded, rain does not fall and desertification is reinforced.

With the spread of industrialization, the increased
demand for electric power, and the creation of new
products, the use of the atmosphere as a disposal sink
for industrial wastes has of course increased tremen-
dously. The atmosphere has changed, is changing, and
will change. It is a tremendous machine which has
historically managed to absorb "insults" from volcanic
eruptions to manmade intrusions, without long-term dis-
turbance of an equilibrium.[15]

It is rapidly becoming apparent that certain activities of mankind are in the process of altering the world
climatic balance. The implications of such alterations
for a world where climate is an important part of a

nation's well-being and where nations are increasingly
armed with nuclear weapons are also becoming apparent.
At least three issue areas require attention: (1) acid
rain; (2) carbon dioxide and the "greenhouse" effect;
and (3) the effect of chlorofluorocarbons (CFC's) on the
ozone layer of the stratosphere.

Of these three issue areas, only one--acid rain--is
of international concern only because it affects many
countries and the source of the problem is often in
another nation. Acid rain does not appear to involve
worldwide climatic effects. The other two--the increase
of carbon dioxide in the atmosphere and the effects of
CFC's on the ozone layer of the stratosphere--are truly
global issues in that they both threaten change in the
overall world climate and cannot adequately be amelio-
rated by the action of any one or even several countries.
A worldwide response is clearly required.

A. Acid Rain

There is substantial evidence that acidity levels
in precipitation have varied throughout history. Many
natural sources such as volcanoes and forests increase
the atmospheric loading of sulphur oxides, especially
sulphur dioxide (SO_2) and nitrogen oxides (NO_x) which,
on chemical reaction in the atmosphere, precipitate as
rain or snow containing higher acidity levels.

We have, however, come to realize two important
sets of facts. On one hand, the greater the acidity of
precipitation in an area, the more likely it is to cause
erosion of stone surfaces of buildings and other structures, to harm crops, and to kill fish in ponds, lakes,
and streams.[16] On the other hand, it now seems clear
that many human activities--the burning of coal and oil,
other industrial pursuits such as smelting, automobile
exhaust, even farming--are adding substantially in
various regions to the already present natural causes of
acid precipitation or are creating new areas of acid
precipitation damage.[17] Many of the effects of these
activities are felt in countries other than the source
of the pollution.[18]

There is already widespread national and international concern about the effects of acid precipitation
and about ways of dealing with them. As the United
States moves increasingly to the use of coal to generate
power, for example, increases in emissions may be anticipated unless steps are taken immediately to forestall
adverse effects. Furthermore, remedies must be carefully
evaluated. The introduction of very tall smokestacks
may lead to a lessening of pollution in the immediate
vicinity of the pollutant source, but it also places
particulates higher in the atmosphere and makes it easier

for them to travel great distances.

Before great strides can be expected internationally, countries with an avowed interest in pollution problems must be prepared to put "their own houses in order." Many nations have begun this process. The United States, among many other countries, has extensive legislation and regulations concerning the basic pollutants involved in acid rain. However, much more could be done. Permissible atmospheric releases of both sulphur oxide (SO_x) and NO_x could be lowered. Research efforts could be increased. Coal washing could be made mandatory where appropriate. Use of tall stacks could be restricted. The worst offending plants could be phased out.

On the international level, an agreement between the United States and Canada, signed in August 1980, includes plans for major studies and recommendations for dealing with perceived perils.[19] The United States and Canada share major geographic areas where the underlying bedrock has a low capacity to buffer acids and is therefore susceptible to damage. John Fraser, Canada's Minister of the Environment, has called acid rain "the most serious environmental problem that Canada faces."[20] President Carter's 1979 Environmental Message recognized acid rain as a global threat of great importance and set up a ten-year Federal Acid Rain Assessment Program.[21] In 1977, the United States Clean Air Act was amended to make it clear that air pollution from the United States causing problems abroad could lead to a requirement of action by the states.[22] Thus, a beginning has been made on the North American continent.

In 1979, the Economic Commission for Europe (ECE), a United Nations regional organization with thirty-four members including the United States and Canada, promulgated the Convention on Long-Range Transboundary Air Pollution.[23] This Convention recognizes the necessity of international cooperation in monitoring and research. It is the first major direct acknowledgement of the issues. Despite the absence of a mechanism for compelling pollution abatement, the Convention calls for the joint development of air pollution control strategies. The parties pledge to make efforts "to limit, and as far as possible, gradually reduce and prevent air pollution."[24] This is a first step for Europe. It should be followed, in time, by additional agreements to establish the liability of nations for damage caused and to award compensation where appropriate.[25]

B. Carbon Dioxide

While the magnitude of our lack of knowledge and understanding about the chemical and other processes which take place in the upper atmosphere is appallingly large, the last few decades have witnessed dramatic gains in this area. Satellite probes, computers and computer modeling, and vast cooperative scientific programs covering large areas of the globe now make possible a better understanding of what the atmosphere is and how it functions. Such research has also made it possible to estimate the inroads and changes in the atmospheric commons which humans have made. Of the immediate insults to the environment (and to a decent life for humans), we can readily recognize the prevalence of such problems as smog in our cities and harmful acid rain. There are other, larger-scale effects which may be even more deleterious over time than these more visible, immediate examples.

For several decades, scientists have noted an increase in atmospheric carbon dioxide (CO_2). It is predicted that carbon dioxide in the atmosphere will about double in the period 1960 to 2030 (perhaps even to 2050).[26]

Since carbon dioxide tends to prevent the escape of heat from the earth, if this doubling occurs it could raise the global mean temperature of the earth some 1.5 to 4.5 degrees Celsius, with less warming at the Equator and more at the poles.[27] Shifts in the location of the earth's rain belts could also occur. While some nations might find their weather improved, others are certain to be worse off, and at this stage, no one can predict with certainty that anyone will be better off overall. Any improvements are hard to forecast and there might not be net national benefits at all. Local gains might be overbalanced by planetary disasters.

Carbon dioxide enters the atmosphere from many natural sources, In addition, however, the advent of the industrial revolution led to a demonstrable increase in the atmosphere's CO_2 load. It is estimated that approximately three-fourths of the CO_2 in the atmosphere comes from the industrialized nations.[28] Less developed countries contribute a limited share by their own industrial processes. To a larger degree these countries contribute to CO_2 increases in the atmosphere by removing forests and burning the wood.

A CO_2-induced warming of the planet (in fact, any warming of the planet) would cause changes in the environment. Some areas may become more usable for farming. Other areas may lose warmth and moisture or may have too much heat for traditional crops. Increased heating at the poles may be enough to cause polar ice to melt with unpredictable climatic consequences. The West Antarctic ice sheet is considered less stable than other land-based ice and might melt, raising the earth's water level by perhaps ten feet. If this and the other

Antarctic and Greenland ice sheets were to melt, water
levels might rise as much as eighty feet worldwide.
These are true catastrophes in the making. It is not
that they are likely. It is simply that we can no longer ignore these possibilities.

A relatively limited number of countries are the
major contributors to CO_2 emissions. They are also the
primary beneficiaries of the industrialization which is
based on the use of fossil fuels. The United States,
the Soviet Union, and China are also the great sources
of coal, the use of which will increase because of petroleum shortages. Only a few countries, such as Brazil,
are the major holders of vast forest resources. Determined action by a relatively few states, therefore,
could make a major contribution to changing the rate of
CO_2 loading in the atmosphere. Individually, several of
these nations have accepted the need to act. All question what steps should be taken. Few support any kind
of international management or controls. Although the
results of the "greenhouse effect" might not be observed
for a century, the process having already begun may lead
inexorably to unacceptable, perhaps even unforeseen consequences if actions are not taken in the immediate
future. Without a beginning now, the processes may become irreversible.[29]

C. Chlorofluorocarbons

Chlorofluorocarbons (CFC's), perhaps best known
under DuPont's trade name "freon," are a class of wonder
chemicals. They are made up of extremely inert molecules which do not readily bond with others. They are
versatile, nontoxic to humans, and are long lived. They
have been widely used in aerosol spray cans, as industrial solvents, in air conditioning and refrigeration,
and in foams used for cushioning, insulation, and pack-
aging. They are the blowing agents used to make the
cups and trays used by fast-food chains, for "plastic"
egg cartons, and the like. They are also relatively
inexpensive. The United States has accounted for about
thirty percent of the world's emission of CFC's.[30] In
1976, this amounted to approximately 250 millions pounds
from nonaerosol applications.[31]

With all their good qualities, why are CFC's of
current concern? In 1974, certain scientists first
advanced the theory that CFC molecules, because of their
inertness, rise to the stratosphere essentially unchanged. Once in the stratosphere, the sun's rays cause
them to change and combine with molecules of ozone in a
manner which lessens the ozone in the stratosphere.
Since it is the ozone layer which shields humans, crops,
animals, and life near the surface of the waters from

damaging ultraviolet radiation, a decrease in ozone
could lead to increases in skin cancer in areas of the
earth where meteorological conditions and skin color
make this disease an existent threat, not to mention
damage to crops and other life forms. Moreover, another
predicted result of CFC's in the stratosphere is an
increase in the earth's temperature by the middle of the
next century. By itself, CFC temperature increases are
modest. When added to a CO_2 temperature-induced increase (an increase perhaps four times greater than that
produced by CFC's alone), it assumes a far more serious
potential for disruption.

One additional point warrants consideration. The
escape of CFC's into the atmosphere is not limited to
the time of their manufacture. Some escape slowly as
the product is used, as in the case of rigid foams.
Others are stored and released only when the product is
discarded, as in the case of home refrigerators. This
"bank" of CFC's is expected to grow rapidly over the
decades unless a halt occurs now. While waiting, the
quantity of CFC's is growing and will become increasingly
more costly to police and control.

Reaction to the perceived long-range effects of CFC's
remains mixed internationally. Some scientists suggest
that further proof needs to be produced. This reluc-
tance to act exists despite identification of the problem
in authoritative reports issued by the National Academy
of Sciences in 1977 and 1979, by the World Meteorological
Organization, and by the staff of the United Nations
Environment Programme (UNEP).[32]

D. Present International Safeguards Against Pollution

Action to date has been primarily national, with the
United States taking the lead by banning the use of
CFC's in aerosol spray cans and by proposing overall
limits on production. A few other nations, such as Canada, have acted as well. The Common Market countries
have moved slowly. Scandinavian countries are taking
action. The British and French have noted their doubts
that there is as yet a demonstrable problem. There is
a UNEP program in place for studying and monitoring the
ozone layer. The critical question is whether these
actions are adequate.

In the future, nations might enter into accords to
set rules, to ban CFC's where appropriate, to use taxes
and other incentive systems to limit their use, to
regulate imports and exports, to encourage makers and
users to find substitutes, and to use those CFC's which
cause the least damage to the ozone layer. However, even
before a worldwide consensus on this issue is developed,
an agreement among the industrialized nations could

dramatically change the outflow of CFC's.[33]

With both CO_2 and CFC's, the problem is truly global. The activities of one or even a small number of countries can have an immediate impact, but amelioration or a cure is ultimately the responsibility of all states. In each case, while the source of the problem exists in both present and future activities, actual "visible" proof of deleterious change may not be available for decades. Thus, for both CO_2 and CFC's, if preventative action is not begun at once, and on a broad scale, it is probable that the feared consequences will have occurred, or at least that the trend toward such consequences will be irreversible when they become widely perceived.

IV. CLIMATE MODIFICATION AND THE POTENTIAL FOR INTERNATIONAL CONFLICT

A common feature of all of the types of climate modification noted here is their potential for causing international tension and conflict. International modification of local weather, if it involves a border area, and of large scale storms (hurricanes, for example), is likely to be viewed as a "zero sum game,"[34] where one party loses if another gains. This may or may not be scientifically accurate, but any change may be perceived as a loss by some party. If the Chinese and Japanese governments advise the United States that a proposed typhoon suppression experimental program to be based on Guam is a potentially dangerous experiment, it is probably appropriate for the United States not to proceed, even if American scientists are certain that no effects could be felt in China or Japan. Once a typhoon was seeded, the United States would be blamed for all of its eventual damages regardless of whether the seeding could have contributed to it.[35] With an operational experiment in the Gulf of Mexico, even unseeded and uninvestigated hurricanes led to claims by some Mexican politicans that the United States is "stealing" Mexico's rainfall.

Perhaps only a highly visible, truly internationalized experimental program could eliminate or dampen such a clamor. But what if it is proved that at least some modification efforts do cause certain losses? There is no mechanism for decision at the international level. Are states free to make choices having domestic benefit regardless of the effects of such choices on other nations? Who speaks in defense of the international "commons" -- the seas, the atmosphere?

A. Present International Legal Standards

Although international law to date is embryonic at best, there is law in these areas. It is generally recognized as law that no nation may permit activities on its soil which will cause harm in another nation. In the classic case on this issue, the Trail Smelter Arbitration,[36] the tribunal was asked to deal with a smelter in British Columbia, and the effect of its pollution on properties in the state of Washington. Finding that damage was in fact being caused, the tribunal assessed damages and required that the pollution be monitored and diminished. While it did not, and could not, order the smelter to cease operations (a point worth noting for future cases), the tribunal did state that:

> [N]o State has the right to use or permit the use of its territory in such a manner as to cause injury by fumes in or to the territory of another or the properties or persons therein, when the case is of serious consequence and the injury is established by clear and convincing evidence.[37]

A similar but broader statement was made by the International Court of Justice in a dissimilar situation in The Corfu Channel Case[38] when the Court said that a state has an obligation "not to allow knowingly its territory to be used for acts contrary to the rights of other States."[39]

These ideas have been increasingly included in international instruments in the past several decades.[40] The 1972 Declaration of the United Nations Conference on the Human Environment in Stockholm gave us several directly relevant principles relating not only to damage to another state but to the environment generally.[41]

For all sources of atmospheric modification, therefore, the basic norms have been stated and generally accepted. These norms apply regardless of whether the modification is intentional or not and whether it affects another nation specifically or the world's environment in general. No state may permit activities on its territories which seriously injure another state or its citizens, nor may it permit serious damage to the environment as a whole. Despite these principles and except for limited bilateral and special multilateral arrangements, there are now no widely accepted international mechanisms for resolving disputes as to scientific facts, for evaluating claims of injury and making binding awards, or for dealing with activities which affect the environment generally. In each case, some start has been made. Before reviewing progress to date and offering some suggestions for the future, however, one vitally important stumbling block in the path of any effective international control of pollution must be considered. This relates to the tension between development and the use of the atmospheric commons to dispose of the waste products of development.

B. Industrialization in the Developing Countries

Just as the United Nations has recognized the damage of pollution both to the human environment and to peace between neighbors, it has also firmly and repeatedly recognized a "right" to development. Although this right is often asserted by the less developed nations, the more developed nations also support the goals of development. While the more industrialized nations acknowledge the inherent instability caused by tensions between rich and poor, they seemingly trust the apparent efficacy of development and industrialization as the "invisible hand" in the eventual self-limitation of population growth, and hope that development will help in the alleviation of disease, starvation, infant mortality, and short life expectancy.

Scientists and decisionmakers in many of the more developed countries have, however, become increasingly aware of the dangers to the environment the industrial revolution has created. Through the traditional free use of waters, oceans, and the atmosphere as dumps for our wastes, we endanger not only our countries and ourselves, but also our neighbors and, potentially, the very survival of human life. We are thus presented with a dichotomy. Industrial development has resulted in vastly increased health, well-being, and life expectancy for most humans in those countries which are already well on the path of industrialization. Conversely, industrialization also brings threats to those it helps and to the world environment.

Since it is clear that countries will industrialize, we need to devise strategies immediately to begin to cope with potential consequences even if they are decades away. We need to understand, to accept, and to plan for a world in which there are tensions between development (which means burning more fossil fuels, cutting more forests, using marvelous products like CFC's) and the more general but eventually overwhelming need of environmental survival.

V. FUTURE WORLD ORDER

A. Protection of the International "Commons"

As we turn to the future, it seems clear, at least in principle, that the international "commons" must be protected from harmful activities arising in any state. The effects of large-scale industrialization, the omnipresence of the automobile, the increasing knowledge of the deleterious effects of many waste materials, acid rain, smog, high level atmospheric pollution -- all this has led not only to discussion and studies but to legislation and the creation of domestic and international mechanisms for problem solving. The efforts thus far are limited. Not all countries are concerned. Not all problems are recognized as problems. Nevertheless, while it would be unwise to assume that, internationally, all nations are realistically assessing the potential problems or even that they have moved forcefully to cope with existent and demonstrated perils, it would also be foolish to ignore the important steps that have already been taken.

In the United States, activities have included the creation of and the decade of work by the Environmental Protection Agency (EPA). Water and air quality are monitored, research is intense, and standards have been set. From its origins, the EPA has been concerned with international issues. As Senator Henry Jackson, the principal author of the National Environmental Policy Act, said on the Senate Floor, the Act is a "congressional declaration that . . . we will not intentionally initiate actions which will do irreparable damage to the air, land and water which support life on earth."[42] The Act applies to the entirety of the "human environment," including "international aspects."[43]

On the issues of potential international concern, efforts have been focused on the amelioration of CO_2 and acid rain problems, and vigorous action has been taken with respect to CFC's. The use of CFC's in aerosol spray cans has been prohibited and regulations limiting overall production are being developed.[44] Several other countries have also taken action to limit the escape of the chemical contributors to acid rain and to cut back air and water pollution.[45] Several countries have followed the United States' lead to limit the movement of CFC's into the stratosphere.[46]

Bilaterally, the United States has been working with Mexico on water and air quality problems,[47] and with Canada on the problems of water use, water pollution, and acid rain.[48] The United States, France, and the United Kingdom are parties to an innovative treaty on monitoring the stratosphere.[49] European countries have entered into several bilateral and multilateral agreements to curb pollution, especially in multinational lakes and rivers.[50] As discussed above, the ECE promulgated a treaty on transfrontier, long-range, airborne pollution.[51] The Scandinavian countries are not only cooperating nationally with respect to transborder pollution, but have also opened their courts and administrative mechanisms to citizens of neighboring states affected by pollution.[52]

B. Progress in International Institutions

At an even broader level, the United Nations, while stressing the right of each nation to develop, has adopted resolutions pointing out the need to limit the dangers from pollution.[53] The U.N. Environment Programme (UNEP) has been given a special role as overseer of the international programs concerning the ozone layer. Other agencies, including inter alia the World Meteorological Organization (WMO), the World Health Organization (WHO), and the Food and Agriculture Organization (FAO), have special assignments as part of the effort to assess the state of the upper atmosphere and to find indications of change while there is still time to act. Such nongovernmental scientific agencies as the International Council of Scientific Unions (ICSU)[54] have also played important roles in advancing our knowledge and, therefore, in contributing to issue identification and potential resolution.

VI. CONCLUSIONS

Despite these signs of progress, the international record in preserving and sharing resources is not good. The potential loss of the great whales due to human rapaciousness, despite international efforts to preserve them, is a case in point. Perhaps what is now needed is a dual strategy, one which would press forward along the lines of observation, monitoring, fact-finding, standard setting and, eventually, enforcement at an international level, while at the same time we search for techniques which would permit humanity a decent environmental future.

We should press forward vigorously in each nation to continually set the highest standards of environmental protection consonant with decent survival and progress. We should press for a growth of international activities in monitoring and, in time, in developing stringent rules for national action. Uniform rules may well help an enterprise avoid a competitive disadvantage if other enterprises are not obligated to take steps to avoid pollution. Over time, effective rules should be

developed and upheld by national courts and, perhaps, by
the International Court of Justice or by a new environmental law tribunal for assessing facts and awarding
recompense.[55]

It must be noted, as some scientists are now pointing out, that climatic change is inevitable. If humanity disappeared, climate would still change over time.
Mankind may be benefited or harmed by a particular
change, and it is appropriate to prevent where possible
human-induced damaging change. However, change is the
order of the universe. Because of this fact, it is appropriate to urge decisionmakers in all nations to give
present and continuing attention to strategies which
accept very longterm change in climate as certain, and
to work to reduce the risks of damage to humanity from
such changes. Cooperation in developing weather modification techniques, strong, more resistant crops,
cattle with better tolerance for temperature and moisture changes, programs for improved storage of crops,
cooperation in distribution of necessities worldwide,
and assistance in alternative programs of development,
could make nations more immune from climatic change.

There is clearly room for the wider use of international agencies (UNEP, WMO, WHO, FAO, and others)
while a general agreement or agreements could be promulgated through the United Nations General Assembly or at
special conferences. This is not a plea for a technological "fix" which would obviate the need for the control of pollution, for preserving the atmosphere, or for
trying to cope directly with insults to the environment.
Indeed, we need to develop international regulation and
control as rapidly as we can. The rate and magnitude
of man-made changes in the world environment may already
be exceeding our capacity to cope effectively. What is
proposed is a dual strategy. Solutions to our environmental problems will come slowly. We need to move to
protect against human impacts on the environment and to
ameliorate future conditions regardless of the cause.

In general, we can point with pride to certain
major national and international efforts to identify
dangers to the human "commons" and, primarily on a
national basis, to cope with them. Since the problems
are global, multinational efforts to control transfrontier pollution and assaults on the atmosphere are essential. No single nation can do it alone. These efforts
have begun, but the conflicts of interest are very real.

International cooperation must be forcefully pur-
sued with assurance for the less developed nations (or
for any nation especially affected) of favorable terms
for pollution-free or pollution-moderating technology,
for substitute goods, or for whatever it takes to encourage development while safeguarding the human future.

Perhaps then we can face the future with some degree of certainty. Still, if there comes to be recognized a true crisis of the environment, threatening the lives of all or most humans or at least requiring strict rationing of the right to industrialize, then major changes in the present world system would be required. We would in that case need something like a responsible world government with the ability to assure the equitable distribution of the rights to life, to material welfare, and to security.

NOTES

1. Langmuir, Schaefer, and Vonnegut, addresses to the American Physical Society, reported in N.Y. Times, Jan. 31, 1947, at 16, col. 1; Schaefer, "Man-made Snow," 69 Mech. Eng. 32 (1947); Schaefer, "Production of Ice Crystals in a Cloud of Supercooled Water Droplets," 104 Science 457 (1946); see generally Ball, "Shaping the Law of Weather Control," 58 Yale L. J. 213 (1949).
2. See generally G. Breuer, Weather Modification, Prospects and Problems (1980); Danielson, Sherk & Grant, "Legal System Requirements to Control and Facilitate Water Augmentation in the Western United States," Den. J. Int'l L. & Pol'y 511 (1976); Samuels, "Prospective International Control of Weather Modification Activities," 21 U. Toronto L. J. 222 (1971); Sigel, "International Control of Weather Modification in a Regime of Long-Range Weather Forecasting," 19 Harv. Int'l L. J. 535 (1978); Wood, "The Status of Weather Modification Activities Under United States and International Law," 10 Nat. Resources Law. 367 (1977-78); Note, "Weather Genesis and Weather Neutralization: A New Approach to Weather Modification," 6 Calif. W. Int'l L. J. 412 (1976)
3. Samuels, "International Control of Weather Modification Activities: Peril or Policy?," 13 Nat. Resources J. 327 n.1 (1973); Taubenfeld, "International Environmental Law: Air and Outer Space," 13 Nat. Resources J. 315, 321 (1973).
4. Legal and Scientific Uncertainties of Weather Modification (W. Thomas ed. 1977). See generally Hassett, "Weather Modification and Control: International Organizational Prospects," 7 Tex. Int'l L. J. 89 (1972-72); Samuels, note 3 supra.
5. Taubenfeld, "Weather Modification and Control: Some International Legal Implications," 55 Calif. L. Rev. 493 (1967). See also Hassett, note 4 supra; Samuels, note 2 supra; Wood, note 2 supra.
6. Example would include the storm that helped save England from the Spanish Armada and the determination of D-Day for Europe in 1944 by the weather outlook. The

possibility of using weather to deny information to an
enemy, to create battlefield hazards, and to destroy
crops have all been considered.

7. 13 Nat. Resources J. 315, 323 n.23 (1973).

8. Convention on the Prohibition of Military or any
Other Hostile Use of Environmental Modification Techniques, done at Geneva, May 18, 1977, entered into force
for the United States, Jan. 17, 1980, T.I.A.S. No. 9614.

9. A revew of the impacts of a number of human
activities on the atmosphere can be found in Inadvertent
Climate Modification: Report of the Study of Man's
Impact on Climate (SMIC) (1971) [hereinafter referred to
as Inadvertent Climate Modification]. See also Coppoc,
"The Environment: No Respecter of National Boundaries,"
43 Alb. L. Rev. 520 (1979); Dickstein, "National Environ-
mental Hazards and International Law," 23 Int'l & Comp.
L. Q. 426 (1974); Jackson, "The Dimensions of Interna-
tional Pollution," 50 Or. L. Rev. 223 (1970-71); Joyner
& Joyner, "Global Eco-Management and International Org-
anization: The Stockholm Conference and Problems of
Cooperation," 14 Nat. Resources J. 533 (1974); Muir,
"Legal and Ecological Aspects of the International
Energy Situation," 8 Int'l Law. 1 (1974).

10. Taubenfeld, supra note 3, at 322; Wood, supra
note 2, at 385 n.67.

11. Taubenfeld, supra note 5, at 501 n.43.

12. See Taubenfeld, note 3 supra.

13. Id.

14. See, e.g., Gatz, "An Investigation of Pollutant
Source Strength--Rainfall Relationships at St. Louis,"
in Seventh Conference on Inadvertent and Planned Weather
Modification 9 (1979) (American Meteorological Society,
Banff, Alberta, Canada, Oct. 8-12, 1979).

15. This does not mean, of course, that atmospheric
norms have not changed drastically over the countless
years of the existence of the atmosphere.

16. See Ferenbaugh, "Acid Rain: Biological Effects
and Implications," Envt'l Aff. 745 (1975).

17. Other sources add to the quantities of both
sulfur oxides and nitrogen oxides released into the
atmosphere.

18. There are at present substantial emissions in
the northeastern United States, in southeastern Canada,
and in northern Europe, Jackson, supra note 9, at 226-27.

19. Acid rain agreement, signed Aug. 5, 1980, by
Secretary of State Edmund Muskie and Ambassador to the
United States Peter Towe; discussed in 209 Science 890
(Aug. 22, 1980).

20. Speech of Nov. 2, 1979, Action Seminar on Acid
Precipiation, Toronto, Canada.

21. 15 Weekly Comp. of Pres. Doc. 1353. 1372-73
(Aug. 2, 1979).

22. 42 U.S.C. §§ 7401 et seq. (1977) (amending 42 U.S.C. §§ 7401 et seq. (1967)).

23. Convention on Long-Range Transboundary Air Pollution, done Nov. 13, 1979, 1 U.N. ECE, Annex 1, U.N. Doc. E/ECE/HLM.1/2 (1979), reprinted in 18 Int'l Legal Mats., 1442 (1979).

24. Id. art. 2.

25. A number of authorities have considered both the legal and biological causes and effects of acid rain. See Babich, Davies, & Stozky, "Acid Precipitation: Causes and Consequences," Environment, May 1980, at 6; Coppoc, note 9 supra; Ferenbaugh, note 16 supra; Graves, "Rain of Troubles", Science 80, July/Aug. 1980 at 75, (includes Rosencranz, "International Forecast: More Acid Rain," at 79); Likens, Wright, Galloway, & Butler, "Acid Rain," Scientific Am., Oct. 1979, at 43.

26. Becker, "Does a CO_2 Catastrophe Impend?," 38 Pub. Power 24, 25. See generally Council on Environmental Quality, Global Energy Futures and the Carbon Dioxide Problem (1981); W. Kellogg & R. Schware, Climate Change and Society: Consequences of Increasing Atmospheric Carbon Dioxide (1981).

27. Council on Environmental Quality, supra note 26, at 45.

28. M. Tolba, The State of the World Environment 1980: The 1980 Report of the Executive Director of the United Nations Environment Programme (1980).

29. See also Inadvertent Climate Modification, note 9 supra; Bleicher, "An Overview of International Environmental Regulation," Ecology L. Q. 1 (1972); Joyner & Joyner, note 9 supra.

30. See National Academy of Science, Halocarbons: Effects on Stratospheric Ozone (1976); see also National Academy of Science, The National Research Council in 1977 (1977).

31. Id.

32. Note 28 supra.

33. A range of activities resulting in impacts on the stratosphere is considered in chapter 9 of Inadvertent Climate Modification, note 9 supra.

34. Taubenfeld, supra note 5, at 49 n.10.

35. Id. at 496 n.19, 498-99 n.33.

36. The Tribunal gave a preliminary award on April 16, 1938, and the final award on March 11, 1941. Trail Smelter Arbitration (United States v. Canada), 3 R. Int'l Arb. Awards 1911 (1938); id. at 1905 (1941). The decisions of the Trail Smelter Arbitral Tribunal are also reported in 33 Am. J. Int'l L. 182 (1939) and 35 Am. J. Int'l L. 684 (1941). For an in-depth discussion of the case, see Rubin, "Pollution by Analogy: The Trail Smelter Arbitration," 50 Or. L. Rev. 259 (1971).

37. 3 R. Int'l Arb. Awards at 1965.

38. The Corfu Channel Case (Albania v. United Kingdom), [1949] I.C.J. 4.

39. Id. at 22.

40. The Helsinki Rules on the Uses of the Waters of International Rivers, for example, state that no nation can pollute so as to cause "substantial injury" to another nation and that the injured nation could call for abatement or compensation for damages. U.N. Doc. A/CN. 4/274, reprinted in Yearbook of the International Law Commission, U.N. Doc. A/CN.4/SER.A/1974/Add.1(Part 2), at 357; also reprinted in International Law Association, Report of the Fifty-second Conference, Helsinki 484, (1966). See generally Bleicher, note 29 supra. Several other shared river and lake treaties are in accord. See, e.g., The Indus Waters Treaty, Sept. 19, 1960, India-Pakistan-I.B.R.D., 419 U.N.T.S. 125; Agreement for the Full Utilization of the Nile Waters, Nov. 8, 1959, U.A.R.-Sudan, 453 U.N.T.S. 51; Treaty Relating to the Uses of the Waters of the Niagara River, Feb. 27, 1950, United States-Canada, 1 U.S.T. 694, T.I.A.S. No. 2130; Treaty Relating to the Utilization of the Waters of the Colorado and Tijuana Rivers, and of the Rio Grande, Feb. 3, 1944, United States-Mexico, 59 Stat. 1219, T.S. No. 994.

41. Principle 6, for example, expressly states that:
The discharge of toxic substances or of other sub-stances and the release of heat, in such quantities or concentrations as to exceed the capacity of the environment to render them harmless, must be halted in order to ensure that serious or irreversible damage is not inflicted upon ecosystems . . . .
This concept is later reinforced in Principles 21 and 22:
Principle 21. States have, in accordance with the charter of the United Nations and the principles of international law, the sovereign right to exploit their own resources pursuant to their own environ-mental policies, and the responsibility to ensure that activities within their jurisdiction or control do not cause damage to the environment of other States or of areas beyond the limits of national jurisdiction.
Principle 22. States shall co-operate to de-velop further the international law regarding lia-bility and compensation for the victims of pollution and other environmental damage caused by activities within the jurisdiction or control of such States to areas beyond their jurisdiction.
Report of the United Nations Conference on the Human Environment (Stockholm, 5-16 June 1972), 1 U.N. GAOR (21st plen. mtg.), U.N. Doc. A/CONF.48/14 Rev.1 (1972) reprinted in Int'l Legal Mats. 1416 (1972) [hereinafter

cited as Stockholm Conference on the Human Environment].
See also Sohn, "The Stockholm Declaration on the Human
Environment," 14 Harv. Int'l L. J. 423 (1973).

42. Cong. Rec. 40416 (1969).

43. The National Environmental Policy Act § 102(2)
(C) (1969) (current version at 42 U.S.C. §§ 4321 et seq.)
(1976 Supp. III 1979). See also H. R. Rep. No. 378, 91st
Cong., 1st Sess. 7 (1969).

44. In March 1978, the EPA and the FDA issued bans
on the use of CFC's in aerosol applications. The ban
became effective Oct. 15, 1978. Exemptions from the
general prohibition on manufacture, processing and distribution as well as essential use and special exemption
are discussed in 40 C.F.R. §§ 762.45 et seq. (1981).
The FDA has promulgated separate regulations on the use
of CFC's in articles at 21 C.F.R. § 2.125 (1978).

45. Bleicher, supra note 29, at 44-45 nn.177-78,
where various reports and problems of Norwegian "black
snow" are discussed.

46. Sweden, Norway and Canada have enacted the most
comprehensive limitations on the manufacture of CFC's.
Concern has been expressed in Germany and the Netherlands.

47. Agreement of Cooperation Regarding Pollution of
the Marine Environment by Discharges of Hydrocarbons and
Other Hazardous Substances, July 24, 1980, entered into
force Mar. 30, 1981, United States-Mexico, noted in 81
Dep't State Bull. 61 (June 1981); Memorandum of Under-
standing for Cooperation on Environmental Programs and
Transboundary Problems, June 14-19, 1978, United States-
Mexico, 30 U.S.T. 1574, T.I.A.S. No. 9264; Agreement on
the Permanent and Definitive Solution to the Interna-
tional Problem of the Salinity of the Colorado River,
Aug. 30, 1973, United States-Mexico, 24 U.S.T. 1968,
T.I.A.S. No. 7708; Convention on the Prevention of Marine
Pollution by Dumping of Wastes and Other Matter, opened
for signature Dec. 29, 1972, 26 U.S.T. 2403, T.I.A.S.
No. 8165 entered into force for the United States,
Aug. 30, 1975.

48. Agreement on Great Lakes Water Quality, Nov. 22,
1978, United States-Canada, 30 U.S.T. 1383, T.I.A.S.
No. 9257; Agreement on Contingency Plans for Spills of
Oil and Other Noxious Substances, June 19, 1974, United
States-Canada, 25 U.S.T. 1280, T.I.A.S. No. 7861.

49. Agreement on Monitoring of the Stratosphere,
May 5, 1976, United States-France-United Kingdom, 27
U.S.T. 1437, T.I.A.S. No. 8255 reprinted in [1978 Refer-
ence File] 1 Int'l Envir. Rep. (BNA)¶ 21:2501.

50. Convention for the Protection of the Rhine
Against Chemical Pollution, done at Bonn, Dec. 3, 1976,
reprinted in 16 Int'l Legal Mats. 242 (1977); Convention
on the Protection of the Rhine Against Pollution by

Chlorides, <u>done</u> <u>at</u> Bonn, Dec. 3, 1976, <u>reprinted</u> <u>in</u>
16 <u>Int'l Legal Mats</u>.265 (1977); The Nordic Convention on
the Protection of the Environment, <u>done</u> <u>at</u> Stockholm,
Feb. 19, 1974, <u>reprinted</u> <u>in</u> <u>The Nordic Environmental</u> Pro-
<u>tection Convention, with a Commentary</u> (Swedish Royal
Ministry for Foreign Affairs and Royal Ministry of Agriculture), <u>also</u> <u>reprinted</u> <u>in</u> 13 Int'l Legal Mats.591
(1974) [hereinafter cited as The Nordic Convention].

    51. Note 23 <u>supra</u>.

    52. The Nordic Convention, <u>supra</u> note 51, art. 3.

    53. Stockholm Conference on the Human Environment,
note 42 <u>supra</u>.

    54. The International Council of Scientific Unions
together with the World Meteorological Organization are
partners in preparing, coordinating and directing a
major international study, the Global Atmospheric Research Program. Taubenfeld, <u>supra</u> note 3, at 323. For
a discussion of the 9 scientific committees and 16 scientific unions within ICSU, see Joyner & Joyner, <u>supra</u>
note 2, at 576.

    55. For a discussion of incidents involving
transnational airborne pollution that have been referred
to the International Court of Justice, see Bleicher,
<u>supra</u> note 29, at 44 n. 174.

11
A Resource Management Approach to Carbon Dioxide During the Century of Transition

Edith Brown Weiss

ABSTRACT

The increasing accumulation of carbon dioxide (CO_2) in the atmosphere needs to be viewed as a problem in developing the appropriate transition strategies for moving from a fossil fuel to a non-fossil fuel economy in the next fifty to one hundred years. Processes need to be developed for managing carbon dioxide emissions which will sufficiently delay the warming of the earth's temperature to give time to develop new technologies for storing and recycling the carbon dioxide and to adapt to any changes in climate. Central to this management strategy are scientific determinations quantifying the extent of carbon dioxide input necessary to produce measurable variations in the global environment.

The carbon dioxide problem is foremost a problem in the management of fossil fuels. States have the sovereign right in international law to control the exploitation of their natural resources, and will resist measures which are perceived as intruding upon this sovereignty. Thus, the feasibility and desirability of establishing an international regime for setting a global ambient air quality standard for carbon dioxide, and for implementing it at the national/regional level through emission limitations designed to meet this standard, needs to be explored. This regime could involve measures for allocating emissions between competing producers and perhaps contain provisions for the lease and sale of emission allocations.

Presently the major contributors to carbon dioxide pollution are a handful of developed countries. The OECD, the European Economic Community, and the Convention on Long-Range Transboundary Air Pollution offer appropriate forums for initiating discussions regarding strategies for monitoring, limiting, and allocating carbon dioxide emissions.

The private sector should also be directly involved in the discussion of strategies for mitigating carbon

167

dioxide emissions. The formulation of appropriate business incentives for developing controls on emissions and for developing new ways to store carbon dioxide must be - a process of which the private sector is an integral part.

The increase in CO_2 is also a deforestation problem. The precise contribution of deforestation to this increase has not been scientifically determined, but it does not appear to be nearly as significant a contributing factor as that of fossil fuels. Problems of deforestation involve a wide community of states, including many in the developing world, and a number of multinational corporations. The problem for the international community is much broader than limiting the increasing amounts of CO_2 being released into the atmosphere by the effects of deforestation. It involves also development and implementation of environmentally sound management strategies of the forests and the soils for sustained yield. Any progress in controlling CO_2 release is likely to be a by-product of progress in this area. Limitations on CO_2 emissions would not be a feasible approach while, on the other hand, efforts to raise "international consciousness" about the implications of forest and soil management for carbon dioxide levels and global temperatures are both a necessary and useful step.

The atmosphere is a global resource that states need to manage. International law indicates a growing obligation of states to develop processes for an equitable use of common natural resources and for preventing harm to other states from activities which arise within their own jurisdiction or under their control. It is essential that processes are developed for minimizing the impact on the global temperatures of the production and development of fossil fuels during the transition period from a fossil fuel to a non-fossil fuel economy. This is what is meant by references to the "CO_2 transition strategy" for managing the atmosphere.

INTRODUCTION

Partly as a result of the world's increasing use of fossil fuels, carbon dioxide is accumulating in the atmosphere at a rate estimated to double the present concentrations by the year 2050.[1] Carbon dioxide in the atmosphere traps infrared radiation coming from the earth's surface and prevents it from excaping into outer space, thereby raising the temperature of the earth's surface. This phenomenon is commonly known as the "greenhouse effect." If the present atmospheric concentration of carbon dioxide doubled, world climate models predict an average global surface warming between 2°C and 3.5°C, with greater temperature increases at higher latitudes.[2]

This increase in the global surface temperature
would have a major impact on the world's climates, ocean
currents, and growing seasons. It would significantly
disrupt agricultural production and water supplies in
some areas.[3] At some point, increased concentrations of
carbon dioxide could cause the floating ice in the Arctic
to disappear and could trigger the disintegration of the
West Antarctic Ice Sheet, consequently raising the sea
level as much as fifteen to twenty feet.[4] The President's
Council on Environmental Quality has concluded that this
projected increase in carbon dioxide poses "one of the
most important contemporary environmental problems" and
"threatens the stability of climates worldwide and therefore, the stability of all nations."[5]

The rapid increase in the atmospheric concentration
of carbon dioxide is well documented. Scientists do not
agree, however, on the rates of projected increases and
their climatic effects, the sources of a carbon dioxide
build-up, or the capacity of existing reservoirs in the
global system to absorb future increases in carbon dioxide. Yet there is a clear warning from the scientific
community that the process of managing the carbon dioxide
build-up must be initiated, and that strategies for
adapting to its impact must be designed and implemented.
The problem becomes particularly important in light of
the nation's new policy favoring rapid development of
coal resources. The President's Commission on Coal concluded that in order to reduce dependency on foreign oil,
coal must replace oil and natural gas as the primary
energy source.[6] Coal releases much more carbon dioxide
than oil or natural gas.[7]

The carbon dioxide problem challenges the international community to break new ground to handle its
unique blend of political, economic, legal, and scientific issues. How, in the face of serious scientific uncertainties, should states manage the emission and release of carbon dioxide into the atmosphere, when many
states contribute to the problem in widely varying
degrees, when all states will be affected by the resulting climate change but in different ways, when the
activities contributing to a carbon dioxide build-up are
central to the energy and land-use practices of states,
and when costly preventive strategies, to be effective,
would have to be initiated at least a decade or more
before the full effects of CO_2-induced climate change
would be felt? As a preliminary approach to the problem,
this article briefly reviews international law as it is
concerned with transboundary environmental pollution and
shared resources, and discusses both is usefulness and
its limitations as precedent for handling the carbon
dioxide problem. It then suggests possible strategies
for managing the increasing emissions of carbon dioxide

into the atmosphere.

I.   DESCRIPTION OF THE CARBON DIOXIDE PROBLEM

Conceptually, the global increase in carbon dioxide is a problem in the management of scarce natural resource: the quality of the global atmosphere. Part of this is an international pollution problem: states dump carbon dioxide pollutants into the atmosphere; this can lead to a decrease in the quality of global resources. Since fossil fuel resources are limited and likely to be replaced by alternative energy supplies in the future, the steady build-up of carbon dioxide is a phenomenon which will take place only for the next fifty to one hundred years. The problem is thus one of managing the atmosphere during the transition from a fossil fuel economy to a non-fossil fuel economy.

Carbon dioxide is a gaseous by-product of the use of fossil fuels, of deforestation, and of other activities. It may be viewed as a pollutant.[8] In economic terms, contries that develop fossil fuels and emit carbon dioxide into the atmosphere are using the atmosphere as a free good in developing their own resources. They are not internalizing the cost of the diseconomies they are inflicting upon the atmosphere by developing these resources. One can approach this problem either be regulatory mechanisms which seek to limit the amount of emissions or by economic incentives, including taxes, which prompt contributors to take measures to limit the amount of emissions. Domestically, the United States has had some experience in managing air,[9] water,[10] noise,[11] and other forms of pollution.[12] Internationally, various countries and organizations have had experience in dealing with pollutants which destroy the ozone layer,[13] with ocean,[14] river,[15] outer space,[16] and air pollution[17] Conceptually, the issues are not completely new. What makes the carbon dioxide problem so uniquely difficult is that it is caused by many point sources of pollution and that the pollutants emerge as by-products of the use of critical natural resources--the consumption of fossil fuels, and to an extent yet unknown, the harvesting of forests and misuse of soils. Moreover, the problem develops slowly with no immediate health or environmental effects, making it all the more difficult to convince decision-makers to take immediate action.[18] Approaching the CO_2 problem as a pollution problem reveals its basic nature: it is a problem in energy management.

There appear to be two major sources for the build-up of carbon dioxide: (1) fossil fuels; and (2) deforestation. The first is will documented, but there is considerable uncertainty about the net contribution of the

latter.[19] To the extent that the CO_2 build-up is primarily attributable to the use of fossil fuels, the
problem is one arising mainly from the activities of
developed countries. To the extent that deforestation
is involved, a wider community of states are contributing
actors. Identification of those states that are sources
of carbon dioxide is important in fashioning the appropriate international regime. Rotty has estimated the
percentage contribution of various areas of the world to
atmospheric carbon dioxide emissions, as of 1974 and
projected to the year 2025. In 1974, the United States,
the Soviet Union, Eastern Europe, and Western Europe
accounted for seventy percent of all carbon dioxide emissions, with the United States and Western Europe alone
accounting for forty-five percent of the atmospheric
CO_2 emissions.[20] This suggests that at present it is both
appropriate and potentially feasible for a relatively
small handful of countries to join together to make
multilateral initiatives aimed at curtailing carbon
dioxide emissions.[21]

II.   INTERNATIONAL LAW AND CARBON DIOXIDE POLLUTION

International law embodies two principles which
apply to the management of carbon dioxide accumulations:
(1) a principle of "equitable use," applicable to
countries using a shared natural resource; and (2) a
principle which makes states responsible for damage
caused to the environment of other states in areas beyond
their jurisdiction. The Stockholm Declaration on the
Human Environment, adopted in 1972, provides that "States
have, in accordance with the Charter of the United Nations
and the principles of international law . . . the responsibility to ensure that activities within their jurisdiction or control do not cause damage to the environment of other States or of areas beyond the limits of
national jurisdiction."[22] These principles have been
adopted in some international agreements governing air
and water pollution and the use of international rivers.[23]
They have been used to develop processes for information
exchange, coordination, consultation, and compensation
for harm suffered.[24]

A.   International Rivers

The underlying legal standard embodied--either
explicitly or implicitly--in arrangements for managing
international rivers and river basins is that of "equitable utilization." The principle is implemented primarily through water allocation and quality control mechanisms and compensatory schemes.

The Helsinki Rules on the Uses of the Waters of
International Rivers, adopted by the International Law
Association in 1966, impose a duty on states to prevent
future pollution of international drainage basins[25] and
require violators to cease the wrongful conduct and
compensate the injured co-basin state.[26] The rules also
suggest that states should take "all reasonable measures"
to abate existing problems[27] and enter into negotiations
to achieve this end.[28] The 1909 Treaty between the
United States and Great Britain Relating to Boundary
Waters and Questions Arising Between the United States
and Canada, which is designed to prevent boundary water
disputes, also prohibits transboundary water pollution.[29]
The 1978 Agreement Between the United States and Canada
on Great Lakes Water Quality carries this provision forward and requires the parties to use "best efforts" to
ensure water quality standards are met.[30] The International Joint Commission, a fact-finding body established to implement the 1909 Treaty,[31] assists in implementing the 1978 Agreement.[32]

As between the United States and Mexico, an 1889
convention[33] and a 1944 treaty[34] govern water allocation
and boundary line disputes. An International Boundary
and Water Commission implements these agreements.[35] The
United States and Mexico are expanding their efforts to
include measures for water quality control. A memorandum of understanding between the Sub-secretariat for
Environment Improvement of Mexico and the United States
Environmental Protection Agency, signed on June 6, 1978,
provides for consultation and an exchange of experts to
resolve environmental problems.[36] It calls for periodic
meetings and parallel efforts toward research and monitoring of pollution. These two agencies are also to
devise an early warning system for potential environmental problems.[37]

There are a number of river basin agreements designed to promote the harmonious development of a region,
such as the Treaty on the Plate River Basin of 1969,[38]
to which Argentina, Bolivia, Brazil, Paraguay and Uruguay
are contracting parties. Such agreements traditionally
provide for a committee to coordinate use of the water
resources.[39] The problem is that these provisions
usually exist only in form.

Several Western Europe countries--France, West
Germany, Luxembourg, Switzerland and the Netherlands--
have undertaken measures to prevent and abate pollution
of the Rhine.[40] Under the Convention on the Protection
of the Rhine Against Chemical Pollution, the parties
agree to eliminate or reduce the discharge of certain
enumerated pollutants to specified emission standards.[41]
The International Commission for the Protection of the

Rhine Against Pollution coordinates the implementation
of the agreement.[42] A more recent agreement, the Convention on the Protection of the Rhine Against Pollution
by Chlorides, has not yet entered into force.[43] This
convention calls for the reduction of the chloride content in the Rhine waters along the Dutch/German border,
which has resulted from the injection of chloride wastes
into the sub-soil in the Alsace region.[44] Potassium
mining in that region is the primary source of this
pollutant.[45] The French safeguard is its unilateral
right to cease injections when they appear to pose a
"serious danger to the environment."[46] Nevertheless,
this convention has met with considerable opposition in
France. Consequently, the French government has been
unable to ratify the agreement in Parliament, much to the
distress of the Dutch.[47]

Experience with international rivers and river basin
agreements suggests that it will be difficult to negotiate effective arrangements to manage carbon dioxide
accumulations. In general, these agreements have shown
that upstream users put downstream users at their mercy.
Experience with the Rhine conventions demonstrates the
political obstacles that confront the implementation of
multilateral efforts to control water pollution.

B.   Air Pollution

Existing conventions concerned with air pollution,
like the water pollution agreements, break down into two
basic groups. The first impose an obligation on a
contracting party to inform and consult with another
state when activities within the jurisdication of the
former may adversely affect the environment of the latter.
These agreements also typically contain arrangements for
coordinated research programs and data exchanges.
Examples include the 1979 Convention on Long-Range Transboundary Air Pollution[48] and the 1976 tripartite Agreement on Monitoring of the Stratosphere.[49] The second
kind of agreement goes one step further to include provisions for dispute resolution, such as a right of access
to domestic courts or administrative bodies, or establishment of an impartial fact-finding commission. The
Nordic Convention on the Protection of the Environment[50]
and the United States-Canadian International Joint Commission's Michigan-Ontario Air Pollution Board[51] are good
examples of the latter kind.

The most recent international agreement concerned
with air quality is the Convention on Long-Range Transboundary Air Pollution, which has been signed by thirty-
five countries including the United States, Canada, and
most of the countries in Eastern and Western Europe.[52]

The agreement imposes an obligation on contracting parties to consult upon request about activities which affect or pose a "significant risk" of long-range trans- boundary air pollution.[53] The legal duty to combat the discharge of air pollutants is admittedly weak. States are merely required to act "without undue delay."[54] To its credit, the Convention contains lengthy provisions on research, monitoring, and information exchange, which are aimed at mitigating sulphur dioxide (SO_2) emissions.[55]

The 1976 Tripartite Agreement on Monitoring of the Stratosphere--to which the United States, France, and the United Kingdom are the contracting parties-- concen- trates solely on increasing scientific understanding of the ozone layer.[56] It requires the parties to collect, exchange, and analyze information on the stratosphere, and to fully integrate their activities with the existing international networks of the World Meteorological Organ- ization and the U.N. Environment Programme.[57] One pur- pose of the agreement is to demonstrate the feasibility and utility of collaborative international action in this area.[58]

The Nordic Convention, in contrast to the above- mentioned agreements, provides a framework for abatement and for compensatory relief for persons injured by trans- boundary air and water nuisances.[59] It requires the contracting parties--Denmark, Finland, Norway, and Sweden--to accord to non-citizens equal access to admin- istrative agencies and domestic courts and non-discrimin- atory treatment.[60] It gives to any person who is affected or may be affected "by environmentally harmful activities" the right to ask for measures to prevent damage,[61] and provides for compensatory relief.[62] Although this pro- cess could conceivably be applied to enjoin activities until carbon dioxide standards are met, it is probably not practical as a workable solution to the carbon dioxide situation.

Coordinated monitoring and emission regulations, on the other hand, are not only viable but have been utilized in other transboundary air pollution situations. The International Joint Commission (IJC) between the United States and Canada undertook in the early 1970's to mitigate air pollution problems between Michigan and Ontario.[63] To assist its efforts, the IJC established, in 1976, the International Michigan-Ontario Air Pollution Board.[64] The function of this board is to coordinate the implementation of air pollution control programs, including setting a minimum basis for emission standards.[65] As a result of this effort, the air quality in the area seems to have improved, with the percentage of those air quality readings failing to meet the IJC objectives declining throughout the region.[66]

International agreements concerned with managing
air pollution offer at least some limited positive
experiences to draw upon in developing a framework for
managing carbon dioxide accumulations. Certainly, they
suggest that international scientific cooperation in the
gathering and exchange of data and in monitoring CO_2
accumulations would be a desirable and feasible step.
The monitoring of CO_2 might even be included in the
existing networks for monitoring sulphur dioxide, chlorofluorocarbons, and other air pollutants.

In addition to the formal agreements concerned with
air and water pollution, there are a number of arbitral
decisions and negotiated settlements which incorporate
the principles of equitable use and state responsibility
for environmental harm. The Trail Smelter Arbitration
is one of the most frequently cited cases.[67] In this
case Canada was held liable for damage in the State of
Washington from the fumes emitted from a Canadian smelting company. Even though Canada had admitted liability
in the compromise establishing the Tribunal, the final
decision in 1941 declared that:

> [t]he tribunal, therefore, finds [that]
> . . . under the principles of international
> law, as well as of the law of the United
> States, no state has the right to use or
> permit use of its territory in such a
> manner as to cause injury by fumes in or
> to the territory of another or the pro-
> perties or persons therein, when the case
> is of serious consequences or the injury
> is established by clear and convincing
> evidence.[68]

A number of diplomatic settlements at least implicitly recognized the state responsibility for the consequences of pollution inflicted upon other countries.
For example, Mexico complained to the United States that
the water it received from the Colorado River was too
saline to be useful to Mexico and hence in violation of
the 1944 treaty between the two countries. The Mexicans
argued that the treaty included a water quality standard,
a point disputed by the United States. In settling this
dispute with Mexico, the United States agreed to provide
compensation in the form of assistance to rehabilitate
the Mexicali Valley from the damages suffered from the
saline pollution, although it did not actually acknowledge any obligation to do so in international law.[69]

The resolution of the United Nations General
Assembly on natural resources shared by two or more states
calls for an exchange of information and for prior consultation in the use of shared resources.[70] States

engaging in activities which potentially could cause pollution harmful to other states may have a duty to consult with those states or at least offer them an opportunity to engage in consultation. The value of consultation is that it offers a process by which to minimize harm and political conflict and, in the best of cases, to negotiate mutually acceptable arrangements between the concerned states.

III. POLLUTION MANAGEMENT STRATEGIES

A.   Introduction

The increasing concentration of carbon dioxide in the atmosphere may be viewed as a global pollution problem caused primarily by point sources of pollution. If it turns out that the main pollutors (that is, the main producers of CO_2) are also the countries that would be most hurt by a change in climatic conditions triggered by a CO_2 build-up, then it would be in their interests to jointly develop an allocation regime for CO_2 emissions in order to delay or avert such climatic change. If, on the other hand, there are important contributors to the CO_2 concentration in the atmosphere that stand to benefit from CO_2-induced climate changes, it will be very difficult to develop an effective allocation regime.

This is complicated by the fact that most of the scientific factors are still unclear: the relative importance of different sources for the higher CO_2 concentration in the atmosphere, the eventual fact of CO_2 in the global system, and the impact of a given level of CO_2 on the climate of specific regions and countries. Moreover, the elucidation of these underlying phenomena will probably require at least a decade of scientific research.

For this reason, predictions of the political consequences of future climatic changes can be useful as illustrations of the kinds of political alignments that could take place as the world grapples with the carbon dioxide problem. Fortunately, the impact of carbon dioxide accumulation is still distant enough that we can wait for better scientific information before taking political action.

Bearing this caveat in mind, preliminary data indicate that the United States and Europe are at once major contributors to the carbon dioxide increase and potential victims of CO_2-induced climate change.[71] In particular, U.S. agricultural production is predicted by some calculations to decrease as a result of warmer, drier weather in the grain belt,[72] while other portions of the country could be permanently submerged in the less likely event of the melting of the polar ice caps.[73] These predictions depend on uncertain scientific theories and do not take into account the ability of the United States to respond by technological innovation, for example, by developing new crop varieties or species adapted to the new climatic conditions. The United States and other developed nations may be able to adapt far more easily than other countries to adverse climatic change because of greater technical capabilities. Still, the possibilities enumerated above to suggest that the United States has considerable incentive to reduce CO_2 accumulations. From this projection, it appears to be in the interest of at least the United States and Europe to explore strategies for managing carbon dioxide emissions during the coming century.

Under some calculations, countries located in monsoon regions would benefit as warmer global temperatures trigger more favorable rains with accompanying improved crop production.[74] If these predictions are accepted, the possibility of such benefits can significantly affect the formation of an international consensus to control CO_2 emissions. Moves by the United States to limit CO_2 "pollution" would understandably be seen as another example of "environmental imperialism," especially to those beneficiaries who would not view the problem as "pollution" at all. Moreover, as noted earlier, Rotty has predicted that those countries currently in the development stage may become the major sources of CO_2 emissions by the year 2025.[75] Unless the United States and the other developed countries presently responsible for most of the CO_2 emissions have initiated measures to limit the CO_2 build-up in the atmosphere, maximum U.S. remedial initiatives later could result in only a minimum effect, if any, on abating the problem.

One of the major contributors of CO_2 emissions today, the U.S.S.R., is a possible net gainer. Warming global temperature is predicted to increase agricultural productivity by lengthening the growing season for some presently unproductive land.[76] China, which holds a major share of the earth's coal, could also benefit agriculturally. Rice yields are predicted to increase and multiple seasons are possible.[77] If these predictions are accepted, there may be some incentives for the Soviet Union and China to engage in international cooperation to manage CO_2 accumulations.

Predictions as to the likely effect of a given increase in carbon dioxide on specific regions are still far from certain and more research is needed. If it can be assumed that the United States and other developed countries in the northern hemisphere either would benefit from the climatic change or could easily adapt to it and that areas in the developing world will become increasingly arid and agriculturally unproductive, then there may be significant incentives for international cooperation flowing from the demands of the developing world for a redistribution of the wealth.[78]

A complete analysis of the possible effects of an increase in carbon dioxide on key CO_2 contributors--those emitting now and in the future--is essential to an elimination of the shroud of uncertainty surrounding this issue.

In order to devise appropriate strategies for managing carbon dioxide emissions, data which will demonstrate who the important actors are and what proportion they are contributing to the pollution problem are needed. Such data must give a breakdown by states or major contributors to the increased carbon dioxide pollution, both now and projected into the future, and a breakdown which shows how much of the pollution is from fossil fuels, how much from deforestation, and how much from still other sources. Within the fossil fuel category, it is necessary to know which fuels contribute most to the carbon dioxide build-up. While Rotty's data shows global carbon dioxide production by world segments for the year 1974 and projected to the year 2025,[79] Steinberg, Albanese and Vi-Doung have prepared a table showing carbon dioxide generation as a function of fuel source.[80] Such tables are essential for later assessments of appropriate institutional arrangements. It will also be useful to have a breakdown in the use of fossil fuel as to residential heating, gasoline, petrochemicals, and other fossil fuel products, and what part of this use, current and projected, involves coal.

Carbon dioxide as a pollution problem is foremost an energy policy problem. This means that it is important to analyze the workings of the current oil economy, to investigate the private sector's and the public sector's outlook for the development and marketing of coal resources and to consider and involve the private sector in the management of the carbon dioxide problem. The international oil companies have substantial investments in coal and oil shale and thus they will continue to be important actors in the future. More importantly, the feasibility of technological innovations to reduce or recycle CO_2 emissions and the incentives needed to stimulate innovation must be explored and developed with the industries that use fossil fuels. To date little attention has been given to the question of how private industry might be involved in a resolution of the carbon dioxide problem.[81]

Much of the literature tends to discuss the problem in policy terms that suggest an immediate switching to a non-fossil fuel economy or leap to a discussion of managing the impacts of future climatic change.[82] Certainly these are policy elements that ought to be evaluated. But the question that has been largely overlooked and that needs to be addressed is how carbon dioxide emissions from fossil fuels are to be limited to a "manageable" amount that will delay the projected warming and allow time to develop new methods for preventing the release of CO_2 or recycling it for mitigating the climatic effects and for adapting to the resulting climatic change. This means that it is necessary to determine what kind of output of carbon dioxide would result in what kind of build-up in the system, and what rate of build-up of carbon dioxide can be absorbed over what periods of time. Action may be taken at that point to determine what measures may be necessary to insure that states do not exceed these amounts in their production and use of fossil fuels. Given these calculations, it would then be possible to prepare for worst case scenarios, as utility companies do in planning for fuel consumption during winter seasons.

The management of carbon dioxide pollution requires porcesses for risk assessment and impact evaluation, and preventive strategies at the national and international level.

B. National Preventive Strategies

Carbon dioxide pollution raises the possibility of significant, adverse, and irreversible climatic impacts which could be catastrophic to certain sectors of the economies of some countries. Yet, as discussed above, most of the important factors are still scientifically unknown and in dispute. This requires states to balance the economic costs of not acting, all in the face of scientific uncertainty. Since the former are usually easier to quantify, decisions are usually struck for the latter. Project Westford, which dispersed very fine copper needles into space, and the early NASA space experiments are examples of situations where officials had to decide what confidence levels they required in assessing risks from the experiments.

The United States can take steps to control carbon dioxide emmissions, if needed.[83] But the costs of these measures are not known and certainly need to be carefully assessed. Substantive measures which might be taken include the following: (a) requiring any federal environmental impact statement[84] concerned with a project that relies on fossil fuels to identify explicitly the impacts of carbon dioxide emissions into the atmosphere; (b) exploring the feasibility of the development

and utilization of scrubbers to reduce carbon dioxide
emissions or of methods to recycle carbon dioxide and
analyzing the experience with the provisions of the
Clean Air Act as they affect innovation in industry;
(c) providing incentives to industry to engage in research and development which could lead to measures to
reduce carbon dioxide emissions, and analyzing the export
market potential for such measures; (d) imposing substantive limits on the production and consumption of coal
(or other fossil fuels) and on the export of this resource to other countries, particularly Western Europe;
(e) investigating other measures, such as provisions in
the terms of lease for development of coal deposits and
oil shale, which could provide for public intervention
if needed, to manage the level of carbon dioxide emissions; and (f) rationing fuels, taking into account
carbon dioxide generating power, with exemptions for
plants with scrubbers or other means of limiting CO_2
emissions. Whether emissions control is a technically
feasible goal is still unclear and controversial. Such
controls will be adopted only if the costs to economic
growth are acceptable, and these costs have yet to be
defined.

C.   International Preventive Strategies

    Since the major contributors to the carbon dioxide
build-up are presently only a handful of developed
countries,[85] it should be possible to focus the initial
discussions among these primary contributors -- the
United States, Western Europe and, if possible, the
Soviet Union and Eastern Europe. Initial consultations
might begin with the United States and Western European
countries under the umbrella of the European Economic
Community or the Organization for Economic Cooperation
and Development (OECD), one component of which is the
International Energy Agency. Again, it would be necessary to analyze the role that private industry could
play. The oil market is an international one, and the
coal market promises to be likewise. Discussions might
focus on emission controls, as has been the case with
air pollution in the United States[86] and in Europe.
Emission controls ought to be keyed to acceptable limits
which have been determined scientifically to be linked
with given levels of temperature increases in the climate. Admittedly this requires considerable advances in
our scientific knowledge, but obtaining sufficient knowledge to establish such limits should be a primary objective.
    The OECD's Environment Committee at its May 1979
meeting recognized the potential concern of a carbon
dioxide build-up from coal production.[87] The OECD's

Council on Coal and the Environment specifically recommended that "member countries, in the light of appropriate research results, seek to define acceptable fuel qualities, emission levels or ambient media qualities, as appropriate for carbon dioxide."[88] This seems to encompass a scheme to control carbon dioxide emissions which would be similar to that employed in the United States: an international ambient standard for carbon dioxide, together with emission limitations designed to meet that ambient standard, which could be implemented at the national level. In considering such a scheme, it would be critical to have an anlysis of the problems in developing and implementing this scheme under the Clear Air Act[89] and of U.S. experience with the federal statutes governing water pollution,[90] which, in different ways, employ the mixed combination of an ambient standard and an emission standard[91] for emissions mix. The scientific input would be essential in establishing what the ambient standards should be. The allocation of emission limitations between countries would be a highly political decision, one which could prove to be intractable. Applying the emission limitations within each country would entail difficult political decisions about who had the right to contribute what amount of carbon dioxide to the atmosphere.

Predictions by Rotty indicate that by the year 2025, forty percent of the carbon dioxide build-up may come from the developing countries, which now contribute less than twenty percent.[92] Even if the projected contributions of the developing countries were considerably less, it would be essential to involve the participation of the rest of the world in any system of ambient standards and controls to be established. Initially this means at a minimum that efforts must be undertaken to build international consciousness of the problem and to elicit participation of other countries at conferences discussing the problem. Any system that is developed for limiting carbon dioxide concentrations in the atmosphere will eventually need to be carried forward with the participation of the developing countries. The issues raised at that point would be similar to those that arose at the Stockholm Conference on the Environment in 1972, at which developing countries expressed legitimate concern over the potential conflict between development strategies appropriate for their countries and the concerns of the international community which would make those strategies either more expensive or would otherwise impede their development.[93]

Several international institutions are concerned with the increased concentration of carbon dioxide in the atmosphere. These include the OECD, the EEC, the World Meteorological Organization, the U.N. Environment Pro-

gramme (UNEP), the U.N. Development Programme, the U.N.
Educational, Scientific and Cultural Organization, the
International Council of Scientific Unions, the Inter-
ational Institute for Applied Systems Analysis and the
NATO Committee on the Challenges of Modern Society. To
date the role of these institutions has been limited to
identifying the problem, monitoring and evaluating scientific data, collecting and exchanging information regard-
ng the build-up, and the facilitation and coordination
of national and international programs related to it. At
least to some extent, these organizations, or an appropriate mix of them, could be employed in analyzing the
impact of various policy choices regarding the management
of carbon dioxide.

D. Preventive Strategies for Deforestation

     In order to develop appropriate management strate-
gies for a carbon dioxide build-up from deforestation,
it is necessary to assess the amount to which deforestation does, in fact, contribute to an increase in carbon
dioxide. The problem is to determine the direction and
magnitude of the biospheric signal. Are the forests of
the world being cut down at a rate that exceeds reforestation and that exceeds the progressively faster growth
rates of forests that may result from increases in carbon
dioxide? The dispute within the scientific community
regarding the contribution of deforestation makes it
especially difficult to develop strategies to manage it.
After the geographical areas of concern have been identified, alternative ways to slow down the rate of deforestation, or to counteract its effects, must be
eveloped and assessed. Some argue that it is not deforestation per se that produced CO_2, but rather the
destruction of the organic matter of the soil that follows misuse of cleared land.
     The problem for international attention is the de-
velopment and implementation of environmentally sound
strategies for sustained yield management of the forests
and the soils. Any success in controlling CO_2 emissions
is likely to come as a by-product of progress on this
general problem. A regime of separate emission limitations for CO_2 from the deforestation of tropical forests
is not likely to be a useful or viable approach.
     Any effort to control deforestation frontally as-
saults cherished notions of national sovereignty over the
exploitation of a state's natural resources. States can
therefore be expected to resist such measures. A first
and necessary step will be to encourage efforts to raise
international consciousness about the implications of
forest and soil management strategies for levels of
carbon dioxide in the atmosphere, the impact of these

levels on global temperature, and the long range implications of a rise in temperature for the economy and
well-being of individual countries.

The community of actors in deforestation differs
from that in the fossil fuel area. Most forests are in
the developing world. Multinational companies and governments of at least some of the developed countries are
frequently responsible for clearing forests. Thus, the
appropriate forum for discussing this problem would be a
broader based community than either the EEC or OECD.
UNEP is a prominent possibility.

Some international attention has already been focused on the problem of deforestation. In 1979, UNEP's
Governing Council adopted a resolution, introduced by
the United States, calling for a meeting of experts to
develop proposals for an integrated international program on the conservation and wise utilization of tropical
forests.[94] UNEP also sponsored a conference on tropical
forests in April 1980 in Kenya.[95]

In the United States, former President Carter's second environmental message to Congress on August 2, 1979,
addressed two global environmental problems: acid rains
and deforestation of tropical forests.[96] The President
referred to estimates that the world forest could decline
by twenty percent by the year 2000 and noted that "[f]or-
est loss may adversely alter the global climate through
the production of CO_2. These changes and their effects
are not well understood and are being studied by scientists but the possibilities are disturbing and warrant
caution."[97] This was followed by the U.S.-sponsored
resolution in the UNEP Governing Council mentioned
above.[98] In a memo to the Secretary of Agriculture, the
President also directed that:

> [H]igh priority be given to: (1) improved monitoring
> of world forests; (2) research on preservation of
> natural forest ecosystems; (3) research on tropical
> forest multiple use management; (4) studies on
> increasing yields of tropical agriculture; (5) dem-
> onstration of integrated projects of reforestation,
> efficient fuel wood use and alternative energy
> sources; and (6) examination of how U.S. citizens
> and corporations can be encouraged to follow sound
> forest management practices.[99]

An interagency task force on deforestation, established in November 1979,[100] recommended that assessments
of deforestation be a component of environmental impact
statements and that any overseas U.S. projects by federal
agencies and private institutions contain assessments of
the effects of the planned activities on tropical
forests.[101]

Efforts can also be made at the regional level to address the problem of deforestation. In South America, for example, the new Amazon Pact[102] offers a possible umbrella for such discussions and for an exchange of data.

E.   Preventive Strategies for Chlorofluorocarbons

The experience of the United States in attempting to limit emissions of chlorofluorocarbons, which damage the ozone layer, offers useful insights into the problems associated with limiting carbon dioxide emissions. In March 1978, the Federal Drug Administration and the Environmental Protection Agency issued regulations banning the manufacturing and shipping of fluorocarbons for nonessential aerosol uses.[103] The ban is expected to reduce total chlorofluorocarbon emissions by considerably less than twenty-five percent globally.[104] The Clean Air Act requires the Environmental Protection Agency, inter alia, to conduct studies of the ozone problem in an effort to determine what further regulation of chlorofluorocarbons is necessary,[105] but to date EPA has taken no action regulating non-aerosol use. Two studies will be the basis of future EPA action: (1) a National Academy of Sciences Report, Protection Against Depletion of Stratospheric Ozone by Chlorofluorocarbons and (2) a study by the Rand Corporation, Economic Implications of Regulating Non-Aerosol Chlorofluorocarbon Emissions from Non-Aerosol Applications.[106] The Clean Air Act also requires the National Oceanic and Atmospheric Administration to establish a continuing program of research and monitoring of changes in the stratosphere and of climate effects resulting from this change.[107] The results to date indicate that chlorofluorocarbon concentration is increasing at five to ten percent per year, but do not show positive evidence of chlorofluorocarbon depletion of the ozone layer.[108] The impact of the aerosol ban may not be visible for a number of years. Two states -- Oregon and Michigan -- have passed legislation banning non-essential aerosol use of chlorofluorocarbon compounds in an effort to protect the ozone layer.[109]

Action has also been taken in the European Community to limit the use of chlorofluorocarbons in aerosol sprays by thirty percent of 1976 levels over the following two years (December 1979 to December 31, 1981), and which would limit production of chlorofluorocarbons F-11 and F-12 to present levels.[110] Several delegations pushed for a stricter standard, since the standard is less strict than in some existing national laws. Support for a stricter standard also came from two other directions: (1) the European Parliament's Environment, Public Health and Consumer Protection Committee, which adopted a resolution at a meeting in Brussels in November 1979 calling for a fifty percent reduction in the use of chlorofluorocarbons by 1981, and a total ban by 1983;[111] and (2) the conclusion of UNEP's International Scientific Committee at its third session in Paris, in November 1979, that aerosol propellants, such as hydrofluorocarbons, could destroy fifteen percent of the ozone layer within one hundred years if present levels were maintained.[112] The European Economic Community called for a reexamination of the problem "in light of available scientific and economic data" in order to adopt necessary and new measures by June 30, 1981.

Some countries have acted unilaterally. Sweden banned aerosol manufacture and importation in December 1977.[113] West Germany, through cooperative government-industry consultation, has been able to get German industries to agree to reduce aerosol chlorofluorocarbon used by twenty-five percent by 1979 and fifty percent by 1981.[114] Canada has initiated "voluntary" reductions of aerosol use of chlorofluorocarbons.[115]

The OECD has limited its involvement to studies of the economic impact of chlorofluorocarbon regulation. UNEP has assumed the rule of coordinating scientific research on the subject for the international community.

Developments in the regulation of chlorofluorocarbons offer some insights into the issues that will be raised in regulating carbon dioxide emissions. On the one hand, it should be possible to develop further and maintain the scientific network necessary for proper monitoring of carbon dioxide. On the other hand, it will be very difficult to obtain the agreement necessary to manage a global pollution problem. The countries that have been most willing to regulate chlorofluorocarbons, except for the United States, have been those which contribute least to the problem. Canada is responsible for only two percent of the world's chlorofluorocarbons and Sweden does not manufacture any.[116]

The central problem in the transnational regulation of chlorofluorocarbons has been the inability of countries to agree upon a strict standard limiting the use of certain aerosol sprays containing these chemical components. In many ways, the chlorofluorocarbon and carbon dioxide problems are the same. The number of countries which are major contributors--the developed countries-- is small. The effect of polluting the ozone layer with chlorofluorocarbons is the depletion of a global resource. The effect of an increase in carbon dioxide is a global rise in temperature. Yet the modest success both in the United States and most recently in the European Community in achieving at least some form of regulation on the emission of chlorofluorocarbons offers some hope for building such measures to control the emission of carbon dioxide. Carbon dioxide poses a much tougher problem. Unlike chlorofluorocarbons, its source is at the heart of a country's economy -- the production and use of fossil fuels for energy or the removal of its forests.

F. Adaptive Strategies for Carbon Dioxide Pollution

If significant climatic changes occur as a result of temperature increases from carbon dioxide, adaptive strategies will be necessary, at least some of which are likely to focus on preventing the problem from worsening. The experience of dealing with problems of air and water pollution suggests that one potential response should be an attempt to diminish the levels of CO_2 pollution. Thus, one component of the adaptive strategy is likely to be an intensified search for technical solutions, such as ways to expand the capacity of oceans to absorb carbon dioxide or to limit carbon dioxide emissions. Nevertheless, the effects of possible climatic change, particularly upon water supplies and migration patterns, and upon the general dislocation of a country's economy, must also be anticipated.

How states adapt to climatic change will depend on whether or not the changes are beneficial or adverse to their economic and strategic interests. Studies are needed in order to determine who is likely to be affected, in what manner, and at what time, by what degree of climatic change. In the absence of hard data, probably the best contribution is to explore the consequences of various credible climate scenarios. It will be in the interest of those countries that are likely to be adversely affected to join together in measures to alleviate the stress and damage caused by climatic changes. The implications of such alternative state responses to climate change for our international economic and monetary system and for international political stability must also be addressed.

CONCLUSIONS

Carbon dioxide accumulation in the atmosphere is a problem during this century of transition from a fossil fuel to a primarily non-fossil fuel economy. Strategies shall be developed for managing the atmospheric concentration of carbon dioxide so that CO_2 levels do not cause either serious adverse climate changes or changes in climate which overwhelm the capacity of countries to adapt to them.

But the management of carbon dioxide must be put into perspective -- many scientifically generated facts concerning projected increases and resulting climate

changes are still unclear. This means that the topic
should not be pushed into high-level political debates
that would cause countries to adopt premature positions
based on inconclusive premises and embedded in national
political rhetoric. On the other hand, international
scientific collaboration on the climatic and societal
impact of increased concentrations of carbon dioxide
should be promoted and systematic assessments of alternative strategies for managing carbon dioxide emissions
should be commenced. It is time to initiate serious discussions with industry about the feasibility of technological innovation to control or recycle CO_2 output,
and about the incentives that would be needed. A dialogue should be initiated with other countries about
developing processes for managing the CO_2 problem,
building upon existing institutional networks.

More fundamentally, the carbon dioxide issue needs
to be treated as an integral part of the international
energy question. As things now stand, decisions as to
whether to shift to nuclear energy, promote renewable
energy sources, or rely on coal and synfuels will likely
be taken largely independently of CO_2 considerations,
but they will have a dramatic impact on the timing and
rate of CO_2 accumulations. It is therefore essential
that strategies for managing the atmospheric concentration of carbon dioxide be integrated into national and
international energy policy. Raising international public consciousness of the problem is a necessary first
step.

NOTES

1. Climate Research Board, National Research Council
U.S. National Academy of Sciences, Carbon Dioxide and
Climate: A Scientific Assessment (1979), [hereinafter
cited as National Research Council Report]; G. Woodwell,
G. MacDonald, R. Revelle & C. Keeling, "The Carbon Di-
oxide Problem: Implications for Policy in the Management
of Energy and Other Resources (1979)," [hereinafter
cited as CEQ Report], reprinted in Senate Comm. on Gov-
ernmental Affairs, 96th Cong., 1st Sess., Symposium on
Carbon Dioxide Accumulation in the Atmosphere, Synthetic
Fuels and Energy Policy 44 (1979)[hereinafter cited as
CO_2 Symposium].

2. National Research Council Report, supra note 1,
at 1. For a general description of the "greenhouse
effect," see CEQ Report, supra note 1, reprinted in CO_2
Symposium, supra note 1, at 45-47.

3. Schneider, "So What If Climate Changes?" reprinted in CO_2 Symposium, supra note 1, at 78. See also S.
Schneider, The Genesis Strategy (1976).

4. S. Schneider & R. Chen, "Carbon Dioxide Warming and Coastline Flooding: Physical Factors and Climatic Impact" (1980) (unpublished paper available from the National Center for Atmospheric Research, Boulder, Colorado).

5. CO_2 Symposium, supra note 1, at iii.

6. President's Commission on Coal, Recommendations and Summary Findings (1980).

7. MacDonald has concluded that coal releases 2.5 (x 10^{15} g) of carbon dioxide per 100 quads of energy, while oil releases 2.0 and gas 1.45. CEQ Report, supra note 1, reprinted in CO_2 Symposium, supra note 1, at 50.

8. While there is evidence that increased CO_2 concentrations in the atmosphere will have a positive impact on agriculture in some parts of the world, the author believes the predicted adverse consequences of the "greenhouse effect" justifies its classification as a pollutant. See also text accompanying notes 4-5 supra, and notes 70-80 infra on incentives for cooperation.

9. Clean Air Act, 42 U.S.C. § 7401 (1980).

10. Clean Water Act, 33 U.S.C. § 1251 (1980); Safe Drinking Water Act, 42 U.S.C. § 300(f)-(10) (1976 & Supp. I 1980).

11. Noise Control Act, 42 U.S.C. § 4901 (1976).

12. See, e.g., Toxic Substances Control Act, 15 U.S.C. § 2601 (1976); Resource Conservation and Recovery Act, 42 U.S.C. § 6901 (1976).

13. See, e.g., Agreement on Monitoring of the Stratosphere, May 5, 1976, United States-France-United Kingdom, 27 U.S.T. 1437, T.I.A.S. No. 8255, reprinted in [1978] 1 [Reference File] Int'l Envir. Rep. (BNA) ¶ 21: 2501. For further discussion, see notes 56-58 infra and accompanying text.

14. See, e.g., International Convention for the Prevention of Pollution of the Sea by Oil, opened for signature May 12, 1954, 12 U.S.T. 2989, T.I.A.S. No. 4900, 327 U.N.T.S. 3, as amended Apr. 11, 1962, 17 U.S.T. 1523, T.I.A.S. No. 6109, 600 U.N.T.S. 332, as amended Oct. 21, 1969, 28 U.S.T. 1205, T.I.A.S. No. 8505; reprinted in [1978] 1 [Reference File] Int'l Envir. Rep. (BNA) 21:0301; Convention on the Prevention of Marine Pollution by Dumping Wastes and Other Matter, done Dec. 29, 1972, 26 U.S.T. 2403, T.I.A.S. No. 8165, reprinted in [1978] 1 [Reference File] Int'l Envir. Rep. (BNA) 21:1901.

15. See, e.g., Helsinki Rules on the Uses of the Waters of International Rivers, U.N. Doc. A/CN.4/274, vol. 11, at 29 (1966), reprinted in The Report of the Fifty-second Conference of the International Law Association 484, Aug. 20, 1966 [hereinafter cited as Helsinki Rules]; Treaty Relating to Boundary Waters Between the United States and Canada, Jan. 11, 1909,

United States-United Kingdom, 36 Stat. 2448, T.S. No.
548 [hereinafter cited as 1909 U.S.-Canada Treaty];
Convention on the Protection of the Rhine Against Chemical Pollution, done Dec. 3, 1976, reprinted in 16 Int'l
Legal Mats. 242 (1977) [hereinafter cited as Rhine Chemical Convention]. For further discussion, see notes
25-47 infra and accompanying text.

16. Treaty on Principles Governing the Activities
of States in the Exploration and Use of Outer Space
Including the Moon and Other Celestial Bodies, done
Jan. 27, 1967, art. IX, 18 U.S.T. 2410, T.I.A.S. No.
6347, 610 U.N.T.S. 205.

17. Convention on Long-Range Transboundary Air
Pollution, done Nov. 13, 1979, 1 U.N. ECE, Annex I,
U.N. Doc. E/ECE/HCM-1/2 (1979), reprinted in 18 Int'l
Legal Mats. 1442 (1979) [hereinafter cited as TBAP
Convention]; Convention on the Protection of the Environ-
ment, done Feb. 19, 1974, reprinted in 13 Int'l Legal
Mats. 591 (1974) [hereinafter cited as Nordic Convention].
For further discussion, see notes 48-66 infra and accom-
panying text.

18. In contrast, the fact that scientific studies
linked depletion of the ozone layer to increased inci-
dence of skin cancer undoubtedly contributed to prompt
adoption of legislation banning the use of chlorofluorocarbons in aerosol spray cans. See text sec. IV(E)
infra.

19. See generally, Adams, Mantovani & Lundell,
"Wood Versus Fossil Fuel as a Source of Excess Carbon
Dioxide in the Atmosphere: A Preliminary Report," 196
Science 54-56 (1977); Bolin, "Changes of Land Biota and
Their Importance for the Carbon Cycle," id. at 613-15;
Stuvier, "Atmosphere Carbon Dioxide and Carbon Reservoir
Changes," 199 Science 253-58 (1978); Woodwell, Whittaker,
Reiners, Likens, Delwiche & Botkin, "The Biota and the
World Carbon Budget," id. at 141-46.

20. CO_2 Symposium, supra note 1, at 158. Rotty
projects that by the year 2025, the primary contributors
of carbon dioxide accumulation will shift from developed
to developing countries. He estimates that, in 50 years,
the LDC's will comprise 40% of the global emissions of
carbon dioxide while the emissions from the U.S.,
U.S.S.R., and European nations will total 28%. Id. For
detailed analysis of projected rates of energy use by
region, see R. Rotty & G. Marland, Constraints on Carbon
Dioxide Production from Fossil Fuel Use (May 1980) (Institute for Energy Analysis, Oak Ridge).

21. The total picture narrows when the carbon wealth
of nations is viewed exclusively in terms of coal. In
such an analysis, the U.S., U.S.S.R., and China are the
main contributors.

22. Stockholm Declaration of the United Nations Conference on the Human Environment, Principle 21, adopted June 16, 1972, U.N. Doc. A/CONF.48/14 (1972) reprinted in 11 Int'l Legal Mats. 1416 (1972) [hereinafter cited as Stockholm Declaration]. The final report of the Stockholm Conference is conveniently reprinted in a Senate Foreign Relations Committee publication: Senate Comm. on Foreign Relations, 92d Cong., 2d Sess., United Nations Conference on the Human Environment -- Report to the Senate by Senator Claiborne Pell and Senator Clifford Case 12-90 (Comm. Print 1972). A House Public Works Committee print includes a summary of the Conference's recommendations and outlines the position taken by the United States on the matters discussed at the Conference. Staff of House Comm. on Public Works, 92d Cong., 2d Sess., Report on the United Nations Conference on the Human Environment (Comm. Print 1972).

23. See Handl, "The Principle of 'Equitable Use' as Applied to Internationally Shared Resources: Its Role in Resolving Potential International Disputes over Transfrontier Pollution," Revue Belge de Droit International (1978-79). See also, Agreements for the Full Utilization of the Nile Waters, Nov. 8, 1959, U.A.R.-Sudan, 453 U.N.T.S. 51; The Indus Water Treaty, Sept. 19, 1960, India-Pakistan-I.B.R.D., 419 U.N.T.S. 125; Treaty Relating to the Uses of Waters of the Niagara River, Feb. 27. 1950, United States-Canada, 1 U.S.T. 694, T.I.A.S. No. 2130, 132 U.N.T.S. 223; Treaty Relating to the Utilization of the Waters of the Colorado and Tijuana Rivers, and of the Rio Grande, Feb. 3, 1944, United States-Mexico, 59 Stat. 1219, T.S. 994, 3 U.N.T.S. 313.

24. Weiss, "International Liability for Weather Modification," 1 Climate Change 267 (1978).

25. Helsinki Rules, supra note 15, art. X(1)(a).

26. Id. art. XI(1).

27. Id. art. X(1)(b).

28. Id. art. XI(2).

29. 1909 U.S.-Canada Treaty, supra note 15, art. IV.

30. Agreement on Great Lakes Water Quality, Nov. 22, 1978, United States-Canada, art. II, T.I.A.S. No. 9257 [hereinafter cited as 1978 Great Lakes Agreement].

31. 1909 U.S.-Canada Treaty, supra note 15, art. VIII.

32. 1978 Great Lakes Agreement, supra note 30, art. VII.

33. Convention to Facilitate the Carrying Out of the Principles Contained in the Treaty of November 12, 1864, Mar. 1, 1889, United States-Mexico, 26 Stat. 1512, T.S. No. 232 [hereinafter cited as 1899 U.S.-Mexico Convention].

34. Treaty Relating to the Utilization of Waters, Feb. 3, 1944, United States-Mexico, arts. 2, 3, 59 Stat.

1219, T.S. No. 944 [hereinafter cited as 1944 U.S.-Mexico Treaty].

35. 1899 Convention U.S.-Mexico, supra note 33, art. II; 1944 U.S.-Mexico Treaty, supra note 34, art. 1.

36. Memorandum of Understanding for Cooperation on Environmental Programs and Transboundary Problems, June 19, 1978, United States-Mexico, T.I.A.S. 9264.

37. Id.

38. Treaty on the Platé River Basin, signed at Brasilia, Apr. 23, 1969, art. 1, reprinted in 8 Int'l Legal Mats. 905 (1969).

39. The Platé River Basin Treaty establishes the Inter-Government Committee to perform this function. Id. art. III.

40. Rhine Chemical Convention, note 15 supra; Convention on the Protection of the Rhine Against Pollution by Chlorides, done at Bonn, Dec. 3, 1976, reprinted in 16 Int'l Legal Mats. 265 (1977) [hereinafter cited as Rhine Chloride Convention].

41. Rhine Chemical Convention, supra note 15, arts. 1-4.

42. Id. art. 2.

43. [1979] 2 Int'l Envir. Rep. (BNA) 975.

44. Rhine Chloride Convention, supra note 40, art. 2.

45. [1979] 2 Int'l Envir. Rep. (BNA) 975.

46. Rhine Chloride Convention, supra note 40, art. 2.

47. The Dutch, the downstream recipients of pollution in the Rhine, recalled their ambassador from Paris after the French government withdrew its bill for ratifying the Convention from Parliament. Moreover, the Dutch requested the EEC to pressure the French to ratify the agreement. [1979] 2 Int'l Envir. Rep. (BNA) 975.

48. TBAP Convention, note 17 supra.

49. Agreement on Monitoring of the Stratosphere, note 13 supra.

50. Nordic Convention, note 17 supra.

51. 1974 Michigan/Ontario Memorandum of Understanding on Transboundary Air Pollution Control (June 26, 1975) (available from the International Joint Commission);

52. [1979] 2 Int'l Envir. Rep. (BNA) 976-77.

53. TBAP Convention, supra note 17, art. 5.

54. Id. art. 3.

55. Id. arts. 6-9.

56. Agreement on Monitoring of the Stratosphere, supra note 13, arts. II-IV.

57. Id. art. VI.

58. Id. art. I.

59. Nordic Convention, note 17 supra. See also OECD Council Recommendation on the Equal Rights of Access to Information, Participation in Hearings and Procedures

by Persons Affected by Transfrontier Pollution, adopted
May 11, 1976, reprinted in 15 Int'l Legal Mats. 1218
(1976).

60. Id. art. 3.

61. Id.

62. Id.

63. See note 51 supra.

64. International Joint Commission, Second Annual
Report on Michigan/Ontario Air Pollution 2 (1977) (available from the IJC).

65. Id. at 1-2.

66. Id. at 2-4.

67. Trail Smelter Case (United States v. Canada),
3 R. Int'l Arb. Awards 1905 (1941).

68. Id. Decisions of such arbitral tribunals are
binding only on the parties to the arbitration, yet
nevertheless remain important indicators of international
law and derive much of their force from the extent to
which principles enunciated therein are incorporated in
future decisions or agreements.

69. Agreement Confirming Minute 242 of the International Boundary and Water Commission, Aug. 30, 1973,
United States-Mexico, 24 U.S.T. 1968, T.I.A.S. No. 7708.

70. G.A. Res. 3129, 28 U.N. GAOR, Supp. (No. 30)
49, U.N. Doc. A/9030 (1973), reprinted in 13 Int'l Legal
Mats. 232 (1974).

71. R. Rotty, Growth in Global Energy Demand and
Contribution of Alternative Supply Systems (Institute
for Energy Analysis, Oak Ridge Associated Universities,
1979); R. Rotty, Past and Future Emission of Carbon
Dioxide (Institute for Energy Analysis, Oak Ridge Associated Universitities, 1980).

72. W. Bach, "Impact of World Fossil Fuel Use on
Global Climate: Policy Implications and Recommendations" reprinted in CO_2 Symposium, supra note 1, at 121;
Cooper, "What Might Man-Induced Climate Change Mean?"
56 Foreign Aff. 500, 513 (1978).

73. Schneider, note 3 supra.

74. Cooper, supra note 72, at 507. For a complete
analysis, see Bryson, "A Perspective on Climate Change,"
184 Science 753 (1974).

75. See note 20 supra and accompanying text.

76. Cooper, supra note 72, at 505. While Canada
will experience a similar lengthening in its growing
season, this change will be less beneficial since much
of the land affected would be located on the Laurentian
Shield. Id. at 513. See Rotty, note 71 supra.

77. Bach, reprinted in CO_2 Symposium, supra note 1,
at 138; Cooper, supra note 72, at 514-15.

78. See Report of Thomas C. Shelling, Ad Hoc Study
Panel on Economic and Social Aspects of Carbon Dioxide
Increase, to Philip Handler, National Academy of Sciences

(Apr. 18, 1980).

79. CO_2 Symposium, supra note 1, at 158.

80. Id. at 159.

81. No representatives from private industry were invited to the Senate Governmental Affairs Committee's carbon dioxide symposium. The West German government, however, is pursuing intensive research in conjunction with the German coal industry to develop a technical fix, scrubbers, for the carbon dioxide problem. CO_2 Symposium, supra note 1, at 28. In a study for the U.S. Department of Energy, Albanese & Steinberg, of Brookhaven National Laboratory, investigated the practicability of alternative CO_2 control systems. They concluded that most potential CO_2 control systems reduce power generation efficiency and require significant energy input. Of the several options studied, the most promising is to store CO_2 in the deep ocean. Albanese & Steinberg, Environmental Control Technology for Atmospheric Carbon Dioxide (May 1980) (Brookhaven National Laboratory).

82. See, e.g., Cooper, note 72 supra.

83. Some action has already been taken, for example, the July 30, 1979, Senate Committee on Governmental Affairs hearings exploring the relationship between carbon dioxide accumulation and synthetic rules production. CO_2 Symposium, note 1 supra. As a result of these hearings, Senator Ribicoff introduced an amendment authorizing the National Academy of Science to undertake a two-year study of the carbon dioxide problem. That amendment, with the bill, is now part of the Synthetic Fuels Act.

84. On the requirement of federal environmental impact statements, National Environmental Policy Act of 1969, 42 U.S.C. § 4332(2)(c)(1976).

85. The Soviets have moved to convene a ministerial meeting of the United Nations Economic Commission for Europe (ECE) to discuss the world energy situation. A similar Soviet initiative last November resulted in the Convention on Long-Range Transboundary Air Pollution. While such a meeting would be an appropriate forum for discussing the carbon dioxide problem (the U.S., Canada, and East and West Europe are all members of the ECE), the chances for such a meeting are probably slim as long as Afghanistan and other situations remain unresolved. [1980] 339 Envt'l Users Rep. (BNA) 15. See note 20 supra and accompanying text. See also note 21 supra.

86. Clean Air Act, 42 U.S.C. § 7401 (1980).

87. OECD Environment Comm. Press Release (Paris, May 8, 1979).

88. Recommendation of the Council on Coal and the Environment, id. at 12.

89. 42 U.S.C. § 7401 (1980).

90. <u>E.g.</u>, Clean Water Act, 33 U.S.C. § 1251 (Supp. I 1976).

91. The U.S. Clean Air Act embodies a two-step approach to maintaining and enhancing air quality. First, the federal government establishes a primary (for the protection of public health) and a secondary (for the protection of public welfare) national ambient air quality standard for each pollutant listed in the Act. 42 U.S.C. § 7409(b)(1980). Second, the states, through state implementation plans, formulate emission standards defining specific quantitative limits on the amount of the pollutants individual sources may release. 42 U.S.C. § 7410 (1980). For a discussion, see Rodgers, <u>Environmental Law</u> 254-59 (1977).

92. <u>See</u> note 71 <u>supra</u> and accompanying text.

93. <u>See</u> Stockholm Declaration, note 22 <u>supra</u>.

94. [1979] 2 <u>Int'l Envir. Rep.</u> (<u>BNA</u>) 841.

95. <u>Id</u>. The UNEP meeting in Kenya advocated that the global community should give "urgent consideration" to the building up of alternative energy supplies such as solar power and windpower, which should take over from the carbon dioxide producing fuels. [Current] <u>Int'l Envir. Rep.</u> (<u>BNA</u>) 241.

96. 15 Weekly Comp. of Pres. Doc. 1353, 1371-73 (Aug. 2, 1979).

97. <u>Id</u>. at 1371.

98. [1979] 2 <u>Int'l Envir. Rep.</u> (<u>BNA</u>) 841.

99. <u>Id</u>.

100. <u>Id</u>.

101. [Current] <u>Int'l Envir. Rep.</u> (<u>BNA</u>) 49.

102. Treaty for Amazonian Cooperation, done <u>at</u> Brasilia July 3, 1978, <u>reprinted in</u> 17 <u>Int'l Legal Mats.</u> 1045 (1978).

103. 43 <u>Fed. Reg.</u> 11,301-26 (1978).

104. Stoel, Compton & Gibbons, "International Regulation of Chlorofluoromethanes," 3 <u>Env. Pol'y & Law</u> 130 (1977).

105. 42 U.S.C. § 7453 (1980).

106. [1979] 10 <u>Envir. Rep.</u> (<u>BNA</u>) 1521-22.

107. 42 U.S.C. § 7454 (1980).

108. Conversation with Dr. Lester Machta, Director of Air Resources Laboratories, NOAA (Jan. 13, 1980).

109. <u>Or. Rev. Stat.</u> §§ 468.605, 468.996(6); <u>Mich. Comp. Laws. Ann.</u> §§ 336.103, 336.107 (effective Mar. 31, 1977). Maine and Minnesota also enacted legislation prohibiting aerosol sprays containing chlorofluorocarbons for certain uses. [1977] 8 <u>Envir. Rep.</u> (<u>BNA</u>) 179, 666. The New York Department of Environmental Conservation adopted regulations requiring warning labels on aerosols with chlorofluorocarbons. <u>Id</u>. at 135. At one time, 20 states were considering some type of regulation. <u>Id</u>. at 1693-94.

110. [1980] 3 <u>Int'l Envir. Rep.</u> (<u>BNA</u>) 3.

111. <u>Id.</u>

112. <u>Id.</u>

113. Amendment of Ordinance 1973-334 on Products Hazardous to Health and the Environment adding Section 486, [1977] Swedish Fed. Stat. 1095, <u>codified</u> <u>in</u> [1973] Swedish Code of Statutes 329.

114. T. Stoel, International Regulation of Fluoro-carbons V-(1-2) (Apr. 17, 1979) (draft paper available from the Natural Resources Defense Council).

115. II <u>Can.</u> <u>Stat.</u> Ch. 72 (1975).

116. Stoel, <u>supra</u> note 114, at VII-(6-7).

12
The International Law and Politics of Acid Rain

Armin Rosencranz

I. INTRODUCTION

The Environmental Law Institute, headquartered in Washington, D.C., has conducted an international comparative study of transboundary air pollution since early 1979. This study focuses on sulfur oxides (SO_x) and acid rain. Its findings and conclusions, however, may also apply to carbon dioxide (CO_2),[1] another airborne pollutant which crosses national boundaries, even though sulfur dioxides are primarily regional pollutants,[2] whereas carbon dioxide envelops the entire globe. But CO_2 and SO_x both have been amendable to abatement primarily for scientific and economic reasons.[3] This article will be limited to a discussion of transboundary air pollution by SO_x and acid rain,[4] and leave to others to draw any comparison with CO_2.

The major thesis of the article is that, notwithstanding the legal doctrines clearly recognized by the Trail Smelter Arbitration[5] and Principle 21 of the 1972 United Nations Conference on the Human Environment in Stockholm,[6] international law is ineffective in the field of transboundary air pollution, and invariably gives way to considerations of national and international politics. Nations control pollution only if and when it is in their national interest to do so, and not because of any obligation under international law to do so.

II. INTERNATIONAL LAW AND TRANSBOUNDARY POLLUTION

At the 1972 Stockholm Conference on the Human Environment, the problem of Scandinavian lake acidification from airborne sulfur compounds originating outside Scandinavia was first brought to international attention. The Conference produced a Declaration of Principles. Principle 21, the most pertinent to this discussion, provides that "States have, in accordance with the Charter of the United Nations and the principles of international law . . . the responsibility to ensure that activities within their jurisdiction or control do not cause damage to the environment of other States. . . ."[7]

This principle has impressive antecedents. In 1949, the International Court of Justice held in The Corfu Channel Case[8] that Albania had an obligation to warn British users of its waters that those waters contained minefields. The court recognized "every State's obligation not to allow knowingly its territory to be used for acts contrary to the rights of other States."[9]

With respect to transboundary pollution, the Trail Smelter Arbitration,[10] which helped to resolve a protracted air pollution dispute in the 1920's and 1930's between Canada and the United States, is particularly relevant. Canada conceded that fumes from a smelter at Trail, British Columbia, were causing damage in adjacent areas in the state of Washington, and a tribunal was created to determine, inter alia, the amount of damages. In widely quoted dictum, the tribunal asserted that "[n]o State has a right to use or permit the use of its territory in such a manner as to cause injury by fumes in or to the territory of another . . . when the case is of serious consequence and the injury is established by clear and convincing evidence."[11]

Long before the Trail Smelter Arbitration the United States Supreme Court had declared through Justice Holmes, in Georgia v. Tennessee Copper Co., that:

> [I]t is a fair and reasonable demand on the part of a sovereign that the air over its territory should not be polluted on a great scale by sulphurous acid gas, that the forests on its mountains, be they better or worse, and whatever domestic destruction they have suffered, should not be further destroyed or threatened by the act of persons beyond its control, that the crops and orchards on its hills should not be endangered from the same source.[13]

Generally, these principles derive from the Roman legal maxim sic utere tuo, ut alienum non laedas.[14] Unfortunately, neither principles nor maxims are of much consequence in the case of transboundary air pollution.[15] Nations rarely relinquish jurisdiction over cases of pollution emanating from their territory, and even more rarely admit liability for such pollution. The Trail Smelter Arbitration[16] is, in fact, sui generis: Canada admitted liability and agreed to allow United States courts to assess damages. When the United States courts declined to do so, both countries agreed to let a special binational tribunal "arbitrate" the amount of damages. There has been no case like this before or since, and the circumstances of the case are unlikely to rise again.

Nations today are exceedingly protective of both their sovereignty and their pollution prerogatives. They are especially resistant to suggestions that they add pollution control costs to the already high cost of producing electric power, even though they may admit that the production of that power causes unintended but real damage in other countries.[17] In the words of one international diplomat, "one can't expect Europe to reduce its sulfur emissions just to save some Scandinavian fish."[18] Scandinavian environmental officials themselves concede the temerity and impracticality of their request for abatement of European sulfur pollution.

III. MULTILATERAL AGREEMENTS

The recent Convention on Long-Range Transboundary Air Pollution (ECE Convention)[19] seems to be the perfect solution to the victim countries' need for international recognition of the acid rain problem and the polluting countries' need to continue to pollute. The ECE Convention dutifully invokes Principle 21 of the Stockholm Declaration in its preamble, but the West German government reportedly stipulated that preambles have no force of law and that in any case it does not hold itself legally bound by Principle 21.[20] The ECE Convention is the first international accord on air pollution and was hailed by its chairman, Olog Johansson of Sweden, as "a breakthrough in the development of international environmental law."[21] However, it provides merely for the sharing of information, collaborative research, and continued monitoring of pollutants and rainfall. It contains no numerical goals, limits, timetables, abatement measures or enforcement provisions. Signatories have merely undertaken to "endeavor to limit, and, as far as possible, gradually reduce and prevent air pollution, including long-range transboundary air pollution."[22] They have also agreed to adopt "the best available technology economically feasible."[23] No country has to alter its status quo unless it chooses to. To date, there are few indications that any but the victim countries (Sweden, Norway, Canada, and the United States) are considering further sulfur pollution control measures.

The European Community, whose member-states include Western Europe's major polluters (Britain, West Germany, France, Italy, Denmark, the Netherlands and Belgium), enacted on July 15, 1980, its long-awaited SO_2 Directive.[24] The resolution accompanying this directive incorporates verbatim the ECE Convention formula "to endeavor to limit, and, as far as possible, gradually reduce and prevent air pollution. . . ."[25] The Direc-

tive is so weak that at least two environmentally progressive countries, the Netherlands and Denmark, were
reluctant to approve it. The senior air pollution
official in the Dutch Ministry of Health and the Environment estimated that in less than five percent of the land
area of European Community member states would fail to
conform to the new SO_2 standard at the time of its enact-
ment.[26] Member states can apparently with virtually no
change in present practices and with no appreciable
impact on SO_2 emissions or on the total sulfur load in
the atmosphere over Europe.

IV. BILATERAL NEGOTIATIONS: CANADA AND THE UNITED STATES

Multilateral action is necessary to cope with the
problem of transboundary SO_x pollution in Europe since
numerous countries contribute to the sulfur load. In the
context of North American SO_x emissions and the resulting
acid rain, however, a bilateral arrangement between the
United States and Canada would be both more efficient and
easier to enforce than would a multilateral treaty. Both
countries are "victims" of acid rain since both have
large acid-sensitive regions.[27] The United States sends
three times as much sulfur pollution to Canada as it
receives from that country, but Canada exports far more
SO_x per capita than does the United States.[28] Thus, acid
rain is a mutual problem and the two countries have a
mutual interest in abating its flow across their common
border. But Canadian and American negotiators are still
far away from a formal agreement after three years of
talks. Moreover, both countries are now contemplating
energy programs which would increase their SO_x pollution[29] in the face of this supposed mutual interest and,
more importantly, in abrogation of the ECE Convention
which they both so recently signed.

In the waning days of the Carter presidency, presumably in anticipation of a new administration even less
disposed to controlling power plant emissions than were
their predecessors, the Canadian Parliament enacted legislation authorizing its federal government to reduce
pollution from sources contributing to problems (viz.
acid rain) in other countries.[30] The immediate and perhaps sole effect of this legislation was to give life to
section 7415 of the U.S. Clean Air Act,[31] under which the
U.S. Environmental Protection Agency (EPA) can compel
states to reduce air pollution when such pollution has
been found by a duly constituted international agency[32]
to endanger public health and welfare in a foreign country, if and only if the foreign country has the legal
ability to take reciprocal action under the same circumstances. The effectiveness of section 7415 has been at
stake because it was unclear whether Canada, whose

federal government has generally deferred to its pro-
vinces in pollution control matters, could reciprocate.
The recent Canadian legislation apparently removed that
cloud, but in actuality it has accomplished little more
than to enable the then EPA Administrator to issue a
hortatory statement saying that his staff would examine
the issue and recommend that the offending state be
formally notified. Such recommendations must come before
President Reagan's EPA Administrator, and prompt or significant remedial action seems highly unlikely.

The above example serves as one indication that the
whole subject of transboundary air pollution is fraught
with political and economic considerations which have
little to do with international law and agreements, and
which may effectively neutralize domestic law with international purposes.

V. THE LIMITS OF INTERNATIONAL LAW AND INSTITUTIONS

Numerous agreements, most notably the 1979 ECE Convention, promote international consultation and cooperation in research, monitoring, and assessment of the
environmental impacts of present or planned sources of
pollution.[33] However, nothing in the present international legal framework effectively fosters preventive
action. General principles concerning the responsibilities of nations to compensate for the damages caused by
transboundary pollution may occasionally be useful in
allocating expenses and may have some deterrent value,
but they do little to avoid the permanent environmental
damage that can be expected from acid rain and perhaps
from the greenhouse effect of increased CO_2 production.[34]
These general principles are no help in describing the
point at which a nation's interest in industrial development must yield to concerns over the effects of transboundary pollution.

Moreover, there is no mechanism to enforce any international legal doctrine that is not made part of a
sovereign nation's domestic law. No international agency
is ceded the power to enforce international environmental
principles or, indeed, "binding" international treaties
and agreements.[35] The most respected of international
adjudicatory bodies, the International Court of Justice,
may rule on a case only after the involved countries
have consented to a referral, which is a rare occur-
rence.[36] In the only two major international environmental cases where the involved nations consented to be
bound by the decision of a neutral tribunal,[37] the
claimants were required to demonstrate specific causes of
specific environmental injury.[38] Unfortunately, because
of the incomplete scientific understanding of both the
atmospheric chemistry and the effects of transported
sulfur pollutants, one cannot yet establish that specific

sources are responsible for acidification of distant
lakes and soils.[39] If action had to await a clear link
between emissions and distant environmental effects, or
the full determination of the damage by acidity, irreversible damage would almost certainly take place in
various parts of the world.[40]

VI. DOMESTIC PROCEDURES TO RESOLVE TRANSBOUNDARY
     DISPUTES

     Domestic procedures are sometimes successfully en-
listed to resolve international environmental disputes,[41]
especially when there are no difficult choice of law
questions and where the source of the injury and amount
of damages are determinable. The effects of increased
acidification such as loss of fish stocks, enhanced
corrosion, and reduced agricultural productivity, are
compensable types of injury; but judgments for damages
are poorly suited to disputes arising from transboundary
acid rain pollution. The multiplicity of sources and
their relative contribution to atmospheric loadings make
it difficult to prove a claim, assign liability, or
provide effective remedies.
     If polluters' national courts were willing, for
example, to apply Principle 21 of the Stockholm Declaration or any of its predecessors or successors[42] against
their own offending citizens, then such principles of
international law would have teeth. Thus far, no country's courts have been so aggressive, although several
courts have entertained suits invoking extraterritorial
damage.[43] Attitudes of self-interest and national
autonomy regarding environmental problems are shared by
judges as well as by legislators and bureaucrats, and
these attitudes seem unlikely to change in the foreseeable future.

VII. PROGNOSIS: LIMITED ABATEMENT BUT INCREASED
      AWARENESS

     Current controls, including general principles of
international law and the ECE Convention, are not adequate to abate SO_x emissions sufficiently to remedy the
transboundary acid rain problem.[44] Numerous control
strategies, policies, and technologies are available and
could be extremely effective, but few nations seem willing to bear the cost.[45] Indeed, the pressures today are
in the opposite direction, viz., to relax air quality and
emissions standards to thereby make coal-generated electric power more efficient and economical.[46]
     The prospects for timely action look bleak. Sweden
and Norway will undoubtedly call on the ECE Convention
signatories to implement its principles. The polluting

countries will probably continue to call for proof of
damage, identification of specific sources, and resolution of scientific uncertainties. The polluters may propose to bear the modest costs of liming acidified lakes,
an offer which the recipient countries will undoubtedly
reject as an inadequate substitute for abatement and as
potentially dangerous to aquatic ecosystems.

The Stockholm Declaration stimulated the creation of
numerous national institutions to protect the environment
and promoted world awareness of the acid rain phenomenon,
if not of its danger. The ECE Convention, like multilateral agreements on water quality and marine pollution,[47]
may at a minimum help maintain the environmental status
quo and perhaps bring about voluntary improvements in the
environment. Nevertheless, no international principles
or practices, and certainly not the qualified language
of the ECE Convention,[48] can compel remedial action.

The most likely area for progress may come through
implementing the ECE Convention's provisions for exchanging available information on "major changes in
national policies and in general industrial development,
and their potential impact, which would be likely to
cause significant changes in long-range transboundary
pollution."[49] Aggressive implementation by victim
countries of this provision and of its attendant notice
and consultation requirements would afford an opportunity
to attract media and citizen attention in the polluting
countries. This could exert a salutary influence on the
polluters' plans for sulfur control.

The projected dissemination by the Secretariat of
the Economic Commission for Europe of member states'
energy scenarios could offer another wedge for victim
countries to influence the policies of the polluting
countries. Information exchanges among ECE countries on
developing coal-utilization technologies should guarantee
rapid dissemination of new technological developments.
Broad multilateral subscription to such technologies may
yield economies of a scale sufficient to make them af-
fordable. Finally, ECE-mandated multilateral research on
crop damage and health effects from sulfate aerosols and
acid rain may sooner or later demonstrate clearly both
the cost-effectiveness and the necessity of controlling
and abating sulfur emissions throughout the industrial
world. Ultimately, that should induce responsible officials to revise upward their estimates of what is
economically feasible.[50]

Transboundary air pollution is governed not by international law but by national self-interest. That
self-interest, however, combined with the consciousness-
raising effect of vigorous international discussion and
negotiation about sulfur and carbon pollutants and their
potentially irreversible effects, can induce thoughtful
and enlightened public officials to show concern and try

to abate acid rain and CO_2 for their own nation's future.

In this respect, 1980 was an important year. With government support, West German scientists began ambitious research programs on the effects of acid deposition[51] on conifer forests and on buildings and monuments, including the Cologne Cathedral. The United States committed large sums to research the effects of acid deposition and to develop new pollution control technology. Significant progress has been made in developing a unique "low NO_x" boiler to drastically reduce nitrogen oxide emissions from coal burning facilities.[52] The Ontario Ministry of the Environment ordered the INCO smelting plant at Sudbury, Ontario--the single largest pollution source in the world, emitting one million tons of sulfur pollutants annually into the atmosphere--to reduce SO_2 emissions by more than fifty percent by December 1982.[53] Finally, most Western European countries reduced their annual SO_2 emissions by efficiently employing low-cost sulfur control strategies, such as burning low-sulfur coal and oil, washing coal before combustion, and producing more electricity from sulfur-free nuclear power.[54]

VIII. CONCLUSION

International organizations and agreements serve the essential function of educating the international political community. They help to build a consensus about a transnational problem and to develop a context in which sovereign states pursue pro-international policies by perceiving that it is in their own interest to do so. By making and keeping issues like transboundary air pollution or world climate change salient topics for international investigation, discussion, and negotiation, they create a ripple effect. International monitoring, data gathering, and scientific research help to form a consensus among scientists that a problem is serious and deserves remedial action. Sooner or later these ripples are bound to reach policymakers and concerned citizens and to influence national agendas. In this lies the main hope for progress in international environmental protection generally, and in long-range transboundary air pollution specifically.

NOTES

1. CO_2 is the most likely cause of world climate
change in the next century, and SO_x is the main cause of
acid rain. Both enter the atmosphere and can be carried
across national boundaries. The continuing increase of
both compounds is due largely to the increased combustion
of coal and oil to produce electric power in industrial
countries. Coal and oil are carbon-based and contain
significant quantities of sulfur. The Secretariat of the
United Nations Economic Commission for Europe (ECE) estimates that energy consumption in Europe and North America will increase 70% by 1990 and will triple by 2020.
See [1980] 3 Int'l Envir. Rep.(BNA) 101. Even if this
demand were to stabilize at current levels, the environmental changes are likely to be both irreversible and
irremediable. To protect the environment and maintain
current levels and patterns of agricultural productivity,
future power must be generated from renewable, sulfur-
free and carbon-free energy sources, such as solar, wind,
geothermal, or tidal sources. Otherwise, our only hope
is that natural homeostatic processes will somehow buffer
and neutralize the effects of sulfur and carbon compounds.

2. Sulfur oxides originating in the United States
may travel to Canada and those originating in Britain
or Germany may travel to Scandinavia. Sulfur oxides
generally travel hundreds of miles, although some
scientists conjecture that the Arctic haze may consist
of sulfates (SO_4) originating two thousand miles away in
the United States.

3. Both CO_2 and SO_x have not been amenable to abatement for several reasons. First, scientists have been
uncertain about the nature and extent of their effects.
Second, the general public has been largely complacent
about CO_2 and SO_x increases and their supposed effects.
Third, with the exception of sportfishing communities in
acid-sensitive regions, no vocal economic interest group
yet perceives a sufficient economic disadvantage from increased CO_2 and SO_x to compel governmental abatement
action. Fourth, utilities have persistently minimized
the danger of increased CO_2 and SO_x and have steadfastly
resisted costly and energy-intensive abatement pressures.

4. The Convention on Long-Range Transboundary Air
Pollution is not, on its face, limited to acid rain, but
that is what the proposers, Norway and Sweden, and the
signatories, had in mind. The Convention was drawn up
and adopted by the United Nations Economic Commission for
Europe. Done Nov. 13, 1979, 1 U.N. ECE, Annex 1, U.N.
Doc. E/ECE/HLM.1/2 (1979), reprinted in 18 Int'l Legal
Mat. 1442 (1979) [hereinafter cited as ECE Convention].
For a more exact definition of "acid rain," see note

51 *infra*.

5. The Tribunal gave a preliminary award on April 16, 1938, and the final award on March 11, 1941. Trail Smelter Arbitration (United States v. Canada), 3 R. Int'l Arb. Awards 1911 (1938); id. at 1905 (1941). The decisions of the Trail Smelter Arbitral Tribunal are also reported in 33 Am. J. Int'l L. 182 (1939) and 35 Am. J. Int'l L. 684 (1941). For an in depth discussion of the case, see Rubin,"Pollution by Analogy: The Trail Smelter Arbitration," 50 Or. L. Rev. 259 (1971).

6. Report of the United Nations Conference on the Human Environment (Stockholm, 5-16 June 1972), 1 U.N. GAOR (21st plen. mtg.), U.N. Doc. A/CONF.45/14 Rev. 1 (1972), reprinted in 11 Int'l Legal Mat. 1416 (1972) [hereinafter cited as Stockholm Declaration].

7. Id. For a general discussion of other principles of the Stockholm Declaration dealing more specifically with transboundary pollution, see J. Barros & D. Johnston, The International Law of Pollution (1974).

8. The Corfu Channel Case (Albania v. United Kingdom), [1949] I.C.J. 4.

9. Id. at 22.

10. 3 R. Int'l Arb. Awards 1905 (1941).

11. 3 R. Int'l Arb. Awards at 1965.

12. 206 U.S. 230 (1907).

13. Id. at 238.

14. "Use your own property in such a manner as not to injure that of another." Black's Law Dictionary 1238 (5th ed. 1979).

15. Transboundary water pollution is more susceptible to international adjudication and dispute settlement referring to these principles because the sources of water pollution are more determinable than the sources of air pollution, especially long-range air pollution. For the prevailing view in the international community regarding transboundary water pollution, see Helsinki Rules on the Uses of the Waters of International Rivers, art. X, U.N. Doc. A/CN. 4/274, reprinted in Yearbook of the International Law Commission, U.N. Doc. A/CN.4/SER. A /1974/Add.1 (Part 2), at 357; also reprinted in International Law Association, Report of the Fifty-Second Conference, Helsinki 484 (1966) [hereinafter cited as Helsinki Rules.] The Helsinki Rules provide for abatement of pollution causing "substantial injury" to another state for any damages. For a general history of international efforts, see R. M'Gonigle & M. Zacher, Pollution, Politics and International Law (1979); L. Telclaff & A. Utton, International Environmental Law (1974).

16. 3 R. Int'l Arb. Awards 1905 (1941).

17. See Bird, "Environmental Policy Making: Liability for Externalities in the Presence of Transaction Costs," 20 Nat. Resources J. 487 (1980); d'Arge & Kneese,

"State Liability for International Environmental Degradation: An Economic Perspective," id. at 427.

18. Interview with Henri Smets, Organization for Economic Cooperation and Development, Environment Directorate (Apr. 20, 1979).

19. ECE Convention, note 4 supra. The Economic Commissions for Europe is a United Nations regional organization with 34 member states, including Eastern and Western European countries, Canada, and the United States.

20. Reported from an interview with Henri Smets, Organization for Economic Cooperation and Development, Environment Directorate (Nov. 20, 1979).

21. Official remarks of the Chairman of the High Level Meeting within the Framework of the United Nations Economic Commission for Europe on the Protection of the Environment (Nov. 15, 1979).

22. ECE Convention, supra note 4, art. 2 [Emphasis added].

23. Id. art. 6 [Emphasis added].

24. Directive on SO_2 and Suspended Particulates, O.J. Eur. Comm. (No. L 229) 779 (1980), reported in [1980] 2 Comm. Mkt. Rep. (CCH) ¶ 3315.281.

25. ECE Convention, supra note 4, art. 2.

26. Interview with Albert Adriaanse, Dutch Ministry of Health and the Environment, The Hague (Apr. 26, 1979).

27. Typically, these are regions with granite bedrock which have no capacity to neutralize or "buffer" any acid introduced to the water or soil above the bedrock. Much of eastern Canada and the northeastern United States is acid-sensitive.

28. Sierra, May-June, 1980, at 41.

29. For example, during 1980, at President Carter's urging, the U.S. Congress considered legislation under which 80 oil-fired power plants will be converted to coal. Coal-fired plants in the United States emit considerably more sulfur oxides than oil. No provision was to be made to install scrubbers or other pollution-reducing technology in these converted plants. Similarly, in June 1980, President Carter conferred in Venice with the leaders of six other industrial countries (Britain, Canada, France, Italy, Japan, and West Germany), and all conferees determined to double coal use during the next 10 years, notwithstanding the fact that six of the seven conferees are signatories of the ECE Convention.

Finally, Canada has gone ahead with its pre-ECE Convention plans to build two new large power plants adjacent to pristine willderness areas in Montana and Minnesota. Responding to suggestions that these plants could result in significant deterioration in the air quality of adjacent areas in the United States, John Messer, the former Saskatchewan Minister of Energy, declared: "It is our position that we don't have to abide by the laws of other countries." Interview with Robert Sugarman, Former Chairman, United States Section, International Joint Commission (Mar. 20, 1981).

30. Clean Air Amendment Act, [1981] C.C.L. 706, at 9.

31. 42 U.S.C. § 7415 (1976 & Supp. III 1979).

32. The agency is the United States-Canada International Joint Commission, which has repreatedly found that acid rain results from the long-range transport of air pollutants originating from sources in both countries. See Seventh Annual Report on Great Lakes Water Quality of the International Joint Commission (Oct. 1980).

33. This discussion primarily addresses transboundary air pollution, but may also apply to transboundary water pollution.

34. See generally texts cited in notes 7 & 15 supra.

35. Directives of the Council of the European Communities are incorporated into the domestic laws of the members states and, accordingly, have a status different from that of other multilateral agreements.

36. I.C.J. Stat. arts. 36, 37.

37. Trail Smelter Arbitration (United States v. Canada), 3 R. Int'l Arb. Awards 1905 (1941); The Lac Lanoux Arbitration (Spain v. France), 12 R. Int'l Arb. Awards 281 (1957).

38. The Trail Smelter Arbitration, for example, refers to a state's obligation not to allow the air pollution to affect another state where injury is established by clear and convincing evidence.

39. See generally the sources cited in note 17 supra.

40. See note 2 supra.

41. See W. Poro v. Houillieres du Bassin de Lorraine, OLGE Bayern, Saarbrucken (1957), where a German motel owner sued a French electric power plant, whose emissions of soot and smoke damaged crops, flowers, and the recreation business in German territory across the border. The German court awarded damages pursuant to French law. Subsequently, the defendant company installed effective pollution control equipment financed by joint French-German government contributions pursuant to a pre-existing French-German treaty dealing, inter alia, with boundary pollution control.

42. See notes 5, 8, 12 & 37 supra.

43. In Ohio v. Wyandotte Chemicals Corp., 401 U.S. 493 (1971), the United States Supreme Court declined to exercise its original jurisdictuion, but implicitly confirmed the competence of Ohio's state courts to deal with the transnational disputes involved. See also Michie v. Great Lakes Steel Division, Nat'l Steel Corp., 495 F.2d 213 (6th Cir. 1974). See generally Restatement (Second)

of Conflict of Laws § 53 (1963); Restatement (Second) of
Foreign Relations Laws of the United States § 18 (1962).
    44. Notes 22 & 29 supra.
    45. Note 17 supra.
    46. See, e.g., note 29 supra, for a discussion of
industrialized nations' decision to switch from oil to
coal.
    47. Probably the most notable are the Convention for
the Protection of the Marine Environment of the Baltic
Sea Area, Helsinki, Mar. 22, 1974, reprinted in 13 Int'l
Legal Mat. 544 (1974); Convention for the Prevention of
Marine Pollution from Land-Based Sources, adopted
Feb. 21, 1974, opened for signature June 4, 1974, reprinted in 13 Int'l Legal Mat. 352 (1974); and the Convention for the Protection of the Mediterranean Sea
Against Pollution, done at Barcelona, Feb. 16, 1976,
reprinted in 15 Int'l Legal Mat. 290 (1976) [hereinafter
cited as Mediterranean Sea Convention].
    In the recent Draft Protocol to the Mediterranean
Sea Convention signatories have for the first time undertaken to change national policies, including industrial
siting policies, to accord with the Protocol's terms.
See [1980] 3 Int'l Envir. Rep. (BNA) 189 for a reprint of
the full text.
    48. See art. 2 of the ECE Convention, quoted in the
text accompanying note 22 supra.
    49. Id.
    50. See notes 3 & 17 supra.
    51. "Acid deposition" is more technically correct
than "acid rain." It encompasses rain, snow, sleet,
mist, hail, fog, dew, and frost, as well as dry deposition of fine sulfate particulates.
    52. Nitrogen oxides are precursors to nitric acid,
which accounts for one-third of the acid in North
American acid rain. See President Carter's Second Message to Congress on the Environment, 15 Weekly Comp. of
Pres. Doc. 1353 (Aug. 2, 1979).
    53. Ontario and Canadian federal officials made it
clear that the INCO control order was designed to
strengthen Canada's position in the United States-Canada
negotiations and to pressure the United States to take
corresponding measures against U.S. sources of aid rain.
See [1980] 3 Int'l Envir. Rep. (BNA) 234-35. Environmental officials in both countries seem to be telling one
another, in effect, "If you lean on us more, we'll be
able to justify stronger control measures."
    54. It is, of course, impossible to know whether the
same strategies would have been employed in the absence
of international discussion ("consciousness-raising") of
transboundary air pollution and the effects of acid rain.
The net result, however, is to reduce the total sulfur
load in Europe's atmosphere. There are indications,

however, that increased emissions from Eastern Europe
may have offset any Western Europe reductions. But
Eastern European countries, all signatories of the ECE
Convention, became conscious of the long-range transboundary air pollution problem much more recently than
Western Europe, where the Europe-dominated Organization
for Economic Cooperation and Development has been discussing transboundary air pollution for almost a decade.

13
Options for Public Control
of Atmospheric Management

Ray Jay Davis

INTRODUCTION

Intentional modification of weather is a goal which has been partly reached by treating the atmosphere with chemicals. Clouds have been "seeded" to trigger changes in their behavior. Although much needs to be learned before weather resources can be managed to the extent scientific theories postulate, several types of weather phenomena can now be influenced by weather modification technologies:

(1) Supercooled fog and stratus clouds can be treated to improve visibility;

(2) Snowpack, and the resulting runoff, can be augmented by modifying winter clouds rising over some mountain barriers;

(3) Rain can be increased from some kinds of summer cumulus clouds, and their potential for precipitation can be enhanced by increasing the size of clouds; and

(4) Hail suppression is attempted in many places, and although experiments are not conclusive, evaluations of some projects suggest that hail damage in some kinds of storms can be reduced.[1]

Because the atmospheric environment deeply affects the quality of life,[2] management of atmospheric resources has been subjected to legal control by governmental institutions. In the United States, courts have been employed in a number of instances to provide public means for control of weather modification activities.[3] There is cloud seeding legislation in several countries including South Africa,[4] Canada,[5] Australia,[6] and the United States.[7] In some nations there are administrative rules and regulations concerning weather resources management.[8]

Some governmental control over intended weather alteration activities takes place at a local level.[9] However, in the United States, it is more common to regulate cloud seeding through agencies of state governments.[10] In many countries public control of atmospheric management takes place at the national level.[11]

Various legal options are available for public control of atmospheric management. Among those which have been employed and which will be considered herein are:

I. Incidental Control
    A. Delivery of Seeding Materials
    B. Water Resource Rights
    C. Liability Claims
II. Informational Control
    A. Technological Expertise
    B. Disclosure
III. Administrative Control
    A. Project Registration
    B. Operational Permits
    C. Professional Licensing
IV. Contractual Control
    A. Authorization Laws
    B. Appropriation Statutes
    C. Procurement Laws and Regulations
V. Governmental Operations
VI. Prohibition of Weather Modification Activities
    A. Partial Ban
    B. Complete Ban

I. INCIDENTAL CONTROL

Prior to the time of scientific cloud seeding there were no statutes, administrative regulations, or judicial decisions concerning weather modification activities. Many jurisdictions, including forty percent of the states in the United States, still have no legislation relating specifically to weather resources management.[12] This does not mean, however, that weather modification is un-controlled by governmental agencies in such places. Control incidental to the use of other kinds of govern-mental power is widespread. Regulation of the delivery of seeding materials into the atmosphere is one type of control. Allocation of atmospheric water rights is another control device. A third type is legal response to liability claims.

A. Delivery of Seeding Materials

Flight control regulations in statutes and adminis-trative rules are intended to protect the public conven-ience and safety. They include rules concerning transportation of hazardous materials. Carriage on board aircraft of inflammables in the United States is subjected to Federal Aviation Administration (FAA) rules.[13] Some cloud seeding materials dispensed from aircraft are inflammable. Examples are pyrotechnics, which are mounted on racks on aircraft wings, and mixtures of silver iodide (the major cloud seeding chemical) with acetone, which are burned in wing tip generators. The FAA has given exemptions from its hazardous materials rules to weather modifiers.[14] In doing so, or refusing to grant permission to drop pyrotechnics or burn generators, that agency regulates weather modification incidentally to its role as the guardian of aircraft safety.

In some parts of the United States over half of the opportunities for treating the atmosphere take place at night. The occupation of cloud seeding pilot thus involves unusual hours. Pilots can spend many days grounded because no seedable clouds are available, and when there are seedable events it may be necessary for them to work many successive hours. Aviation control agencies, such as the Australian Department of Civil Aviation, have flight time rules. These restrictions are, however, waived for seeding aircraft operations. It is not necessary to employ duplicative pilots who actually work only when atmospheric conditions require seeding beyond the time set for usual aircraft piloting.[15] Authority to make flight-time rules and then to grant or withhold waivers therefore constitutes the power to control airborne weather resources management.

Cloud seeding flights take place in and near storm clouds, and involve problems of air traffic control. There must be coordination of flight instructions relayed from project managers on the ground who have weather radar information and traffic instructions from governmental air traffic controllers who direct commercial and general aviation movements. The formal agreement on flight control between the North Dakota state-operated weather modification managers and the FAA is an example of air traffic control cooperation.[16] The administrative power to determine flight patterns can, however, be used to regulate seeding from aircraft.[17]

Much weather modification activity takes place on the ground. Persons who control access to ground facilities can exercise incidental control over treating clouds. Many of the prime areas for American seeding projects are on or in the atmosphere above federally-owned lands. Some National Forest Service units have asserted that persons wishing to use ground based seeding generators or monitoring equipment must obtain special land use permits for those activities in the national forests.[18] Issuance or denial of permits would be a form of control over cloud seeding incidental to the general permit granting authority.

In order to preserve certain areas from human development, the United States Congress has designated nationally-owned areas of primitive character and ecological significance as part of the national wilderness system.[19] Both cloud seeding and the collection of hydrometeorological data needed to evaluate its impact may intrude upon wilderness areas. Through use of their power generally to prevent uses inconsistent with the wilderness character of such areas, some administrators of national forests and parks have taken the position that mechanized access to data collection instruments in wildernesses will not be allowed.[20] Proposals to reduce the impact of this sort of incidental control by setting up a procedure for approval of various means of data collection have not been enacted into law.[21]

B. Water Resource Rights

Precipitation enhancement is advocated by persons and organizations wishing to obtain additional water. They may not, however, be able to use the water unless they have a legal right to exclude others from its use. Who owns the water in the atmosphere? The meager case law on this point is scattered, comes from lesser courts, and reaches differing conclusions.[22] Montana has a constitutional provision asserting state ownership of atmospheric waters;[23] some states have statutes reaching the same result.[24] These provisions, however, do not allocate water rights. They, like similar laws concerning surface and underground waters,[25] are merely intended to be a basis for exercise by states of the power to regulate the use of water rights.

Of more importance to sponsors of rain and snow augmentation projects than rights in the skies is the right to use additional waters on the ground and in the streams. Case law does not deal with this issue; three American states have statutes addressing it. Colorado's law provides that water flow generated by weather modification activities will be treated like other water. Seeding project sponsors can obtain a legal right of use if, but only if, they file to appropriate it.[26] A somewhat similar Utah statute has been interpreted to give the right of use to the added water to the appropriator whose unfilled water priority stood the highest in rank.[27] North Dakota by law rules that artificially induced precipitation will be treated the same as natural precipitation.[28] By granting or withholding inducements to mount projects, these rules form a type of control over atmospheric water resources management.

C. Liability Claims

When most persons think of law and weather modification their attention turns first to liability claims by land owners and others against weather modifiers. In spite of its fears about litigation the industry has been

very successful in liability lawsuits. Plaintiffs have
won only one case.[29] Judicial control through use of tort
law has been more of a threat than a reality. Of course,
assessment of damages and imposition of injunctions
could be an effective means of control when plaintiffs
manage to prove the elements of their tort claims.

Various liaibility theories have been advanced. For
example, in a Michigan lawsuit, a farmer whose crop had
been damaged by a storm sued a weather modification
company and sponsoring farmer groups asserting theories
of trespass, negligence, nuisance, and ultrahazardous
activity.[30] Although the jury found for the defendants,
this multiple theory approach to litigation seems to be
the best way of getting before the courts a theory upon
which liability can be based.[31]

Probably the basic reason for failure by most com-
plainants in weather modification litigation has been
their inability to prove a causal relationship between
the cloud seeding activity and their harm. For example,
in a Pennsylvania case,[32] plaintiffs alleged that hail
suppression efforts had brought about a drought. They
proved that there had been seeding and that there was a
drought; but they could not establish any connection
between the two. It is not surprising that this should
be the case. Even scientists who use sophisticated
statistical analyses of long-term projects debate findings.[33] Proof of a causal connection in a single instance of seeding is obviously more difficult.

If liability claims are proven, defendants still can
prevail by proving an affirmative defense. The privilege
of public necessity is one such defense. Anglo-American
common law gives persons a right to protect the public
from an imminent disaster by performing acts which might
otherwise be tortious. For example, a firefighter may
pull down buildings to form a fire break to stop a con-
flagration.[34] So too, it might be argued, could a cloud
seeder bring about an innundation of forest lands to stop
a fire. Public necessity and other defenses diminish the
number of cases in which the judiciary would be able to
control weather modification efforts.

II. INFORMATIONAL CONTROL

Information about weather modification is freely
exchanged among scientists, cloud seeding companies, and
nations.[35] A professional organization, the Weather
Modification Association, holds semi-annual meetings
during which cloud seeders exchange information on techniques and activities. The organization also publishes a
journal.[36] Other meteorological publications, such as the
Bulletin of the American Meteorological Society and the
Journal of Applied Meteorology, contain articles relating

weather management technologies.[37] Numerous official
reports are also available.[38] Consequently, persons
knowledgeable in the field can keep current.

In spite of this cooperation and information exchange, much remains to be learned about the properties,
dynamics, and behavior of the atmosphere and about its
response to different seeding techniques. Additionally,
there are many persons interested in weather resources
management who are not well versed in the science and
technology. Withholding information from such persons,
or requiring information disclosure by people who propose
and carry out experimental or operational projects, has
impeded proper seeding operations.

A. Technological Expertise

Persons who seek to launch cloud seeding projects
in Australia usually have become aware of weather modification through reading of the activities of the Commonwealth Scientific and Industrial Research Organization
(CSIRO). This science agency of the Australian government has been successfully involved in weather modification research and development for over thirty years.
Although they share their expertise with state governments,[39] CSIRO scientists do not assist in private
projects.[40] Through informational control the government
has kept the private sector from performing cloud seeding.

B. Disclosure

The National Environmental Policy Act of 1969
directs that all agencies of the federal government shall
include in every recommendation or report on proposals
for legislation and other major Federal actions significantly affecting the quality of the human environment, a
detailed statement by the responsible official on the
environmental impacts and consequences of the proposed
action.[41] Federal projects, which include a large portion
of experimental projects in the United States,[42] must not
be conducted without complying with this advance disclosure requirement if they will have a significant environmental impact. Preparation of adequate impact statements
requires analysis of meteorological and hydrologic
records and consideration of the "natural and social
sciences and the environmental design arts in planning
and decisionmaking."[43] Public access to environmental
impact statements gives people a means of ascertaining
whether environmental considerations have been adequately
incorporated into the projects.

When there are laws and rules mandating that cloud
seeding records be kept and that reports be based upon
them, the public also has access to information about

weather resources management. The federal government in
Canada has a record keeping and reporting statute[44] which
is supplemented by administrative regulations.[45] Weather
modification cannot legally be practiced without public
and official knowledge. Adverse publicity can have a
very real impact upon an industry.[46]

III. ADMINISTRATIVE CONTROL

Weather modification activities are now regulated by
state administrative agencies in about half of the United
States.[47] Agencies, acting under statutory authority, use
a variety of administrative control techniques. Among
them are project registration, operational permits, and
professional licensing.

A. Project Registration

In Idaho persons doing cloud seeding must register
with the state Department of Agriculture.[48] Although the
department has no discretion to reject attempted registration of inappropriate seeding projects, it at least
has an official register of operations in the state.
The World Meteorological Organization (WMO) also has
a register of projects.[49] Member nations in the organization pass along to WMO information as to what projects
are being carried out in their jurisdictions. One of the
rather hesitant steps toward international legal control
over weather modification is the recommendation by
experts designated by member governments that the register be maintained by WMO and that members report the
required information needed for it.[50]

B. Operational Permits

Use of the power to issue operational permits is a
more effective form of administrative regulation.
Illinois has a law under which state officials have the
power to impose conditions upon persons who desire to
carry out weather modification operations in the state.[51]
The time and place of seeding, materials and amounts,
radar, kinds and numbers of personnel, target and control
areas, and other particulars of proposed operations are
reviewed by the regulators. They can shape permits to
fit their perception of the public interest as well as
that of the project sponsors.
Interim administrative modification of permits
allows for adjustments required by unforeseen or changed
circumstances. The Council of State Governments' recommended weather control law delegates to administrators
such power.[52] There are also provisions for emergencies
when permits can be suspended, for revocation and

refusals to renew permits and for hearings to project the
rights of permitees.[53] In order for these requirements
to be effective it is necessary to have competent administrative personnel who monitor projects so they can
know when administrative intervention is needed.[54]

C. Professional Licensing

People selling their services as cloud seeders
should be both competent and honest. The Weather Modification Association has a system for certification of
weather modification managers and operators. They must
demonstrate competency to be certified.[55] Unfortunately,
some cloud seeders are not members of the Association.
It is necessary, therefore, for governments wishing to
check on the qualifications of seeders to set up a
licensing system. California, as an example, requires
minimum levels of educational and practical experience
as a prerequisite to being licensed.[56]

In addition to competency, there is a need for integrity by weather modifiers. Literature is full of
stories of swindling "rainmakers," boastful "experts,"
and athletic "rain dancers."[57] Arizona, in order to
protect the public from persons who promise much and
deliver somewhat less, requires that persons seeking
authority to modify the clouds file with the regulatory
agency copies of their advertising.[58] Revelation of
dishonesty can be a step in the direction of its prevention.

IV. CONTRACTUAL CONTROL

Mr. Justice Holmes once remarked that "men must turn
square corners when they deal with the government."[59] By
requiring people who use government monies to meet conditions imposed by contract, officials can exercise very
extensive control over publicly funded weather resource
management.[60] Three types of laws relate to such contractual control: authorization laws, appropriations
statutes, and procurement laws and regulations.

A. Authorizations Laws

Under the Anglo-American system of jurisprudence,
government spending programs cannot be undertaken without
prior legislative approval. Such authorization legislation in some jurisdictions takes the form of giving power
to agencies which are already in existence to carry out
cloud seeding. Thus in New York there is a law which
authorizes incorporated municipalities to spend money on
weather modification;[61] in California the law stipulates
that any agency empowered to develop water resources can

seed clouds;[62] and a 1980 Illinois law grants the state
water survey authority to evaluate cloud seeding.[63]

In the Great Plains states, statutes authorize the
creation of special weather modification districts which
may levy and collect taxes and then spend their funds on
weather resources management.[64] These authorization laws
stipulate procedures for ceration of the districts, outline procedures for them to follow, and provide means for
their dissolution. In North Dakota, for example, a
petition process has been used to set up and dissolve
weather modification authorities.[65]

B. Appropriation Statutes

In addition to authorization legislation, it is
necessary that expenditure of governmental funds be
carried out in accordance with appropriation of monies
earmarked for the purpose for which they are used. When
appropriations are not forthcoming, government supported
programs must shut down. For example, in South Dakota,
which was the first state to have a statewide weather
modification program, failure by the legislature to
continue funding killed the program.[66] The appropriations
power is a double-edged sword: the public can use it to
encourage cloud seeding by paying the bill, or can use it
to halt government funded weather resources management.

C. Procurement Laws and Regulations

In addition to the sort of fiscal arrangements found
in most contracts, government contracts contain clauses
inserted because of the requirements of procurement
legislation. Bidders also must comply with negotiated
terms of the agreement. The manner of cloud seeding can
thereby be controlled. Accordingly, federal agencies,
which are the major source of research and development
funds, have been able to control weather modification
experimentation in the United States. They use the power
of the purse and of contract to get their way.[67]

V. GOVERNMENTAL OPERATIONS

At one time the Utah cloud seeding law permitted
only the Utah Division of Water Resources to perform
atmospheric water resource development in the state.[68]
In the Australian state of Victoria, seeding permits are
given only to governmental entities.[69] In communist and
many socialist countries cloud seeding is a government
monopoly.[70] At least in theory, government operation of
atmospheric alteration programs is a complete form of
public control over them.

VI. PROHIBITION OF WEATHER MODIFICATION ACTIVITIES

A. Partial Ban

One of the most intrusive forms of control over atmospheric management is a partial ban of cloud seeding activities. The ban could be partial in that it bars seeding unless some condition is met. The Illinois law provides that there shall be no cloud seeding in the state unless it is done under the authority of a permit and carried out under the supervision of a licensed cloud seeder. [71] Such conditional bans form the basis for administrative controls.

Another type of partial ban is a prohibition of a particular kind of activity. Minnesota, for example, bans delivery of cloud seeding materials from ground based generators.[72] Pennsylvania disallows seeding for the purpose of suppressing lightning.[73]

B. Complete Ban

The most intrusive type of regulation of atmospheric alteration is a complete ban. Maryland is the only jurisdiction which has enacted such a law. The ban there, however, is no longer in effect.[74]

VII. SUMMARY AND CONCLUSION

Intentional weather modification is partially attained by treating the atmosphere with chemicals. Government institutions at all levels and within each branch control atmospheric resources management because the atmospheric environment deeply affects the quality of life. Various legal options available for public control of atmospheric management have been considered in this article.

Incidental control includes regulation of delivery of seeding materials and allocation of atmospheric and ground water rights. Rules governing carriage on board aircraft of inflammable and other hazardous materials, flight time, flight patterns, access to ground facilities and activities, and the use of water rights have proved effective means of control. Judicial control through the use of civil liability claims has been rendered ineffective by plaintiff's inability to prove a casual relationship, and by defendant's ability to prove the affirmative defense of public necessity.

Informational control of technological expertise curtails improper seeding operations, and the National Environmental Policy Act of 1969 requirement of advance disclosure by a responsible official concerning environmental impact provides public knowledge of seeding operations. Adverse publicity insures incentives for self regulation of the cloud seeding industry.

Administrative agencies use a variety of control techniques including project registration, operational permits and professional licensing. State and national requirements to register projects within the respective jurisdictions provide observation of activities. Member nations of the WMO pass along this information to maintain international coordination of weather modification. Operational permits impose conditions on the time, place, and manner of seeding, while governmental licensing encourages competent and honest weather modifiers.

Governments exert control over seeding programs through authorization by legislative approval and evaluation of weather resource management districts. These districts secure control through negotiated terms of the contract and through expenditure of governmentally appropriated funds. Some governments grant permits only to governmental entities or prohibit weather modification activities. Although no complete ban is in effect now, governmentally imposed conditions provide one of the most intrusive forms of control over atmospheric management.

Many routes have been taken for public control of atmospheric management. Control strategy usually relies upon a mix of options. It is important that there be careful consideration of control devices so that a proper combination of them will protect against indiscriminate weather modification programs, and secure an atmospheric environment favorably affecting the quality of life.

NOTES

1. Weather Modification Advisory Board, U.S. Dep't of Commerce, The Management of Weather Resources 5 (1978) (Report to the Sec'y of Comm.). See also A. Dennis, Weather Modification by Cloud Seeding (1980); L. Battan, Harvesting the Clouds: Advances in Weather Modification (1969); B. Mason, Clouds, Rain and Rainmaking (2nd ed. 1975).

2. See M. Glantz, H. van Loon & E. Armstrong, Multidisciplinary Research Related to the Atmospheric Sciences (1978); W. Sewell Modifying the Weather: A Social Assessment (1973); W. Sewell, Human Dimensions of Weather Modification (1966).

3. See Davis, "Weather Modification Law Developments," 27 Okla. L. Rev. 409, 412-15 (1974).

4. Weather Modification Control Act, Act No. 78, June 12, 1972 (S. Afr.).

5. E.g., An Act Respecting Artificial Inducement of Rain, Bill 6, March 11, 1970 (Que.).

6. E.g., Rain-making Control Act, Act No. 7637, Dec. 19, 1967 (Vict.).

7. 15 U.S.C. § 330 (Supp. 1980).

8. E.g., 15 C.F.R. §§ 908.1-.21 (1980); Rain-making Regulations, 1968, Statutory Rules 2237/68 (Vict.).

9. See, e.g., Pa. ex rel. Township of Ayr v. Fulk, No. 53 (C.P. Fulton County, Pa., Feb. 28, 1968).

10. Davis, "State Regulation of Weather Modification," 12 Ariz. L. Rev. 35 (1970). See also Davis, "Weather Modification Interstate Legal Issues," 15 Idaho L. Rev. 555 (1979).

11. Such efforts at national control have not been very successful in the United States. See Johnson, "Federal Organization for Control of Weather Modification," 10 Nat. Resources J. 222, 237-52 (1970). See also Taubenfeld, "Weather Modification and Control: Some International Legal Implications," 55 Calif. L. Rev. 493 (1967). Legal control over use of weather modification as a weapons system is discussed in Davis, "Weather Warfare: Law and Policy," 14 Ariz. L. Rev. 659 (1972). Proposed international rules respecting weather resources management are noted in Davis, "WMO/UNEP Weather Modification International Law Proposals," 12 J. Weather Modif. 127 (1980).

12. Davis, supra note 3 at 415. See also Davis, "State Regulation of Weather Modification," 12 Ariz. L. Rev. 35, 55-63 (1970).

13. 49 C.F.R. §§ 107.1, -.373, .751-.90 (1980).

14. Exemptions are given under the procedures set forth in 49 C.F.R. § 107.113 (1980), and standardized in F.A.A. Weather Control Exemption, 49 C.F.R. 175.10(12) (1980). They are processed by the Exemption Branch of

the Office of Hazardous Materials Regulation.

15. Division of Radiophysics, Commonwealth Scientific and Industrial Research Organization, Fourth Course of Instruction in Cloud-Seeding Techniques 26 (1968).

16. Interview with John Odegard, Department of Aviation, University of North Dakota (Oct. 30, 1980).

17. Interview with Thomas Henderson, President of Atmospheric Inc., Kenya Tea Growers Association, Department of Civil Aviation (April 1975); interview with Alex Alusa, Meterologist, Department of Agriculture (Kenya).

18. Sterns, "Weather Modification Activities and National Forest Land Use Permits," in Hail Suppression: Society and Environment 241 (B. Garhar ed. 1977) [hereinafter cited as Farhar].

19. 16 U.S.C. §§ 1131-36 (1976).

20. Sterns, "Weather Modification and Collection of Hydrometeorological Data in Wilderness Areas," in Farhar, supra note 18 at 238.

21. Davis, "Legal Response to Environmental Concerns about Weather Modification," 14 J. Applied Meteorology 681 (1975).

22. In Slutsky v. City of New York, 197 Misc. 730, 731, 97 N.Y.S.2d 238, 239 (1950), a trial court judge stated that property owners "clearly have no vested property rights in the clouds or the moisture therein." In Southwest Weather Research, Inc. v. Duncan, 319 S.W.2d 940, 945 (Tex. Civ. App. 1958), however, an intermediate appellate court judge said that the landowner has a right to "such precipitation as Nature deigns to bestow . . . to such rainfall as may come from clouds over his own property that Nature, in her caprice, may provide." Yet another trial judge has declared that "every landowner has a property right in the clouds and the water in them," but that right is subject to "weather modification undertaken under governmental authority." Pennsylvania Natural Weather Ass'n. v. Blue Ridge Weather Modification Ass'n. 44 Pa. D. & C. 2d 749, 759-60 (C.P. Fulton County, Pa., 1968).

23. Mont. Const. art. IX, § 3(3).

24. E.g., La. Rev. Stat. Ann. § 37:2201 (West 1974); Neb. Rev. Stat. § 2-2401 (1) (1977); N.M. Stat. Ann. § 75-3-3 (1978); S.D. Comp. Laws Ann. § 46-3A-2 (Supp. 1980).

25. 1 R. Clark, Water and Water Rights § 39.3 (1967).

26. Colo. Rev. Stat. § 36-20-103 (1973); Colorado Legislative Council, Controlling Weather Modification Activities (Research Publication 147) 10 (1977).

27. 1980 7c Utah Code Ann. § 73-15-4 (Supp. 1979); R. Dewsnup & D. Densen, Legal Aspects of Weather Modification in Utah 72-72 (1977) (Report to Utah Div. Water Resources).

28. N.D. Cent. Code § 2-07-01 (1975).

29. Southwest Weather Research, Inc. v. Rounsaville, 320 S.W.2d 211, and Southwest Weather Research, Inc. v. Duncan, 319 S.W.2d 940 (Tex. Civ. App. 1958), both aff'd sub nom. Southwest Weather Research, Inc. v. Hones, 160 Tex. 104, 327 S.W.2d 417 (1959).

30. Reinbold v. Sumner Farmers, Inc. and Irving P. Krick, Inc., No. 2734-C (Cir. Ct., Tuscola County, Mich., 1974); see Davis & St. Amand, "Proof of Legal Causation in Weather Modification Litigation: Reinbold v. Sumner Farmers, Inc. and Irving P. Krick, Inc.," 7 J. Weather Modif. 127 (1975).

31. See, e.g., Adams v. California, Civil No. 10112 (Sup. Ct., Sutter County, Cal., 1964); Mann, "The Yuba City Flood: A Case Study of Weather Modification Litigation," 49 Bull. Am. Meteorological Soc'y 690 (1968).

32. Pennsylvania Nat. Weather Ass'n. v. Blue Ridge Weather Modif. Ass'n., 44 Pa. D. & C. 2d 749 (C.P. Fulton County, Pa., 1968).

33. See A. Dennis, supra note 1, §§ 6.1-6.5. A defendant who acts to prevent a threatening injury from some force of nature, or some other independent cause not connected with the threat, is said to be acting under necessity.

34. W. Prosser, Law of Torts 124-27 (4th ed. 1971).

35. J. Hobbs, Applied Climatology § 8.3 (1980).

36. The Journal of Weather Modification, published by the Weather Modification Association, P.O. Box 8116, Fresno, California 93747. The association has published a short explanation in lay terms of the processes involved in cloud seeding. Weather Modification: Some Facts About Seeding Clouds (1977). Copies can be obtained from the Association.

37. The bulletin covers meteorology and climatology generally. The journal deals with the application of principles, including cloud physics and cloud seeding. Both are published by the American Meteorological Society 45 Beacon Street, Boston, Massachusetts.

38. E.g., the series of reports by the World Meteorological Organization on its weather modification project, PEP. Through May 1980 there have been twenty reports in the series. Report No. 13, WMO Training Workshop on Weather Modification for Meteorologists: Lecture Notes (1979), is in essence a handbook on cloud seeding science and technology.

39. See Smith, "Cloud Seeding in Australia," in W. Hess, Weather and Climate Modification 444 (1974).

40. See Davis, "The Law of Precipitation Enhancement in Victoria," 7 Land & Water L. Rev. 1. 6-9 (1972).

41. 42 U.S.C. § 4332 (2)(C) (1976).

42. For a number of years a federal Interdepartmental Committee on Atmospheric Sciences made annual

reports on expenditures of national agencies for weather alteration research and development, and since 1972 federal agencies report their activities to the Department of Commerce. See M. Charak, Weather Modification Reporting Program, 1973-78 (1979), which lists, among others, all federal projects.

43. 42 U.S.C. § 4332 (2)(A) (1976).

44. Weather Modification Information Act, 1971, ch. 59 (Can.).

45. See Canada: Weather Modification Information Act and Regulation Administrative Guidelines (1974) (government publication).

46. See Gellhorn, "Adverse Publicity by Administrative Agencies," 86 Harv. L. Rev. 1380 (1973).

47. Davis, supra note 3, at 415; see also Davis, "State Regulation of Weather Modification," 12 Ariz. L. Rev. 35, 55-63 (1970).

48. Idaho Code Ann. §§ 22-3201, 3202 (1977).

49. World Meteorological Organization, Register of National Weather Modification Projects (1979).

50. Davis, "WMO/UNEP Weather Modification International Law Proposals," 12 J. Weather Modif. 127, 129 (1980).

51. Ill. Stat. Ann. ch. 111 § 7391 (d) (1978). See Ackerman, Changnon & Davis, "The New Weather Modification Law for Illinois," 55 Bull. Am. Meteorological Soc'y 743 (1974).

52. 1978 Suggested State Legislation, Weather Modification Control Act, § 409 at 9, 20 (Council of State Governments 1977).

53. Id. § 410.

54. Davis, supra note 3, at 415. There has been effective monitoring in, for example, Illinois, North Dakota, South Dakota, Texas, and Utah. Those states have been given resources necessary to carry out monitoring.

55. The Association's qualifications and procedures for certification are set forth as 12 J. Weather Modif. 142-44 (1980).

56. Cal. Water Code § 408.5 (Supp. 1981).

57. See D. Halacy, The Weather Changes (1968).

58. Ariz. Rev. Stat. Ann. § 45-2405 B (Supp. 1980).

59. Rock Island, A. & L. R.R. v. United States, 254 U.S. 141, 143 (1920).

60. R. Davis, The Legal Implications of Atmospheric Water Resources Development and Management § 13 (1968).

61. N.Y. Gen. Munic. Law § 119 (o) (McKinney Supp. 1980).

62. Cal. Gov't Code § 53063 (West 1966).

63. Ill. H.B. 2841 (1980) (final version).

64. S. Changnon, R. Davis, B. Farhar, J. Haas, J. Ivens, M. Jones, D. Klein, D. Mann, G. Morgan, S. Sonka, E. Swanson, C. Taylor & J. van Blockland, Hail Suppression: Impacts and Issues 146-48 (1977).

65. N.D. Cent. Code § 2-07-06.5 (1975).

66. See Donnan, Pellot, Leblang & Ritter, "The Rise and Fall of the South Dakota Weather Modification Program," 8 J. Weather Modif. 2 (1976).

67. Davis, "State Regulation of Weather Modification" 12 Ariz. L. Rev. 35, 60-62 (1970).

68. Utah Code Ann. § 73-15-1 (Supp. 1973). The law provided that the "State of Utah . . . shall be the only entity . . . that shall have authority to sponsor and develop cloud seeding research or implementation projects to alter precipitation or cloud forms within the State of Utah."

69. Davis, "The Law of Precipitation Enhancement in Victoria," 7 Land & Water L. Rev. 1, 10-11 (1972).

70. See World Meteorological Organization, Register of National Weather Modification Projects (1979).

71. Ill. State. Ann. ch. 111, § 7310 (1978).

72. Minn. Stat. § 42.09 (6) (Supp. 1980).

73. Pa. Stat. Ann. tit. 3, § 1115 (Supp. 1980).

74. Md. Code Ann. art 66C, § 110A (1967).

14
Global Climate Change and International Law and Institutions

Ved P. Nanda

I. THE PROBLEM

Although climatologists have identified numerous causes of variations in climate, they still lack the necessary information and tools to forecast accurately such variations or to account for severe climatic variations such as the ones that occurred in the early 1970's in different parts of the world. There is, however, widespread belief that human activities are interfering with the earth's atmosphere and are inducing global climatic changes.

Major anthropogenic influences on climate include man's contribution of carbon dioxide and particulate matter into the atmosphere.[1] The increasing use of fossil fuels (coal, oil and natural gas) and perhaps deforestation, too, should be held responsible for the steady rise of carbon dioxide in the atmosphere since the industrial revolution, now constituting about .0336 percent of the atmosphere. Climatologists predict that if the use of global fossil fuels continues to rise at 2.5 percent per year -- the average growth rate between 1973 to 1979 -- it will result in a 30 to 50 percent higher concentration of carbon dioxide by the year 2000 than it was in 1900 and the concentration will again double by the middle of the next century.

Since atmospheric carbon dioxide absorbs part of the infrared radiation from the earth and lower atmosphere, it acts like the glass in a greenhouse to retain radiant energy, resulting in the warming of the lower atmosphere and the earth's surface, the so-called "greenhouse effect." A doubling of the present amount of CO_2 is likely to result in average global warming between $1.5°$ centigrade and $4.5°$ centigrade. This increase will be magnified at higher latitudes, especially the north polar region.

This "greenhouse effect" could bring about major alterations of oceanic movements and shifts in rainfall, temperature and agricultural patterns, thus seriously affecting world food production and population settlements, and modifying social, economic and political arrangements. However, in view of the imperfect nature of world climate modeling and the many variables likely to affect the outcome (including the capacity of existing reservoirs in the global system to absorb carbon dioxide), the timing and magnitude are uncertain at present.

It should be noted that although no accurate data exist regarding the net effect of deforestation on the concentration of CO_2, it is widely acknowledged that by modifying the exchange of carbon dioxide among the land, the biota and the atmosphere, deforestation could have serious implications for the global carbon cycle.[2] The destruction of forests results in the release of CO_2 from the biota which no longer acts to absorb CO_2, but instead becomes its source. In contrast with the rise of CO_2 from the use of fossil fuels, which is mainly caused by industrialized states, many developing countries are primarily responsible for the rise in the concentration of carbon dioxide due to deforestation.

Human activities might also lead to a reduction in ozone levels and thereby modify the climate.[3] While studies are presently being conducted on possible effects of ozone depletion on climate, it is generally acknowledged that a reduction and/or redistribution of ozone could alter the distribution of temperature since ozone has a significant role in determining the radiative balance of the atmosphere, especially the stratosphere. Because ozone absorbs solar radiation, a reduction in stratospheric ozone could result in more solar radiation reaching the ground.

Chlorofluorocarbons (CFC's) cause the reduction of ozone levels when they combine with molecules of ozone in the stratosphere. Also, the introduction of aerosols into the stratosphere may disturb the radiative balance. Preliminary studies have shown that there is a "greenhouse" warming of the lower atmosphere by fluorocarbons, carbon tetrachloride and other trace gases. When the warming effects of these gases is added to the warming by CO_2, the global problem of CO_2 pollution is exacerbated.

More recently, a study has provided substantial evidence of a significant increase in global temperature -- .4°C increase since 1900 -- having already occurred. The scientific community is giving the subject considerable attention. To illustrate, the 1979 World Climate Conference in Geneva has "flashed some ominous signals about the number of disturbing trends relating to the world climate which could have disastrous effects on the biosphere and on humanity."[4]

In recognition of the seriousness of the situation, the Eighth World Meteorological Congress in 1979 established the World Climate Programme, one of whose four major components is its Impact Studies Program.[5] The first phase of the program, to last from 1980 to 1983, includes efforts to: (1) reduce the vulnerability of food systems to climate change, (2) anticipate the impact of climate change caused by human activity, (3) improve the size of climate impact studies, and (4) identify human activities that are most sensitive to climate. However, there is no consensus as to the most desirable responses to the challenges posed by the CO_2-induced temperature increases.

As the following discussion will demonstrate, the existing international legal mechanisms are inadequate to provide effective preventative or remedial measures. International environmental law is still in a nascent stage and it seems imperative that legal institutions, norms and procedures be strengthened and new ones fashioned to cope with the problem.

II. INTERNATIONAL ENVIRONMENTAL LAW

A. Overview

Although international environmental law still is in its infancy, there are some pertinent principles which provide guidelines for state conduct. For example, the Roman legal maxim sic utero tuo ut alienum non laedas (use your property in such a manner as not to injure that of another) provides the basis of many agreements related to the use of international rivers.

The Helsinki Conference of the International Law Association in 1966 adopted what it called a "key principle" in the management of international rivers and drainage basins. The principle as part of the Helsinki Rules, reads: "Each basin State is entitled, within its territory, to a reasonable and equitable share in the beneficial use of the water of an international drainage basin."[6] Under the principle of "equitable utilization", states are obligated to prevent future pollution of international drainage basins. Those who violate the preventive prescription are required to cease the wrongful conduct and compensate the injured co-basin state.

Similarly, the 1949 decision of the International Court of Justice in the Corfu Channel Case[7] provides a useful antecedent for the principle subsequently incorporated into the 1972 Declaration on the Human Environment that states are obligated "to ensure that activities within their jurisdiction or control do not cause damage to the environment of other States or of areas beyond the limits of national jurisdiction."[8]

In the Corfu Channel Case, a mine field in Albanian waters caused an explosion harming British vessels. The International Court of Justice held that Albania had an obligation to warn the British that there were mine fields in those waters. The Court specifically stated that it is "every State's obligation not to allow knowingly its territory to be used for acts contrary to the rights of other States."[9]

Earlier, in an air pollution dispute between the United States and Canada which involved the operation of a smelter located in British Columbia which, because of its sulfur dioxide emissions, allegedly caused substantial damage to a number of farms in the State of Washington, the specially created tribunal concluded that:

> [U]nder the principles of international law, as well as of the law of the United States, no State has the right to use or permit the use of its territory in such a manner as to cause injury by fumes in or to the territory of another or the properties or persons therein, when the case is of serious consequence and the injury is established by clear and convincing evidence.
> . . . .
> Considering the circumstances of the case, the Tribunal holds that the Dominion of Canada is responsible in international law for the conduct of the Trail Smelter. Apart from the undertakings in the Convention, it is, therefore, the duty of the Government of the Dominion of Canada to see to it that this conduct should be in conformity with the obligation of the Dominion under international law. . . .[10]

The Tribunal implemented its decision by imposing a detailed regime of controls over the emission of sulfur dioxide fumes from the Smelter. It should be noted, however, that Canada had specifically assumed international liability for damage caused to the United States from activities within Canada and both countries had agreed to let a special binational tribunal "arbitrate" the amount of damages. Thus, the case is unique and perhaps of questionable validity as a precedent.

The principle of State responsibility for transboundary environmental damage has found expression in a number of contemporary diplomatic cases, including the 1954 Japanese Fisherman Case (U.S. responsibility for nuclear tests),[11] the 1957 Lake Lanoux Arbitration French-Spanish river pollution dispute),[12] the 1958 Pacific Tests Case (U.S. nuclear tests),[13] the 1961 Ciudad Juarez Case (U.S. responsibility for river pollution),[14] and the 1973 International Court of Justice

decision in Nuclear Tests Case (France's responsibility
for nuclear testing in the South Pacific).[15] The pre-
cedential value of these cases, however, is uncertain,
both because of their limited context (nuclear testing
or river pollution), and since the results in each case
may be interpreted as a diplomatic modus vivendi rather
than a response to developing customary international
law.[16]

It should come as no surprise that, notwithstanding
the need for international cooperative measures to control transboundary environmental damage caused by state
activities in the course of industrialization and exploitation, the concept of "global management" of the
environment has gained significance only during the last
few decades. Several factors were responsible for this
development, including the accelerated exploitation of
natural resources in much of the world; enhancement of
the ecological concerns as a consequence of an awareness
of the havoc that the "second industrial revolution" was
wreaking on the environment; the recognition and understanding that national environmental protection remedies
alone were ill-equipped to cope with transnational pollution, further confirmed by a number of well-publicized
disasters such as the wrecks of the Torry Canyon and the
Argo Merchant; and the availability of several international organizations such as the United Nations and
the European Economic Community as suitable fora from
which to address the crucial international environmental
concerns.

By the late 1960's, these factors catalyzed a pro-
liferation of bilateral, regional and multilateral conventions on such diverse issues as oil pollution on the
high seas, nuclear transportation and waste disposal,
river pollution, protection of endangered species, acid
rain, weather modification, and transboundary air pollution. To illustrate, by the early 1970's, there were
over twenty institutional arrangements and over 300
bilateral and multilateral conventions covering the
rivers of the world. The second large area of international agreements is in the management of oil pollution on the high seas. By 1974, there were over 30
multilateral conventions and numerous protocols governing the transport of oil, yet, despite these advances,
it was clear by the early 1970's that environmental
efforts were scattered, overlapping, and inadequate to
meet the global environmental challenge.

B. Recent Developments

In 1972, the United Nations responded to the need
for coordination by sponsoring the U.N. Conference on
the Human Environment, held in Stockholm. The Stockholm
conference was the most successful international meeting
on the environment to date, and resulted in the formulation and approval of principles and recommendations to
serve as guidelines for the future conduct of states in
environmental and developmental matters, both nationally
and internationally. It established the framework for
the creation of the United Nations Environment Programme
(UNEP), an organization envisioned to coordinate the
comprehensive goals of global environmental assessment
and management. Despite this grand plan toward consoli-
dation, however, ten years after UNEP's creation, the
task of environmental management is still being attempted by a diverse group of universal, regional,
bilateral and non-governmental organizations.

Any assessment of the institutional progress and
direction of the present environmental "system" will
have to take into account the activities of the United
Nations, including those of UNEP, the International Law
Commission, regional commissions of the United Nations,
U.N. specialized agencies, the inter- and non-governmental organizations, and regional organizations. Only
selected developments will be highlighted here.

Environmental assessment and environmental management constitute the primary areas of UNEP activity.[17]
The environmental assessment activities of UNEP, which
include environmental monitoring, research, evaluation
and review, and information exchange, are primarily
undertaken by the Earthwatch Program which has several
major components including the Global Environmental
Monitoring System (GEMS) and the International Referral
System for Sources of Environmental Information
(INFOTERRA). GEMS encourages and coordinates the
acquisition, analysis, storage and dissemination of data
by governments and international organizations. Projects under the GEMS Program include those related to
resource monitoring; climate-related monitoring; health-
related monitoring, which includes monitoring air
quality, global water quality and food; long-range
transport of pollutants; and ocean monitoring. The
INFOTERRA Program performs the complimentary function of
providing a referral network for the exchange of available environmental information. The INFOTERRA network
has continued to expand -- by the end of 1980, 76 countries had registered information sources with the
INFOTERRA Directory, the number of registered sources
stood at 8,400, and the number of states participating
in the Program had reached 112.

Recent UNEP activities related to environmental management have included the development of frameworks for the preparation of environmental impact assessment statements and for the application of cost-benefit analysis to environmental protection measures. A significant recent development was the signature by nine multilateral development financing institutions in February 1980 at the United Nations Development Program headquarters in New York of a declaration of principles for incorporating environmental considerations into development policies, programs and projects. UNEP has enjoyed its greatest management success in the sponsorship of several regional conferences on the environment, such as the regional conference for the Mediterranean, which adopted a convention and two protocols (in force since February 12, 1978 and ratified by sixteen Mediterranean States and the European Economic Community as of March 1, 1981). Three other regional conferences sponsored by UNEP are on the Red Sea, the Kuwaiti Regional Sea and the West and Central African region.

Aside from the Regional Seas program, UNEP's most significant environmental management work has been in the area of "shared natural resources." In response to the United Nations General Assembly Resolution 3129 of 1973, UNEP established a working group of experts to prepare draft principles for the guidance of states in the conservation and harmonious exploitation of natural resources which they share in common. A set of draft principles was presented by the group in 1978. Subsequently, the General Assembly at its 34th session requested all states to use the principles as guidelines in the formulation of bilateral or multilateral conventions regarding natural resources shared by two or more states.

More recently, a team of experts in environmental law which met under UNEP auspices in Montevideo in October-November 1981 concluded that UNEP should give priority to three areas in developing guidelines, principles or agreements: (1) marine pollution from land-based sources, (2) protection of the stratospheric ozone layer, and (3) transport, handling and disposal of toxic and dangerous wastes.

One of the two revised goals for UNEP for 1982 is to seek agreement on the "principles which should guide States in their relations with each other in respect of shared natural resources, the problems of liability and compensation for pollution and environmental damage, weather modification and risks to the ozone layer." Thus, special attention is being given to issues related to climate change.

In addition to UNEP, the World Meteorological Organ-

ization (WMO) is the primary U.N. agency responsible
for climatic research.[18] WMO has established a Global
Atmospheric Research Program (GARP) which has been
studying the effect of CO_2 on climate. WMO's World
Weather Watch is composed of three parts -- (1) the
global observing system, (2) the global data processing
system, and (3) the global telecommunications system.
Since 1968 it has been active in meteorological research.
WMO also maintains a laboratory for the calibration of
instruments used to monitor CO_2 on a global scale. It
has sponsored many workshops on CO_2 and more recently in
1979 it arranged the World Climate Conference which
addressed questions pertaining to CO_2-induced climatic
change.

The noteworthy accomplishments of the Economic
Commission for Europe[19] include the Convention on Long-
Range Transboundary Air Pollution (ECE Convention),
which entered into force in November 1979, and the adoption of a Declaration of Policy on Prevention and Control of Water Pollution, in April 1980.

III. INTERNATIONAL INSTITUTIONS AND NORMS RELATED
      TO CLIMATE CHANGE

A. Overview

The closest analogy to the management of anthropogenic influences on climate is transboundary air
pollution, especially in the context of acid rain.[20] In
the recent past, several regional and bilateral agreements and national measures have been taken to prevent
such pollution and to provide remedial measures.

In addition, UNEP has established several programs
to compile information registries so that governments
may become aware of the developing treaties and protocols relating to environmental management. UNEP has
also adopted a three-pronged approach to encourage the
growth of environmental law administration abilities in
developing countries by promoting national environmental law, stimulating environmental law education and
research, and promoting wider acceptance and implementation of international environmental agreements.

The 1979 ECE Convention[21] which was hailed by its
chairman as "a breakthrough in the international environmental law," obligates contracting parties (35
countries including the United States, Canada and most
of the East and West European states have signed it) to
consult on request on activities affecting or posing a
"significant risk" of long-range transboundary air pollution. It also provides for information exchange,
continued monitoring of pollutants and rainfall, and
collaborative research, with the objective of mitigating

sulfur dioxide (SO_2) emissions. Critics, however, find the Convention inadequate as it contains no abatement provisions, enforcement mechanisms, numerical goals, limits or timetables, although parties have agreed to adopt "the best available technology economically feasible," they are required to act "without undue delay," and have undertaken to "endeavor to limit and, as far as possible, gradually reduce and prevent air pollution, including long-range transboundary air pollution." Subsequently, on July 15, 1980, the European Community adopted its SO_2 Directive, which implements the Convention but also falls short of providing effective measures to prevent SO_2 emissions.

In 1976, the United States, France and the United Kingdom entered into an agreement on monitoring of the stratosphere, under which the parties are obligated to collect, exchange, and analyze information on the stratosphere, and to integrate their activities with those of the WMO and UNEP.

In contrast, the Nordic Convention on the Protection of the Environment and the United States-Canadian International Joint Commission's Michigan-Ontario Air Pollution Board provide legal frameworks for abatement as well as compensatory relief for persons injured by permitting a right of access to domestic courts or administrative agencies, and by providing for the establishment of impartial fact-finding commissions to coordinate the implementation of air pollution control programs. U.S.-Canada negotiations are continuing on the acid rain problem, which has become a grave issue in both countries.

Although abatement provisions and enforcement mechanisms in these bilateral and regional agreements are deficient, some positive steps are discernible. These include provisions which have led to shared information, coordinated research and continued monitoring of pollutants -- perhaps a useful model for developing appropriate strategies in the management of CO_2 accumulations.

Several countries, including the United States, Canada and West Germany, have undertaken impressive research programs on the effects of acid deposition and the development of new pollution control technologies. Their recent efforts at the reduction of their SO_2 emissions by efficiently employing sulfur control strategies show promising signs.

B. Preventive and Adaptive Strategies to Manage CO_2 Pollution

1. Fossil Fuels   The first important step is the gathering of the necessary data by scientific studies as

to which fossil fuels contribute how much to the build-up of carbon dioxide, who the major contributing states are, what the projected impacts of such build-ups will be in the future, the possible role of private industry and the public sector in ameliorating the situation, and what options are available in either gradually switching to non-fossil fuels or adapting to the build-up of CO_2 in the atmosphere.

The next step would be to explore international, regional, bilateral, and national measures to combat the CO_2 build-up. For example, could there be international, regional or bilateral agreements on ambient CO_2 standards? The obvious conflict between environment and development,[22] a precursor of which was evident at the 1972 Stockholm Conference, is difficult to avoid. Consequently, the political decision has to be faced as to who has the right to contribute what amount of carbon dioxide to the atmosphere. However, it seems essential that the major participants in monitoring and evaluating scientific data, collecting and exchanging information, and coordinating national and international programs, such as UNEP and WMO, the EEC and the OECD, and the International Council of Scientific Unions along with other inter- and non-governmental organizations, assume the responsibility for evaluating the various policy choices nations and international organizations will have to face toward the goals of preventing and remedying the situation.

2. <u>Deforestation</u> Again, the first step will be to gather the necessary data regarding the contribution of deforestation to the CO_2 accumulations. However, since the main contributors to this problem are the developing countries, the pertinent fora for discussion and action on this subject are likely to be UNEP, the U.N. Development Program, and the Food and Agricultural Organization. There is definitely a need for a coordinated international program on the conservation and wise utilization of tropical forests. UNEP has already undertaken preliminary discussions on the subject. Also regional initiatives, such as the 1978 Treaty for Amazonian Cooperation,[23] offer promising prospects.

C. <u>Strategies to Manage Chlorofluorocarbons</u>

Regulatory actions to prevent the pollution of the ozone layer from CFC's have been undertaken by the European Economic Community, several European countries including Sweden and West Germany, and the United States and Canada. To illustrate, in December 1979, the environment ministers of the European Economic Community adopted a proposal to reduce CFC's in aerosol sprays by

30 percent of 1976 levels over a two-year period, from
December 1979 to December 31, 1981.[24] Also, UNEP's International Scientific Committee had warned in its 1979
Paris session that aersol propellants, such as hydrofluorocarbons, could destroy 15 percent of the ozone
layer within a hundred years should present levels be
maintained.[25] West Germany, Sweden, Canada, and the
United States have taken certain measures to reduce
aerosol use of CFC's. UNEP and the OECD have also
undertaken studies on the potential effects of CFC's.

IV. CONCLUSION

The need is apparent to undertake international,
regional, bilateral and national actions to manage CO_2
accumulations. It does not seem likely that an international convention setting CO_2 emission standards,
establishing fact-finding commissions, coordinating
research efforts, providing for public education measures, and mandating the reduction of atmospheric CO_2
levels is a likely prospect in the near future. The
issue is highly political and in the existing international setting, universal prescriptions on abatement
provisions and enforcement mechanisms are not feasible.
The answer now must lie in coordinating the activities
of the primary actors -- scientists and policy makers,
states likely to be adversely affected by CO_2 increases,
and the many inter- and non-governmental organizations
already actively involved in discussions, studies and
evaluations. More work also needs to be done to
heighten public awareness of these global environmental
problems. It is envisaged that the global nature of the
problem notwithstanding, this process will lead to
regional and national measures and initiatives which
will provide the essential first steps for both preventive and adaptive management strategies.

The problem has already reached national and international agendas. It is imperative, however, that
scientific, legal, economic, and political interests and
pressures converge for the fashioning of necessary institutions and norms to influence both national and
international energy policies. In the final analysis,
we in the latter part of the twentieth century must have
the vision and the will to find creative solutions to
this formidable problem.

NOTES

This is an adapted version of a paper the author prepared for a special issue of UNESCO's Impact of Science on Society (1982).

    1. See generally Council on Environmental Quality, Global Energy Futures and the Carbon-Dioxide Problem, Jan. 1981; Robinson, "Effluents of Energy Production: Particulates," in National Academy of Sciences, Energy and Climate 61 (1977).

    2. See generally Bolin, "Change of Land Biota and their importance for the Carbon Cycle," 196 Science 613 (1977).

    3. See generally The Ozone Layer (A. K. Biswas ed. 1979).

    4. U.N. Dept. Public Information, Non-Governmental Organizations Section, World Environment, U.N. Doc. DPI/NGO/SA/80/6 (1980), at 1.

    5. See WMO, Outline Plan and Basis for the World Climate Programme 1980-1983, WMO No. 540 (1979). See also W. Kellogg & R. Schware, Climate Change and Society 125 (1981).

    6. Int'l Law Ass'n, Helsinki Rules on the Uses of the Waters of International Rivers art. IV (1967).

    7. [1949] I.C.J. 4.

    8. Principle 21 of the Declaration. See Report of the United Nations Conference on the Human Environment (Stockholm, 5-16 June 1972), 1 U.N. GAOR (21st plen. mtg.), U.N. Doc.A/CONF. 48/14/Rev. 1 (1972).

    9. [1949] I.C.J. 4, 22.

    10. 3 U.N. Rep. Int'l Arb. Awards 1911, 1925-61 (1941).

    11. For a report, see N.Y. Times, Jan. 5, 1955, at 6, col. 1. For discussion of the incident see Arnold, "Effects of the Recent Bomb Tests on Human Beings," 10 Bull. Atomic Scientists 347 (1954); Margolis, "The Hydrogen Bomb Experiments and International Law," 64 Yale L. J. 629, 637-39 (1955).

    12. See generally 53 Am. J. Int'l L. 156 (1959).

    13. See 4 M. Whiteman, Digest of International Law 78-96 (1965).

    14. See 6 M. Whiteman, Digest of International Law 256-59 (1968).

    15. See [1973] I.C.J. 99, 135; [1974] id. at 252,257.

    16. See, however, Nanda, "The Establishment of International Standards for Transnational Environmental Injury," 60 Iowa L. Rev. 1089, 1100-1101 (1975).

    17. UNEP, The Environment Programme: Programme Performance Report -- Report of the Executive Director, UNEP/GC. 9/5, February 25, 1981; UNEP, Environmental Management -- An Overview, UNEP Report No. 3 (1981).

18. For a summary report of its activities, <u>see</u> Environmental Law -- An In-Depth Review, UNEP Report No. 2, at 82-85 (1981).

19. For a summary report, see <u>id</u>. at 42-47.

20. <u>See generally</u> Acid Rain, Hearings before the Subcomm. on Oversight and Investigation of the House Comm. on Interstate and Foreign Commerce, 96th Cong., 2d Sess., Serial No. 96-150 (1980).

21. The Convention was Done Nov. 13, 1979, 1 U.N. ECE, Annex 1, U.N. Doc. E/ECE/HLM. 1/2 (1979), <u>reprinted in</u> 18 Int'l Legal Mat. 1442 (1979).

22. <u>See generally</u> Almeida, Beckerman, Sachs and Corea, "Environment and Development -- The Founex Report," Int'l Council., Jan. 1972.

23. Done at Brasilia July 3, 1978, <u>reprinted in</u> 17 Int'l Legal Materials 1045 (1978).

24. See [1980] 3 Int'l Envir. Rep. (BNA) 3.

25. See <u>id</u>.

Contributors

ROBERT S. CHEN is Resident Fellow, Climate Board,
National Academy of Sciences. He has been involved in
a variety of national and international climate-
related activities, including several Academy studies
of carbon dioxide, climate variability and change and
climate impacts, the Department of Energy's Research
planning efforts for CO_2/climate impact assessment, and
a number of international climate meetings in support
of the World Climate Program.

RAY JAY DAVIS, B.A., Idaho State University; J.D.,
Harvard Law School; LL.M., Columbia Law School, is a
Professor of Law, J. Reuben Clark Law School, Brigham
Young University, and a former president of the
Weather Modification Association.

EDWARD FRIEDMAN, Ph.D., Wayne State University, has
major career interest in remote sensing of the Earth's
surface and atmosphere with a special emphasis on
detection of climate parameters. During much of 1980
he was a visiting scientist at the National Center for
Atmospheric Research in Boulder, Colorado, during which
time his article was prepared.

WILLIAM W. KELLOGG, B.A.,Yale; Ph.D., U.C.L.A.; is Senior
Scientist at NCAR, and former Head, Planetary Sciences
Department, Rand Corporation; former President, Ameri-
can Meteorological Society; former Advisor to the
Secretary-General of the World Meteorological Organi-
zation on the World Climate Program.

PETER T. MOORE, B.S.F.S., Georgetown University (School
of Foreign Service); J.D., University of Denver, is
associated with the law firm of Greengard, Blackman
and Senter of Denver and is a former Managing Editor
of the Denver Journal of International Law and Policy.

240

VED P. NANDA, B.A., M.A., Panjab University (India);
LL.B., Delhi University (India); LL.M., Northwestern
University; Graduate Fellow, Yale Law School, is a
Professor of Law, and Director, International Legal
Studies Program, University of Denver College of Law.
He was a Distinguished Visiting Professor of Inter-
national Law, IIT, Chicago-Kent College of Law during
Summer-Fall 1981 and has served as consultant to the
U.S. Dept. of Energy.

JOHN S. PERRY is Executive Director, Climate Board,
National Research Council. A graduate of Queens Col-
lege, New York, he received his doctorate from the
University of Washington. He was seconded to the World
Meteorological Organization headquarters, Geneva, in
1976-1978 to support the Global Atmospheric Research
Program and since his return has remained actively
involved in international scientific activities.

WALTER ORR ROBERTS, M.A., Ph.D., Harvard University;
recipient of numerous honorary degrees, is President
Emeritus of the University Corporation for Atmospheric
Research; Vice President, American Philosophical
Society; Senior Fellow of the Aspen Institute; Profes-
sor of Astro-geophysics at the University of Colorado.

ARMIN ROSENCRANZ, A.B., Princeton University; J.D.,Ph.D.,
Stanford, is a lawyer, political scientist and writer.
Dr. Rosencranz is a former fellow of the National En-
dowment for the Humanities, studying the future of
environmental defense. During 1979-80 he directed the
International and Comparative Study of Transboundary
Air Pollution at the Environmental Law Institute,
Washington, D.C.

STEPHEN H. SCHNEIDER, Ph.D., Columbia University, is
currently head of the Visitors Program and Deputy
Director of the Advanced Study Program at the National
Center for Atmospheric Research. Dr. Schneider is
editor of <u>Climatic Change</u> and has served as White House
consultant in the Nixon and Carter administrations.
Also, he has served on numerous national and international committees on climate, food, water, energy
and environmental issues and is a frequent consultant
and participant in numerous UN-sponsored activities.

ROBERT SCHWARE, B.A., Political Science, University of
Colorado; M.A., University of Essex; Ph.D., London
School of Economics and Political Science, is a polit-
ical scientist with the National Center for Atmospheric
Research (NCAR) in Boulder, Colorado. Before joining

NCAR he was with the Food, Climate, and the World's Future Program of the Aspen Institute for Humanistic Studies.

GEORGE WILLIAM SHERK, B.A., M.A., Colorado State University; J.D., University of Denver College of Law, is a staff associate, National Conference of State Legislatures, and is former Attorney-Advisor, U.S. Department of Energy.

HOWARD J. TAUBENFELD, A.B., 1947; LL.B., 1948; Ph.D., 1958, Columbia, is a Professor of Law, Southern Methodist University School of Law. He has served as consultant, U.S. Department of State, National Science Foundation; Environmental Protection Agency; and National Center for Atmospheric Research.

EDITH BROWN WEISS, LL.B., Harvard Law School; Ph.D., University of California at Berkeley, is an Associate Professor of Law, Georgetown University Law Center. She is Associate Editor of Climatic Change; Member of U.S. National Weather Modification Advisory Board; Member of National Academy of Sciences Panel on Intergovernmental Climate Programs, and was Consultant to United Nations Environment Programme, 1975-78.

THOMAS W. WILSON, Jr., is a full-time writer. Formerly he was Director of the Program on Environment and the Quality of Life at the Aspen Institute of Humanistic Studies, and was Political Adviser, U.S. Delegation to NATO.

Selected Bibliography

I. OFFICIAL DOCUMENTS AND REPORTS

An Action Plan for the Human Environment, Report by the Secretary General, U.N. Conference on the Human Environment, U.N. Doc. A/CONF. 48/5 (1972).

Almeida, Beckerman, Sachs and Corea, "Environment and Development -- The Founex Report," Int'l Concil., Jan. 1972.

British-North American Committee, The GATT Negotiations 1973-79: The Closing Stage by Sidney Golt and A Policy Statement by the British-North American Committee (1978).

Center for Environmental Assessment Services, Climate Impact Assessment, United States -- Annual Summary 1980, National Oceanic and Atmospheric Administration, Washington, D.C. (1980).

Climate Research Board, National Research Council, U.S. National Academy of Sciences, Carbon Dioxide and Climate: A Scientific Assessment (1979).

Climate Board, Managing Climatic Resources and Risks, Report of the Panel on the Effective Use of Climate Information in Decision Making (Washington, D.C.: National Academy Press, 1980).

Council on Environmental Quality, The Global 2000 Report to the President: Entering the Twenty-First Century (1980).

C.E.Q., Environmental Quality, Annual reports of the Council on Environmental Quality (U.S. Gov't. Printing Office, Washington, D.C., 1979, 1980).

243

David Davies Memorial Institute of Int'l Studies, Water Pollution as a World Problem (1971).

Developments in the Field of Natural Resources -- Water, Energy and Minerals -- Technical Aspects of International River Basin Development, U.N. Doc. E/C. 7/35, (1972).

UNEP, Report of the Governing Council of the United Nations Environment Programme on the Work of Its Ninth Session, Nairobi, 13-26 May 1981, UNEP/GC. 9/15, 5 June, 1981.

The Atmosphere: Endangered and Endangering, Fogarty Intl. Center Proc. No. 39, Nat'l Inst. of Health, Washington, D.C. (DHEW Publ. No. NIH) 77-1065 (1977).

R. Garcia, "Climate Impacts and Socioeconomic Conditions -- Edited Transcript of Remarks Delivered at the Workshop," in International Perspectives on the Study of Climate and Society, Climate Research Board, National Academy of Sciences, Washington, D.C. (1978).

Gatz, "An Investigation of Pollutant Source Strength -- Rainfall Relationships at St. Louis," in Seventh Conference on Inadvertent and Planned Weather Modification (American Meteorological Society, Banff, Alberta, Canada, Oct. 8-12, 1979).

Henning, A Selected Bibliography on Public Environmental Policy and Administration, 11 Nat. Res. J. 205 (1971); U.N. Doc. A/CONF. 48/13/Rev.1 (1972).

R. Kates, "Improving the Science of Impact Study," proposal by the Scientific Committee on Problems of the Environment, International Council of Scientific Unions, Paris (1980).

Mattei, F., "Climate Variability and Agricultures in the Semi-arid Tropics," Proc. World Climate Conference, (WMO No. 537, World Meteorological Organization, Geneva, 1979).

D. Meadows, D. Meadows, J. Randers and W., Behrens, The Limits to Growth (Report to the Club of Rome, 1972.)

R.E. Munn and L. Machta, "Human Activities that Affect Climate," in Proceedings of the World Climate Conference, World Meteorological Organization Report No. 537, Geneva (1979).

NAS, Carbon Dioxide and Climate: A Scientific Assessment (Report of ad hoc Study Group on Carbon Dioxide and

Climate, Woods Hole, Mass. Climate Research Board, National Academy of Sciences, Washington, D.C. 1979.)

Oguntoyinbo, J.A. and R.S. Odingo, "Climatic Variability and Land Use: An African Perspective," Proceedings of the World Climate Conference (WMO No. 537, World Meteorological Organization, Geneva, 1979).

R. Rotty & G. Marland, Constraints on Carbon Dioxide Production form Fossil Fuel Use (May 1980) (Institute for Energy Analysis, Oak Ridge).

"SCOPE Workshop on Climate/Society Interface" SCOPE Secretariat, International Council of Scientific Unions, Paris, Panel IV (1980), "Social and Institutional Responses" in Workshop on Environmental and Societal Consequences of a Possible CO_2-Induced Climate Change, CONF-7904143, Carbon Dioxide Effects Research and Assessment Program, U.S. Dept. of Energy, Washington, D.C.

Thomas C. Shelling, Ad Hoc Study Panel on Economic and Social Aspects of Carbon Dioxide Increase, to Philip Handler, National Academy of Sciences (1980).

Inadvertent Climate Modification: Report of the Study of Man's Impact on Climate (SMIC) (1971); Sessions 1 and 2 of the Seventh Conference on Inadvertent and Planned Weather Modification (1979) (American Meteorological Society, Banff, Alberta, Canada, October 8-12, 1979.) Cambridge, MA: M.I.T. Press.

M. Tolba, The State of the World Environment 1980: The 1980 Report of the Executive Director of the United Nations Environment Programme (1980).

Weather Modification Advisory Board, U.S. Dep't. of Commerce, The Management of Weather Resources (1978 Report to the Sec'y of Comm.).

G. Woodwell, G. MacDonald, R. Revelle & C. Keeling, "The Carbon Dioxide Problem: Implications for Policy in the Management of Energy and Other Resources," reprinted in Senate Comm. on Governmental Affairs, 96th Cong., 1st Sess., Symposium on Carbon Dioxide Accumulation in the Atmosphere, Synthetic Fuels and Energy Policy 44 (1979).

World Meteorological Organization, Outline Plan and Basis for the World Climate Programme 1980-83. (WMO No. 540, World Meteorological Organization, Geneva, 1980.)

Schaake, J.C., Jr. and F. Maczmarek, "Climate Variability and the Design and Operation of Water Resource

Systems, "Proc. World Climate Conference (WMO No. 537, World Meteorological Organization, Geneva, 290-312, 1979).

WMO Project on Rev. and Monitoring of CO_2, Dept. No. 2, World Meteorological Organization, Geneva (1979).

WMO, Report of the Meeting of CAS Working Group on Atmospheric Carbon Dioxide (Boulder, Colo. 1979).

UNEP, The Environment Programme: Programme Performance Report -- report of the Executive Director, UNEP/-GC. 9/5, February 25, 1981.

BOOKS

Albanese & Steinberg, Environmental Control Technology for Atmospheric Carbon Dioxide (May 1980)(Brookhaven National Laboratory).

Attiga, A.A., Global Energy Transition and the Third World, Third World Foundation, London (1979).

J. Barros & D. Johnston, The International Law of Pollution (1974).

L. Battan, Harvesting the Clouds: Advances in Weather Modification (1969).

Bneuer, Weather Modification: Prospects and Problems (1976), first English language edition published by Cambridge University Press (1979).

H. Burmester, Vessel Source Pollution: The Integration of International and Domestic Responses in the Search for an Effective Legal Framework (Center for Ocean Law and Policy, University of Virginia, June 1978).

Carter, V.G., and T. Dale, Topsoil and Civilization (Revised edition, University of Oklahoma Press, Norman, Okla., 1974).

A. Dennis, Weather Modification by Cloud Seeding (1980).

Garcia, R., Nature Pleads Not Guilty (Pergamon Press, New York, 1981).

M. Glantz, H. van Loon and E. Armstrong, Multidisciplinary Research Related to the Atmospheric Sciences (1978).

Glantz, Desertification: Environmental Degradation in and around Arid Lands. M.H. Glantz (ed.) (Westview Press, Boulder, Colo. 1977).

Kellogg, W.W. and R. Schware, Climate Change and Society: Consequences of Increasing Atmospheric Carbon Dioxide (Westview Press, Boulder, Colo., 1981).

Kouda, V.A., Land Aridization and Drought Control (Westview Press, Boulder, Colorado, 1980).

B. Mason, Clouds, Rain and Rainmaking (2nd ed. 1975).

McCaffrey and Lutz (eds), Environmental Pollution and Individual Rights: An International Symposium (1978).

R. M'Gonigle and M. Zacher, Pollution, Politics and International Law (1979).

S. H. Schneider, with L.E. Mesirow, The Genesis Strategy (New York: Delta, 1979).

S.H. Schurr, J. Darmstadter, H. Perry, W. Ramsay, and M. Russell, Energy in America's Future: The Choices Before Us (Baltimore: Johns Hopkins Univ., 1979).

W. Sewell, Modifying the Weather: A Social Assessment (1973); W. Sewell, Human Dimensions of Weather Modification (1966).

L. Telclaff and A. Utton, International Environmental Law (1974).

Thomas (ed.), Legal and Scientific Uncertainties of Weather Modification (1977).

White, G.F., and J.E. Haas, Assessment of Research on Natural Hazards (Cambridge, MA: M.I.T., Press, 1975).

Carbon Dioxide, Climate and Society, J. Williams (ed.), (Pergamon Press, New York, 1979).

ARTICLES

Adams, Mantovani and Lundell, "Wood Versus Fossil fuel as a Source of Excess Carbon Dioxide in the Atmosphere: A Preliminary Report," 196 Science 54-56 (1977).

Alexander, "Regional Arrangement in the Oceans," 71 Am. J. Int'l L. 84 (1977).

Almond, "The Extraterritorial Reach of United States Regulatory Authority Over the Environmental Impacts of Its Activities," 44 Albany Law Review 739 (1980).

Babich, Davis and Stotzky, "Acid Precipitation: Causes and Consequences," 22 Environment 6 (May 1980).

Ball, "Shaping the Law of Weather Control," 58 Yale L. J. 213 (1949).

Bolin, "Change of Land Biota and Their Importance for the Carbon Cycle," 196 Science 613 (1977).

K. Butzer "Adaptation to Global Environmental Change," Prof. Geographer 32:269-78 (1980).

Coppoc, "The Environment: No Respecter of National Boundaries," 43 Albany Law Review 520 (1979).

"CO_2 and the Effects of Human Activities on Climate," 17 Nature and Resources, No. 3, July-September 1981, 2-5.

Danielson, Sherk and Grant, "Legal System Requirements to Control and Facilitate Water Augmentation in the Western United STates," Den. J. Int'l L. & Pol'y 511 (1976).

d'Arge and Kneese, "State Liability for International Environmental Degradation: An Economic Perspective," Natural Resources Journal 427 (1980).

Davis, "Weather Modification Law Developments," 27 Okla. L. Rev. 409 (1974).

Davis, "State Regulation of Weather Modification," 12 Ariz. L. Rev. 35 (1970).

Davis, "The Law of Precipitation Enhancement in Victoria," 7 Land and Water L. Rev. 1 (1972).

Davis, "Weather Modification, Stream Flow Augmentation, and the Law," 24 Mineral Law Institute 833 (1978).

Davis, "WMO/UNEP Weather Modification International Law Proposals," 12 J. Weather Modif. 127 (1980).

Davis, "Legal Response to Environmental Concerns about Weather Modification," 14 J. Applied Meteorology 681 (1975).

Dickstein, "National Environmental Hazards and

International Law," 23 Int'l and Comp. L. Q. 426 (1974).

Ferenbaugh, "Acid Rain: Biological Effects and Implications," 4 Environmental Affairs 745 (1975).

Frenzen, "Weather Modification: Law and Policy," 12 Boston College Industrial and Commercial Law Review 503 (1971).

Glantz, M.H., "The Value of a Long-Range Weather Forecast for the West African Sahel," Bull. Am. Meteorol. Soc., 58:150-158 (1977).

Graves, "Rain of Troubles," 209 Science 75 (July/-August 1980).

Handl, "State Liability for Accidental Transnational Environmental Damage by Private Person," 74 American Journal of International Law 527 (1980).

Hassett, "Weather Modification and Control: International Organizational Prospects," 7 Texas International Law Journal 89 (1972).

Joyner and Joyner, "Global Eco-Management and International Organization: The Stockholm Conference and Problems of Cooperation," 14 Nat. Resources J. 533 (1974).

Kates, R.W., "Climate and Society: Lessons from Recent Events." Weather, 35, 1, 17-25, 1980.

Lee, "International and Legal Aspects of Pollution of the Atmosphere." 21 University of Toronto Law Journal 203 (1971).

Likens, Wright, Galloway and Butler, "Acid Rain," 241 Scientific American 43 (October 1979).

Madden and Ramanathan, "Detecting Climate Change Due to Increasing Carbon Dioxide," 209 Science 763 (1980).

Margolis, "The Hydrogen Bomb Experiments and International Law," 64 Yale L. J. 629, 637-39 (1955).

Maudlin, W.P., "Population Trends and Prospects," Science 209:148 (1980).

McDougal and Schneider, "The Protection of the Environment and World Public Order: Some Recent Developments," 45 Mississippi Law Journal 1085 (1974).

Mensah, "International Environmental law: International Conventions Concerning Oil Pollution at Sea," 8 Case W. Res. J. Int'l L. 110 (1976).

Meyer-Alrich, K.M., "Socioeconomic Impacts of CO_2-induced Climatic Changes and the Comparative Chances 6f Alternative Political Responses: Prevention, Compensation, and Adaptation." Climatic Change 2 :313 (1979).

Muir, "Legal and Ecological Aspects of the International Energy Situation," 8 Int'l Law. 1 (1974).

Nanda, "The 'Torrey Canyon' Disaster: Some Legal Aspects," 44 Den. L. J. 400 (1967).

Nanda, V.P., "The Establishment of International Standards for Transnational Environmental Injury." 60 Iowa Law Review 1089 (1975).

N. Nicholls, "Long-Range Weather Forecasting: Value, Status, and Prospects," Rev. Geophys. Space Phys. 18:771-788 (1980).

Perry, H. and Landsberg, H., "Projected World Energy Consumption," Energy and Climate (National Academy of Sciences, Washington, D.C., 1977).

R.J. Reed, "Destructive Winds Caused by an Orographically Induced Mesoscale Cyclone," Bull. Am. Meteorol. Soc. 61: 1346-1355 (1980).

Robinson, "Effluents of Energy Production: Particulates," in National Academy of Sciences, Energy and Climate 61 (1977).

Robinson, "Convention for the Protection of the Mediterranean Sea Against Pollution," 2 Earth L.J. 289 (1976).

Rosencrantz, A., "The Problem of Transboundary Pollution." Environment 22 No.5:15-20 (1980).

Rotty, R.M., "Energy Demand and Global Climate Change," Man's Impact on Climate, W. Bach, J. Pankrath and W. Kellogg (eds.), Elsevier, New York, 1979.

Samuels, "Prospective International Control of Weather Modification Activities," 21 U. Toronto L. J. 222 (1971).

Siegenthaler, U. and Oeschger, H., "Predicting Future Atmospheric Carbon Dioxide Levels," 199 Science (1978), 388-95.

Sigel, "International Control of Weather Modification in a Regime of Long-Range Weather Forecasting," 19 Harv. Int'l L. J. 535 (1978).

Smith, "Cloud Seeding in Australia," in W. Hess, Weather and Climate Modification 444 (1974).

Sterns, "Weather Modification Activities and National Forest Land Use Permits," in Hail Suppression: Society and Environment 241 (B. Garhar ed. 1977).

Stuvier, "Atmosphere Carbon Dioxide and Carbon Reservoir Changes," 199 Science 253-58 (1978).

Taubenfeld, "International Environmental Law: Air and Outer Space," 13 Nat. Resources J. 315 (1973).

Utton, "International Environmental Law and Consultation Mechanisms," 12 Columbia Journal of Transnational Law 56 (1973).

Warrick, R.A., "Drought in the Great Plains: A Case Study of Research on Climate and Society in the USA," in Climatic Constraints and Human Activities, IIASA Proceedings Series Vol. 10, J. Ausubel and A. Biswas, Eds, New York: Pergamon (1980).

"Why a World Climate Rrogramme?," 17 Nature and Resources, No. 1, January-March 1981, 2-7.

Wood, "The Status of Weather Modification Activities Under United States and International Law," 10 Nat. Resources Law. 367 (1977-78).

Zalob, "Approaches to Enforcement of Environmental Law: An International Perspective," 3 Hastings International and Comparative Law Review 299 (1980).

Index